ᔐ INSIGHT GUIDES

LAS VEGAS

smart guide

Discovery
CHANNEL

APA PUBLICATIONS L
Part of the Langenscheidt Publishing Group

Contents

Areas

Below: Downtown, where it all began.

A–Z

Left: spin the wheel and take a chance. Will you go home a winner?

Atlas

Below: sarcastic and savvy, a showgirl stops to say "hi."

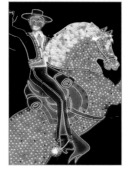

Las Vegas

Unique in the world, Las Vegas is the place where the wildest dreams just might come true. They will probably not, but at least the possibility is there. From its origins as a gangsters' haven to its 21st-century makeover as an unrivalled center of lavish showrooms, world-class restaurants, hair-raising thrill rides, and over-the-top shopping, Las Vegas never ceases to amaze.

Destination Fact and Figures

Population: **545,000 (1,777,500 in metro Las Vegas)**
Area: **7,881sq. miles**
Visitors per year: **38.9 million**
Casino winnings 2006: **$6.6 billion**
Per capita income: **$22,060**
Unemployment: **4.4 percent**
Annual average rainfall: **4.5in**
Average summer high temperature: **101.6°F**
Average winter low temperature: **38.3°F**
Water consumption: **408 million gallons per day**
Electricity consumption: **5.3 million kilowatts per day**

Desert fantasy

Las Vegas is all about illusion. It has more professional magicians and Elvis Presley impersonators than any other city on earth. Its theme resorts employ such architectural tricks as forced perspective to convince you that a fireworks volcano, a not-really-life-size Eiffel Tower and an ersatz Statue of Liberty are, if not the real thing, even better than the real things because they are surrounded by slot machines.

"Now you see it, now you don't" describes how older hotels, like the Stardust in 2007, are demolished with the speed of dynamite blasts to make way for ever bigger resorts that materialize at the drop of a few billion dollars to become the tallest, widest, richest, or best new thing if only for a matter of months. But the biggest magic trick of all is the one that materialized this city in the remote, sunbaked lunar landscape of the Mojave Desert; a desert that seems to now isolate this remarkable city from the "normal world" that its visitors usually inhabit.

Tourist mecca

With virtually no manufacturing industry or agriculture, there is no reason why a city the size of Las Vegas should exist at all out here in a landscape where cattle can barely survive and natural resources are scarce, a landscape the government considered ideal for nothing more than testing nuclear weapons. As recently as the 1930s, even Las Vegas's city fathers did not expect it would ever grow to more than 5,000 people. Yet today 17 of the world's top 20 largest hotels are neighbors along the Las Vegas Strip. Together, they boast 133,000 hotel rooms – 85 percent more than New York City – with another 38,000 to be added over the next three years in anticipation of between 53 and 55 million visitors a year (a growth rate of 150 percent).

Caviar, showguys, and Ferraris

The attractions that draw people to this bright-lit desert oasis are as unique and constantly changing as the Strip itself. A

Below: the desert scenery surrounding Vegas is as magnificent as it is large.

retro revival of Studio 54 and the world's last genuine Playboy Club, a bar made of solid ice where you can order premium vodka and caviar, a bevy of buff male dancers stripping to delight bachelorettes (a reversal of roles for the traditional Vegas peepshow and showgirls), a Ferrari dealership where you can dream impossible dreams right in the hotel…

These are just a few reminders that while you can't take it with you, you can have a lot of fun along the way, so long as you can face the consequences. Despite this, for most visitors, a Vegas vacation is no tougher on the wallet than any other, just quicker.

Three days in "Sin City"

Las Vegas is designed to deliver maximum experience in minimum time. Most Vegas enthusiasts will tell you three days is plenty. In that time, you can win a small fortune at blackjack, then lose it again and more. You can sate your senses on enough extravaganzas to kill any desire to stand in line for another show. You can eat all-you-can-eat at a sprawling international buffet, then dine at another one the next day or choose to go to a five star gourmet restaurant. By day three, you're numb, exhausted, grinning, quite possibly broke. Next year, chances are, you'll want to go back. Almost everybody does. When it comes to Vegas, once is simply not enough.

Highlights

▲ The architectural fantasy that makes up **the Strip** has been attracting the dreamers and the desperate for decades.

▶ **Getting married** in Vegas can still be impulsive, just get the marriage license before midnight.

▲ **Shopping** at resorts such as Caesars Palace or Wynn Las Vegas is some of the ritziest in America.

▶ **World-class dining** has replaced the all-you-can-eat buffet as the centerpiece for the Strip's catering industry.

▲ **Big-budget Shows** from Cirque du Soleil to Céline Dion play nightly.

▶ Vintage neon signs and the world's largest lightshow bring the night to life in the renovated **Downtown**.

Southern Strip

The southern half of Las Vegas's famous Strip, originally known as Arrowhead Highway, runs due south from the Mirage's volcano to the Mandalay Bay and is only a few minutes' drive from the airport. In earlier times, this area was less densely developed than the northern Strip, making it the natural place to build huge new mega-resorts in the 1930s, when the legalization of gambling in Atlantic City threatened to render old-time Vegas casinos obsolete. Today, the southern Strip is a highrise adult fantasyland packed with such spectacles as a fake Statue of Liberty, a faux Eiffel Tower, and the world's largest Coca-Cola bottle.

See Atlas Pages 138-139

Heavy Hitters and False Cities

In recent years, growth along this stretch of the strip has generally been from north to south. The **Flamingo**, toward the north end, was among the first Strip hotels, started by the legendary gangster, Bugsy Seigel, more than half a century ago. It can also claim the first neon sign on the Strip: a parade of pink flamingos on the Flamingo Hotel's façade. Proceeding south, the lineup reads like a list of successive "biggest"

Harrah's, presently the largest casino owner on the strip, owns Caesars Palace, Paris Las Vegas, Flamingo Las Vegas, Harrah's, Bally's, and the Rio All-Suites. The company started in Reno and also owns other casinos in Atlantic City, Lake Tahoe, and elsewhere.

hotels: **Caesars Palace**, **Bally's** (a resurrection of the original MGM Grand), the **Bellagio**, **Paris Las Vegas**, and today's **MGM Grand**, presently the largest hotel in the world.

These five casinos have plenty of attractions in their own right. The exclusive **Forum Shops** in Caesars Palace, which are decorated with supersize replicas of ancient Roman and Renaissance sculptures, are said to form the world's richest retail district.

The Bellagio was inspired by the resort of the same name at Lake Como in Italy. The fountains of "Lake Bellagio" dance to opera and classical ballet music every half-hour during the afternoon and every 15 minutes through the evening until midnight. Paris Las Vegas has the most conspicuous landmark on the southern

Above: in Vegas a fortune can be read before it is won.

Strip, the half-size replica of the Eiffel Tower.

SEE ALSO ACCOMMODATIONS P.20–3; CASINOS P.38–46; SHOPPING P.120

Beyond the Historic Tropicana

The **Tropicana** used to mark the outskirts of town. Beyond its palm-liked grounds lay only bare desert studded with ocatillo and creosote bushes.

Today, these wide-open spaces have been filled in by such luxury resorts as the pyramid-shaped **Luxor**, the towering gold **Mandalay Bay,** and the smaller but more exclusive **Four Seasons**.

Left: the Eiffel Tower at Paris Las Vegas is an exact model of the original, but at half the size.

The Las Vegas Monorail, 3.9 miles long with seven stations, whisks passengers along a route behind the southern Strip casinos, linking them to the Convention Center. For sightseeing, an all-day pass is a must.

This part of the Strip is ideal for sightseeing on foot. Interconnected pedestrian skyways, from which you can watch the traffic congestion below, provide easy passage between Caesars Palace, **Bill's Las Vegas**, Bally's Las Vegas, and the Bellagio.

Another set of skyways links **New York New York**, the MGM Grand, the Tropicana, and the **Excalibur**.
SEE ALSO ACCOMMODATIONS P.20–3; CASINOS 40, 41, 43–45; CHILDREN P.56, 59

Getting Around

If you are driving, the best plan is to park in one of the huge multilevel parking lots behind the hotels. All are free, but beware: while signs inside the hotels helpfully point you toward the central casinos, from which doors opening onto the Strip are only a few steps away, when trying to find your way back to your car you are likely to discover that no signs lead from the casino back to the parking lot.

For purposes of taking in the amazing sights of the southern Strip, as long as you have a car it matters little whether you stay in a Strip hotel or in much cheaper accommodations downtown, on the Boulder Highway, or in Henderson.

If you have reservations for a show or a fine restaurant, though, remember to allow more time than you think you need. Negotiating traffic can take a frustratingly long time, especially if you find it necessary to turn left to reach a hotel on the other side of the street. Then, too, you can wander vast distances through a hotel's shopping mall, lobby and casino en route to the showroom or restaurant you are looking for, and one wrong turn can set you to retracing your footsteps through capacity crowds.

But in the end, you will find that the experience is worth the hassle.

New York New York's Manhattan Express is the oldest and longest roller coaster on the Strip. There are three others – the Sahara's Speed, The Ride, Circus Circus's Canyon Blaster, and the Stratosphere's High Roller.

Right: the New York New York hotel contains replicas of the Empire State Building, the Statue of Liberty, the Brooklyn Bridge, the Soldiers and Sailors Monument, the Whitney Museum, and Grand Central Station.

Northern Strip

With its sky cranes, half-built towers and vacant lots, the northern Strip looks like an ambitious urban renewal zone. In fact, it offers glimpses of both Vegas's seamy past and its towering future. Nothing exemplifies the contrast between past and future like the intersection of the Strip and Desert Inn Road, where the Wynn Las Vegas is the tallest high-rise hotel in town. Catty-corner across the intersection, a construction site has replaced the Strip's original highrise, the nine-story Stardust. Another neighboring property under construction is planned to stand four stories higher than the Wynn, making the block a battleground for monumental egos.

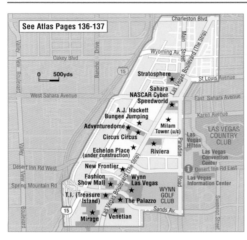

Above: Venetian charms meet American dreams.

From the Rat Pack to Fat Cats

The northern half of the Strip extends from the Venetian and the Mirage at a diagonal for 2 miles, presently anchored at its northern end by the spectacular Stratosphere Tower.

In the old days, this was the main part of the Strip, where Vegas nostalgia buffs may recall that Frank Sinatra and the Rat Pack used to headline at the Sands, entertainer Wayne Newton (known as Mr Las Vegas) sang down the street at the Stardust, and Howard Hughes, one of

the world's wealthiest men, lived in eccentric seclusion in the penthouse of the Desert Inn, where he finally lost control of his business empire.

Today, all three of these venerable hotels are gone. In their place have arisen some of the newest, most elegant and expensive hotels on the Strip, including the **Venetian** and the **Wynn Las Vegas**. The city's large, upscale **Fashion Show Mall** also stands as one of the northern Strip's top landmarks – with 250 classy stores and restaurants, it is the largest shopping mall in Las Vegas as

well as one of the most exclusive.

Nearby, the **Mirage** was once synonymous with magicians Siegfried & Roy who retired from their hit magic-and-animals show after Roy Horn was mauled by a tiger. They – and their tigers – are honored by a statue in front of the casino.

Seeming out of place among such august company, the **Circus Circus** formerly stood as one of the biggest and showiest properties in Las Vegas. Today, dwarfed by other hotels farther south, its image is less impressive than just plain comical. Pink-and-white and shaped like a circus tent with a huge matching tower

Left: the Wynn Las Vegas has many luxuries, including the only public golf course on the Strip, originally built for the Desert Inn in 1950.

Indeed, much of this area seems to be in transition, making it an unattractive place to walk and isolating the northernmost resort, the **Stratosphere** (the only Strip hotel actually within the city limits of Las Vegas), from the rest of the Strip.

To appreciate it, you have to imagine what the future holds. In the ruins of the Stardust, ground has been broken on the $4 billion **Echelon Place** project. It will have four hotels, 25 restaurants, and the city's largest casino when it opens in 2010.

New York and Atlantic City developer Donald Trump is nearing completion of the first phase of his ambitious "twin" Trump Towers, which will stand just slightly taller than rival Steve Wynn's hotel. And neither Trump's nor Wynn's skyscrapers will hold a candle to Texas developer Christopher Milam's planned Milam Tower Condominiums, centered around a 1,888-ft obelisk that will be the tallest building west of the Mississippi.

SEE ALSO ACCOMMODATIONS P.24; CASINOS P.48–9; CHILDREN P.59–60

behind it as well as a vast RV park that can park 399 motorhomes at once with full hook-ups.

People still come to see the famous free acrobatic acts, which take place high above the main casino floor, with the oblivious slot machine players (and the acrobats) protected by a 100,000-sq ft net.

SEE ALSO ACCOMMODATIONS P.23, 25; CASINOS P.47, 50; CHILDREN P.56, 59; SHOPPING P.120–121, 123–4

the hotel of choice for most families with young children. It is still popular with the little ones. **Adventuredome**, the hotel's indoor, air-conditioned amusement park, is still going strong, as is **Sahara's NASCAR Cyber Speedworld**, but other major attractions such as Wet 'n' Wild Waterpark and the Guinness Book of World Records museum have closed to make way for future developments that are less suited for youngsters.

Men at Work

The terrain north of here has traditionally been the Strip's family fun zone, mainly because Circus Circus was

The New Frontier *(right)* hosted Elvis Presley's first Vegas performance in 1958 and Diana Ross and the Supremes' last performance together in 1970.

Beyond the Strip

Most of metropolitan Las Vegas looks nothing like the Strip. It is typical suburbia, in which the western part of the city is home to ordinary people who never go to the tourist zones, while the southern region, a solid sprawl all the way to the former mining town of Henderson, is inhabited mainly by workers in the hospitality industry. But as business booms on the Strip, pushing real estate prices higher and higher (in 2004, Christopher Milam paid $450 million for the Wet 'n' Wild Water Park's 276-acre site, or $17 million an acre), tourism has inevitably spilled over the edges of the Strip into formerly modest neighborhoods on both sides.

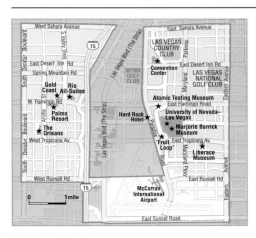

Above: blackjack dealers follow strict rules when deciding when to hit, thereby increasing the house's odds.

Bursting at the Seams

The spillover from the Strip began with the building of the **Las Vegas Convention Center**, originally a domed rotunda built by local government in 1959 to help boost hotel occupancy during the week. Located one very long block east of the north end of the Strip, the old Convention Center was expanded, then imploded to make way for the new one, which is now one of the largest convention centers in the US. Each year it holds the Consumer Electronics Show, the world's largest trade show.

Of course, Las Vegas's ability to accommodate the country's largest expos has ensured that even the largest resort hotels never run short of visitors, even when casino tourism is slow.

SEE ALSO CONFERENCE SURVIVAL P.62–3

UNLV

East of the Strip, bounded by Flamingo Road, Paradise Road (the route to the airport), and Tropicana Avenue, the compact, modern campus of the **University of Nevada – Las Vegas** has become one of the nation's leading metropolitan universities, thanks to steady expansion made possible by enormous contributions from civic boosters and alumni such as the presidents of the Bellagio and Palms hotels. Its **Marjorie Barrick Museum** is a natural history

> Not all Vegas residents work in the hospitality industry. For the past 10 years, the city has led the US in new customer service call centers, usually employing workers at home.

Left: the carnaval-themed Rio All-Suites was one of the first resorts to open off-Strip.

Fabulous Resorts

Another area that is beginning to witness a tourism boom is the formerly desolate part of town that was separated from the Strip when Interstate 5 was built. Some of the best casino resorts in town have been springing up along **West Flamingo Road**. They include the **Rio All-Suites**, known for its fantastic panoramic views of the Strip from a distance sufficient to take it all in, and what some all-you-can-eat connoisseurs claim is the best dinner buffet in Vegas.

Also noteworthy, and just a little way down West Flamingo from the Rio, the self-conciously hip **Palms Resort** has several unique features: the newest, largest concert stadium in town; a professional recording studio that can be used from any guest room; and a neon bunny-head sign that advertises the last surviving Playboy Club on Earth. In its heyday, the Playboy Club had 40 locations in the United States, Europe and Asia.
SEE ALSO ACCOMMODATIONS P.28; CASINOS P.52–3;

museum with an exhibition hall set aside for art.
SEE ALSO MUSEUMS AND GALLERIES P.100

Paradise Road

Anchored by the Convention Center, the university, and the airport, **Paradise Road** has become a center for off-strip commercial activity. Not only does this busy street boast most of the city's business-oriented hotels at the convention center and airport ends, but in between it has developed a popular **"Restaurant Row"** of independent dining establishments and a hip, youngish alternative to the Strip scene. This is typified by the **Hard Rock Hotel**, with one of the major state-of the art rock concert venues in the city, called **The Joint**. This 8,000 sq ft facility has two bars and a balcony VIP area, and two huge video screens help to bring the stage alive.

SEE ALSO ACCOMMODATIONS P.27; CASINOS P.51; LIVE ENTERTAINMENT P.87; RESTAURANTS P.116–8

Fruit Loop

Also along Paradise Road, adjacent to UNLV, is the **"Fruit Loop,"** Vegas's main gay bar district. LGBT bars here host many events during Pride Week, the first full week in May. Popular venues include **Buffalo**, a low-key denim and leather bar, and the funky **Piranha** nightclub.
SEE ALSO GAY AND LESBIAN P.74–5

Below: Manilow and Menopause: things slow down once you leave the strip.

Downtown Las Vegas

Fremont Street, the center of downtown Las Vegas, is packed with history, most of it infamous. It had secret casinos before casinos were legal. It had prostitutes, pimps, con artists, and every form of frontier lowlife imaginable. Then Bugsy Seigel and the boys came to town, and rivalry broke out between "Glitter Gulch" (the old name for Downtown) and the Strip. Though the big bucks wound up on the Strip, Glitter Gulch was where serious gamblers went to gamble seriously, with no showbiz nonsense to get in the way. The city has made great strides toward making Downtown respectable, but the ghosts of the past still haunt Fremont Street.

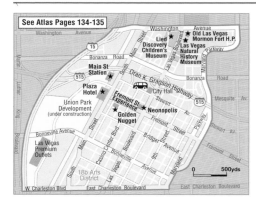

See Atlas Pages 134-135

The most notorious local character in old Las Vegas was not Bugsy Seigel, but Texas bootlegger Benny Binion, who arrived broke after being released from a Texas prison and became the richest casino owner in Glitter Gulch.

Around Fremont Street

The central part of Downtown—in fact, the only part most tourists ever see—lies along just five pedestrians-only blocks of **Fremont Street** and spills over onto **Casino Center Boulevard**

and **South Main Street**. Once, the big attraction was the neon signs of an earlier, pre-plasma-screen era, **Vegas Vic** *(see p.103)*, the 40-ft cowboy with his waving arm and booming welcome; Vic's equally mechanical wife

Vegas Vickie (née Sassy Sally); and the giant good-luck horseshoe above the door of Benny Binion's casino. They are still there as part of the **"Neon Museum,"** which preserves historic Las Vegas signs in place, even though the businesses they advertised may be long gone.

But today, the neon glitz of past times is all but eclipsed by the **Fremont Street Experience**. This term originally referred to the 90-ft high, four block long vaulted sunshade

Below: unlike the ever-modernizing Strip, Downtown celebrates its brash, neon heritage.

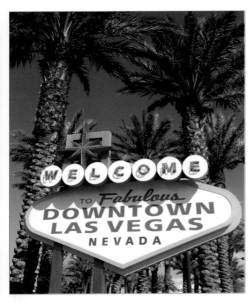

spectacles in the city. Though the Fremont Street Experience folks have made mighty efforts to promote a new, family-friendly image for Downtown, this has not been easy along a street occupied by 10 casinos with disreputable pasts.

SEE ALSO MOVIES P.95; MUSEUMS AND GALLERIES P.102, 103

Arts District

The other part of Downtown that visitors will find good to know about lies about a mile south-east of the Fremont Street pedestrian mall, surrounding the intersecton of South Main Street and West Charleston Boulevard. Officially designated as the **18b Arts District**, this concentration of low-rent, hideaway artists' studios looks unimpressive most of the time, until you peek behind the doors to old warehouses that house the studios. It comes to vibrant life on **First Friday** each month.

SEE ALSO MUSEUMS AND GALLERIES P.96–98

> The 18b Arts District got its name because it encompassed 18 blocks of downtown Vegas.

that kept Fremont Street relatively cool on hot summer days and became the ultimate sound-and-light show after dark. In 2004, the show was revamped with a state-of-the-art LED system, like those TV screen moving signs that line the Strip, but much bigger (the screen is 1,500ft long and stands 90ft above street level, cost: $17 million). The show was renamed Viva Vision, and Downtown boosters made it clear that the "Fremont Street Experience" referred to not just the sound-and-light show itself but also the whole street, including its vintage neon signs, its 10 casinos, and **Neonopolis**, the big shopping, dining, and entertainment complex (it has the city's

largest multiscreen movie theater complex) at the intersection of Fremont Street and Las Vegas Boulevard. Shows are hourly from sundown to midnight, with a completely different show every hour.

Though Neonopolis does not draw the crowds that other showy Vegas malls do – perhaps because you have to pay to park there – Viva Vision is one of the most amazing

> Downtown landmark Vegas Vic had his booming recorded voice silenced after actor Lee Marvin, staying across the street, complained about the noise.

Below: Downtown may lack big live acts, but the edgy crowds and a heavy dose of nostalgia create their own spectacle.

Red Rock Canyon and Mount Charleston

Though many visitors fail to realize it, Vegas is the center of one of the most spectacular desert areas in the south-west. In the old days, locals used to go out there to watch atomic bombs explode, or possibly to bury an inconvenient body. Today they go to hike and ride horseback among the sandstone formations of Red Rock Canyon, or go skiing – yes, snow skiing – on Mount Charleston. Tour companies will take you to any of these places, but exploring them on your own is the best reason to get out of Vegas.

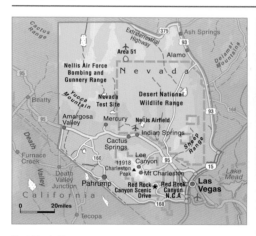

Above: Red Rock Canyon offers nature, pure and simple.

Red Rock Canyon

To reach **Red Rock Canyon National Conservation Area**, follow West Charleston Avenue all the way across town and into the desert. A distance of 18 miles from the Strip (25–45 min depending on traffic), you will come to the visitors' center, which is also the start of the beautiful **Red Rock Canyon Scenic Drive**. Though off-road driving or biking is not allowed, the scenic drive is one of the most popular cycling routes in the region.

There is a campground (bring your own water; closed in summer). Less than half the canyon can be reached by vehicle. To see the rest, hike or rent a horse.
SEE ALSO THE KING, A QUEEN AND COWBOYS P.78–9

Mount Charleston

Though you would think West Charleston Avenue would also take you to **Mount Charleston**, it does not. To get there, go north on US 95 from the Strip for 35 miles and then turn west on state Highway 157. A paved road leads partway up the 11,913-ft peak, where there are several campgrounds and a small lodge, as well as downhill and cross-country ski areas in the winter months.

The higher reaches of Mount Charleston are a designated wilderness area, where all wheeled and motorized vehicles are prohibited.

In summer, there are many miles of hiking and horseback trails through cool ponderosa and aspen forests teeming with wildlife.
SEE ALSO ACCOMMODATIONS P.31

DESERT NATIONAL WILDLIFE REFUGE AND NUCLEAR TEST SITE

If you follow Interstate 15 north from the center of the Strip for about 25 miles and exit on US 93 (exit 64), you will be on your way through the **Desert National Wildlife Refuge**, where bighorn sheep

Left: a magical landscape that even Steve Wynn couldn't buy.

the **Yucca Mountain Nuclear Waste Disposal Facility**, which was designed to house high-grade spent plutonium. Though approved by Congress and the Department of Defense, public opposition has been strong and environmental activists have so far prevented Yucca Mountain from opening.

Their protests are not without warrant. The plutonium waste that the US government wants to bury at Yucca Mountain has a half-life of more than 10,000 years.
SEE ALSO ENVIRONMENT P.65; MUSEUMS AND GALLERIES P.101

Extraterrestrial activity

The third interesting, off-limits thing about the Nevada Test Site is the mysterious **Area 51** – a big attraction for believers in UFOs. To get there follow the uniquely named Highway 375, now designated as the **Extraterrestrial Highway** by the State of Nevada because of its proximity to Area 51.

> More than 1,000 above-ground and underground nuclear weapons tests were conducted at the Nevada Test Site between July 1945 and September 1992.

and rattlesnakes roam. All roads within the refuge are unpaved, and many are only suitable for high-clearance four-wheel-drive vehicles. Most of the visitors here – you will probably not see any others – come for reasons of bizarre curiosity. The main feature of the region is the **Nevada Test Site**, where nuclear weapons tests were conducted. Vegas legend has it that in the 1950s, locals used to pack picnics and drive out to watch the explosions.

More than half the land designated as part of the Desert National Wildlife

Refuge is also part of the Nevada Test Site and off-limits to the public except on organised tours.

By the time the international nuclear test ban went into effect, the Nevada Test Site had been picked for another radioactive purpose:

Right: the ski season at Mount Charleston begins on December 1st and ends in early Spring.

Lake Mead, Valley of Fire, and Hoover Dam

Lake Mead lies just over the hill from the Strip on the other side of Sunrise Mountain. This popular recreation lake has several marinas where pleasure boats are docked, plus swimming and sunbathing beaches, but hot summer weekends aside, you will often find yourself amidst little company, whether on the lake or on the fantastic Lake Mead Scenic Drive. This drive takes in three key sights besides the lake itself: the Lost City Museum in Overton, Valley of Fire State Park, and Hoover Dam.

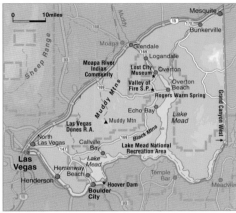

Ringtail cats, which look like skinny raccoons, are common on the rocks around Hoover Dam at night. Stuffed toy versions of them are a favorite dam souvenir.

moved when the original archeological site was flooded by Lake Mead. The village was inhabited for more than 400 years but mysteriously abandoned around AD 1150.

Valley of Fire

Continuing south, you will come to the turnoff for the **Valley of Fire**, a red and white sandstone labyrinth where neolithic hunters left cryptic rock art on the walls of narrow canyons. These petroglyphs are believed to be 4,000 years old, but their significance is unknown.

To fully appreciate the mystery of this unique site, venture along the sandy-floored canyon to **Mouse's Tank**, with its weirdly eroded formations and its intriguing (if exaggerated) legend of a renegade Native american who hid out from the US cavalry there.

The northern half of the Lake Mead drive offers only glimpses of the lake itself, though unpaved side roads lead off to **Overton Beach**

Lake Mead Scenic Drive

There are several entrances to the **Lake Mead Scenic Drive**. Each has an entrance gate where rangers charge a $5 per car fee. The north entrance is at the improbably green farming town of **Overton**, reached by driving 53 miles north of the strip on Interstate 15 to exit 97 and turning south on state highway 169.

This takes you past the **Lost City Museum**, where the ruins of the ancient Native American town called **Pueblo Grande de Nevada** were

Left: a vintage sign from Nevada's early days.

Left: Lake Mead sits in stark contrast to its desert surrounds.

Lake Mead, the largest reservoir in the United States, was created by damming the confluence of the Virgin and Colorado rivers. The lake supplies water to California, but not to Las Vegas.

workers on the Boulder Dam project, keeping them away from the temptations of Las Vegas casinos and saloons. Though property there is now privately owned, gambling is still prohibited in the town. The highlight is a visit to the **Boulder City/Hoover Dam Museum**, located in the town's original **Boulder Dam Hotel**, which also houses a bed-and-breakfast and the local historical society office.

The old, alphabetically lettered residential streets of Boulder City have many houses overgrown with lush gardens, left over from the time when government workers had an unlimited water supply from the dam project.

The outskirts of Boulder City command a spectacular view of Lake Mead.
SEE ALSO ACCOMMODATIONS P.31; MUSEUMS AND GALLERIES P.102

Below: a well-earned rest in the Valley of Fire.

and the marina at **Echo Bay**. Don't pass up a stop at **Rogers Warm Spring**, an idyllic desert oasis lined with palms and teeming with fish.

After winding your way across the barren Black Mountains, you will pass the tip of Las Vegas Bay and come to the road in from Henderson, just a few minutes by freeway from the Las Vegas Strip. This is the entrance used by most visitors to the lake.

There's another place to explore east of Vegas. Follow US 95 across the dam and south for 43 miles to a turnoff marked "Grand Canyon West," where a road takes you north to the hiking and rafting recreation area on the Hualapai Indian Reservation. The reservation includes 108 miles of the Grand Canyon rim. Only two places – Supai and Grand Canyon West – are open to non-Native Americans.

Hemenway Beach, on Lake Mead south of the Henderson entrance, is where kids and university students from Las Vegas go to cool off on hot summer days.

Hoover Dam

Continuing south from the Henderson turnoff, you will reach the end of the scenic drive and join US 93 near Boulder City. The highway makes a steep, winding descent to Hoover Dam, in the depths of Black Canyon on the Nevada-Arizona state line.

The dam has a large visitors' center (entrance charge), and you can walk out on the dam for free or pay for a tour of the interior. Daypacks and large purses are prohibited.
SEE ALSO ENVIRONMENT P.64–5

Boulder City

And finally, there's **Boulder City** itself. The town was built and owned by the federal government to house

South of the City: Ghost Towns

The land south of Las Vegas is some of the most desolate in the Southwest. It wasn't always that way. Several mining towns in the area during the late 19th and early 20th centuries had populations numbering in the thousands, at a time when the town of Las Vegas didn't even exist. Exploring this area presents a startling look at the transitory nature of wealth in the desert. Whether it's worth your while depends on just how much you appreciate local history – or absolute emptiness.

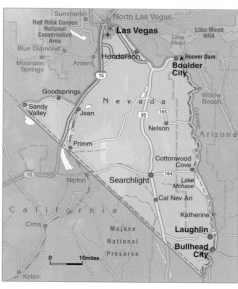

Above: signs warn of common dangers on Nevada roads.

Jean

There are just two ways you can drive south from Las Vegas without crossing the Hoover Dam. If you follow Interstate 15, you'll reach the California state line in about half an hour. Along the way, you'll come to the unique town of **Jean,** which has a total permanent population of 2, yet consists of 3 casinos (at least one of them closed, for now) and a women's prison. Both the casino workers and the prison guards commute from Las Vegas, hence the low number of inhabitants. In 2007, the MGM Mirage Corporation, which owns both open casinos in Jean, announced it would demolish one of them and redevelop the land as affordable housing for Las Vegas workers – an important project because the cost of housing in Las Vegas itself has risen beyond the reach of many hotel employees.

Jean is also the jumping-off point for four-wheel-drive enthusiasts who want to explore the historic mines and ghost towns of the area. Many of these historic reminders lie along unpaved, primitive roads; others no longer have any road to them at all.

Most Clark County, Nevada mines produced silver ore during their heyday. The ores were colorful oxides with mouthful names like chrysocola, heterogenite, and bromargyrite that only a geologist could love.

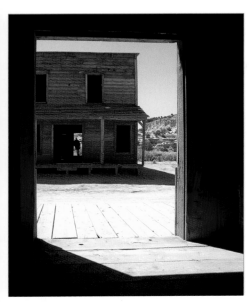

Left: as mines closed, boom towns turned to ghost towns and their remains are still strung across the remote desert regions of Nevada.

tion of the Hoover Dam), all of whom had left by 1935. The town became part of the surrounding ranch, whose owners attempted unsuccessfully to sell it for many years. It still has a few inhabitants, but it is difficult to believe that in the early 20th century, the town was larger than Las Vegas was at the time. Legend says the town was named for the lights used to guide patrons across the desert to houses of prostitution located there.

Nelson

About 10 miles down Interstate 95 from Boulder City, a turnoff leads to the ghost town of **Nelson**. One of the oldest and longest-lived old mining towns in the region, it lasted from 1858 to 1945. Its reason for such a long survival was a wharf and ferry crossing over the Colorado River – the only crossing point within 50 miles. The wharf was ultimately destroyed by a flash flood and never rebuilt, leaving the town to slowly die. Some buildings remain, including an old-fashioned gas station.

Goodsprings

Seven miles west of Jean on the main dirt road, **Goodsprings** was once a mining camp complete with a hotel, a saloon (c. 1898) and a general store. All of these establishments, as well as a few other buildings, are still standing – or at least sagging. The town was completely abandoned after World War I.

Searchlight

Following straight, hilly Interstate 95 south from the turnoff near Boulder City (see p.17) will take you through the town of **Searchlight**, a turn-of-the-20th-century gold mining camp that once reached a population of 5,000 people (coincidentally the maximum projected population for Vegas when energy allocations were allocated during the construc-

Below: Interstate 15 passes through the Mohave Desert and at the foot of the Spring Mountains.

Accommodations

L as Vegas hotel rates vary enormously, but one constant is that hotel rooms cost more on weekends. Rates also tend to go up and down depending on demand, with few bargains available when a big convention or sports event is being held. At other times there are astonishing deals, but you may need to consult the travel pages of a US newspaper to find them. Websites such as vegas.com offer a choice of as many as 100 hotels from $30 per night. As a rule, Downtown Las Vegas and Henderson are cheaper than the Strip, though there are often comparable bargains to be found there too.

Southern Strip

As room rates vary, the dollar signs here are an approximate guide only; sometimes it is possible to bargain on the spot before check-in.

Bally's Las Vegas
3645 Las Vegas Boulevard South; tel: 739-4111 or 800-634-3434; fax: 967-4405; www.ballyslv.com; $$$; monorail: Bally's/Paris Las Vegas, bus: Deuce; map pp.138–139 C3/C4
Bally's is one of the oldest hotels on the Strip, but also one of the most overlooked. Large rooms with a modern flair feature overstuffed furni-

ture and subdued earth tones. The hotel has a beautiful pool area, perfect for hot days.

Bellagio
3600 Las Vegas Boulevard South; tel: 693-7111 or 888-987-6667; fax: 792-7646; www.bellagioresort.com; $$$$; monorail: Bally's/Paris Las Vegas, bus: Deuce; map p.138 B3
One of the city's most lavish resorts, the standard guest rooms are satisfyingly plush. Two key perks are the comfortable beds and huge bathrooms with tubs and showers big enough for two.

Many hotels listed here are, of course, multi-faceted casinos. Here we limit ourselves to reviewing their accommodations. For more information about gaming see their listings in the Casinos chapter (p.38–55). Bars and Cafés (p.32–7) and Restaurants (p.106–19) list their best eating and drinking venues, while information about their live acts can be found in Live Entertainment (p.80–7).

Tip: ask for a room overlooking Bellagio's fountains, as there is in-room music choreographed to the water show.

Bill's Las Vegas
3595 Las Vegas Boulevard South; tel: 737-2100 or 866-245-5745; www.billslasvegas.com; $$–$$$ monorail: Flamingo/Caesars Palace, bus: Deuce; map p.138 C4
The rooms in this small hotel offer a pleasant and comfortable rendition of the "City by the Bay" c.1900, featuring brass beds and etched mirrors.

Caesars Palace
3570 Las Vegas Boulevard South; tel: 731-7110 or 800-634-6661; fax: 731-7172; www.caesars.com; $$$; monorail: Flamingo/Caesars Palace, bus: Deuce; map p.138 B3/B4
A standard-setter since its opening. A recent renovation – including a new tower and pool – raises the level of its already excellent accommo-

Left: Caesars Palace's extensive pools are the finest on the Strip.

Left: high rollers sleep in luxury, and often for free.

dations, where marble and mahogany abound. Baths feature oversize marble tubs, and rooms are tastefully decorated with art and sculpture.

Excalibur

3850 Las Vegas Boulevard South; tel: 597-7777 or 877-750-5464; fax: 597-7009; www.excalibur.com; $$; bus: Deuce; map p.139 C1/C2

Excalibur offers a Renaissance Faire experience aimed at families and budget travelers. Considering the hotel's gaudy exterior, rooms are restrained, with wrought-iron accents over dark wood and contemporary touches of red, blue, and green.

SEE ALSO CHILDREN P.56

Flamingo Las Vegas

3555 Las Vegas Boulevard South; tel: 733-3111 or 800-732-2111; fax: 733-3528; www.flamingolv.com; $$–$$$; monorail: Flamingo/Caesars Palace, bus: Deuce; map p.138 B4/C4

Mobster Bugsy Seigel would hardly recognize the hotel he built in 1946, giving the Las Vegas Strip its start. Little has been left intact to hint at the Flamingo's shady past. Today

the newly refurbished rooms feature king-size beds and soft earth tone decor. A full-wall mirror makes each room seem twice as big as it is.

Four Seasons

3960 Las Vegas Boulevard South; tel: 632-5000 or 877-632-5000; fax: 632-5195; www.fourseasons.com; $$$$; bus: Deuce; map p.139 D1

Quiet, ultra-luxurious accommodations on the upper floors of the Mandalay Bay tower *(see p.22)* are accessed only via a private-lobby elevator. The two-story main building houses the

lobby, four restaurants and bars, a health spa, and meeting rooms. A large pool set in a lush garden is available only to Four Seasons guests.

Harrah's

3475 Las Vegas Boulevard South; tel: 369-5000 or 800-HARRAHS; fax: 369-5008; www.harrahs.com; $$; monorail: Harrah's/Imperial Palace, bus: Deuce; map p.138 B4

Bright colors, light wood, and brass fixtures lend an upbeat feel to the accommodations in this venerable resort, which itself has a light, outdoorsy atmosphere. Jacuzzi tubs are available.

Imperial Palace

3535 Las Vegas Boulevard South; tel: 731-3311 or 800-634-6441; fax: 735-8578; www.imperialpalace.com; $$ monorail: Harrah's/Imperial Palace, bus: Deuce; map p.138 B4/C4

Below: the Bellagio's lobby is decorated with more than 2,000 hand-blown flowers created by Dale Chihuly.

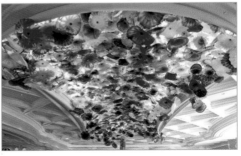

Above: the MGM Grand is the world's largest hotel… for now.

A sprawling complex with comfortable rooms. The adventurous can rent a suite with a mirrored Jacuzzi tub and mirrored ceiling over the bed. The pool area with tumbling waterfall is large and tranquil.

Luxor
3900 Las Vegas Boulevard South; tel: 262-4000 or 800-288-1000; fax: 262-4454; www.luxor.com; $$; bus: Deuce; map p.139 C1
The rooms in the pyramid have one sloping glass wall overlooking the main floor, and most have a shower but no tub (rooms in the towers do have tubs). The rooms feature Art Deco and Egyptian-inspired furnishings, dominated by polished light-and-dark wood headboards, dressers, and armoirs incised with hieroglyphs, and the bathrooms are marble.

There are family-friendly attractions and discount rates are often available.

Mandalay Bay
3950 Las Vegas Boulevard South; tel: 632-7777 or 877-632-7800; fax: 632-7108; www.mandalaybay.com; $$$–$$$$; bus: Deuce; map p.139 C1/D1
Guests at the Mandalay will enjoy an 11-acre tropical environment, including a wave pool, an enormous spa, and a number of trendy restaurants. The decor is lovely and low-key.

MGM Grand
3799 Las Vegas Boulevard South; tel: 891-7777 or 877-880-0880; fax: 891-1030; www.mgmgrand.com; $$$; monorail: MGM Grand, bus: Deuce; map p.139 C3/D2
Four distinct towers result in four different types of room themes. The nicest are in

the Hollywood tower, with gold-speckled walls surrounding maple and cherry furniture. Gilded accents and framed photos of film stars add up to a classy experience.

Monte Carlo
3770 Las Vegas Boulevard South; tel: 730-7777 or 888-529-4828; fax: 730-7250; www.montecarlo.com; $$–$$$; bus: Deuce; map p.138 C2
Striking in its understated European theme, this resort captures an air of continental beauty. The outdoor area is particularly lush, with a wave pool, waterfalls, and a river. Rooms are classically European in flavor and very comfortable. Television sets are concealed in armoires.

New York New York
3790 Las Vegas Boulevard South; tel: 740-6969 or 866-815-4365; fax: 740-6920; www.nynyhotelcasino.com; $$$; bus: Deuce; map p.139 C2
Taking theming to its extreme, rooms here are done in 62 styles, all related to the "Big Apple." Art Deco is the overall inspiration, with round-top furnishings and inlaid wood galore. On average, the rooms are small, but the overall experience is pleasant.

Paris Las Vegas
3655 Las Vegas Boulevard South; tel: 946-7000 or 888-266-5687; fax: 946-4405; www.parislasvegas.com; $$–$$$ monorail: Bally's/Paris Las Vegas, bus: Deuce; map p.138 C3

Prices for a standard double room not including breakfast:
$ $35–60 weekdays
$90–140 weekends
$$ $60–100 weekdays
$140–250 weekends
$$$ more than $100 weekdays
more than $250 weekends
$$$$ The sky's the limit

If you pay a little extra, you can get a room in Paris Las Vegas with windows facing the Strip and enjoy the best possible view of the Bellagio's fountain show *(see p.38–9)* across the street.

Even the lowest-priced rooms here offer luxuriant European decor, with custom-made, vaguely French Regency-style furniture, full-length mirrors and marble bathrooms with separate tubs and showers.

THEhotel at Mandalay Bay

3950 Las Vegas Boulevard South; tel: 632-7777 or 877-632-7800; fax 632-7013; www.mandalaybay.com; $$$; bus: Deuce; map p. 139 C1/D1

The rooms at the Mandalay Bay are among the most spacious on the Strip, even the lowest-priced ones, and feature dining tables, panoramic floor-to-ceiling windows and elegant stonework bathrooms with double sinks and lighted makeup mirrors.

Tropicana Resort and Casino

3801 Las Vegas Boulevard South; tel: 739-2222 or 800-634-4000; fax: 739-2469; www.tropicanalv.com; $–$$$;

monorail: MGM Grand, bus: Deuce; map p.139 C2/D2

Aimed at adult travelers, the Tropicana is one of the few hotels dating back to the "old" Las Vegas of the 1950s and its rates are among the lowest on the Strip. The motif is somewhat Polynesian. The standard rooms are light, plain and functional, accented by bedspreads and draperies in bright tropical designs. Many on the lower floors look out onto lush foliage that surrounds the pool and offers a buffer against the urban clamor. The tropical pool area has swim-up blackjack tables.

Northern Strip

Algiers

2845 Las Vegas Boulevard South; tel: 735-3311 or 800-732-3361; fax: 792-2112; www.algiershotel.com; $$; bus: Deuce; map p.136 B3

This vintage mom-and-pop motel across from Circus Circus *(see right)* offers a quiet haven right on the strip. There are video poker machines in the reception area, a pool fringed with palm trees and a patio café.

Circus Circus

2880 Las Vegas Boulevard South; tel: 734-0410 or 800-

Above: Circus Circus is a long-standing favorite for young families on a budget.

444-2472; fax: 734-5897; www.circuscircus.com; $$ bus: Deuce; map p.136 B2

Circus Circus is Las Vegas's original family-friendly, low-roller hotel-casino. The renovated lobby is classy, but you cannot expect Strip accommodations at this price without compromise. Rooms are typical chain hotel style, with blue carpeting and blonde wood furniture.

Mirage

3400 Las Vegas Boulevard South; tel: 791-7111 or 800-374-9000; fax: 791-7446; www.mirage.com; $$$; bus: Deuce; map p.138 B4

A lovely Polynesian resort, the Mirage was the earliest of the Strip's post-1950s themed additions. The refurbished rooms have a distinctive beach resort feel, with subdued neutral colors, flowery fabrics and gold accents. Most have marbled entries and baths, and there are many canopied beds.

To stay in Circus Circus's newer rooms, request one in the West Tower.

Below: despite the elegant details, check in at the larger resorts can be about as appealing as an airport.

map p.136 B3/B4

Left: the Venetian's extensive canals make for a pleasant, if surreal, stroll.

2121; fax: 791-2027; www.saharavegas.com; $$; monorail: Sahara, bus: Deuce; map p.136 B3/B4

A recent $100-million renovation went the usual Vegas route, replacing a dark and plush atmosphere with lighter decor. The result is one of attractive comfort for tour groups, conventioneers, and mid-budget travelers. The exceptionally spacious rooms are bright, utilizing lots of earth tones and wood, with floral print fabrics and cheerful art on the walls. Suites have separate parlors with mini-bars, and a sofa and chairs arranged around a central table for meetings.

Stratosphere Tower Hotel and Casino
2000 Las Vegas Boulevard South; tel: 380-7777 or 800-998-6937; fax: 383-5334; www.stratospherehotel.com; $–$$$; bus: Deuce; map p.136 B4

Accommodations are located in three of the mid-rise towers. Rooms are surprisingly comfortable, and nicely decorated with Art Deco touches and black lacquer. The least costly rooms are more compact.

TI – Treasure Island
3300 Las Vegas Boulevard South; tel: 894-7111 or 800-944-7444; fax: 894-7414; www.treasureisland.com; $$$; bus: Deuce; map p.136 B1

A recent renovation has ditched the kid-oriented motif in favor of a more grown-up theme. Affordable and comfortable, rooms are housed in a Y-shaped tower, with the cheaper rooms on the lower floors and more expensive ones higher up.

New Frontier
3120 Las Vegas Boulevard South; tel: 794-8200 or 800-421-7806; fax: 794-8445; www.frontierlv.com; $$; bus: Deuce; map p.136 B1

A reincarnation of one of the longest-established hotels on the Strip, with a venerable history – Elvis first played here. While the hotel has a Wild West motif, it doesn't carry over into the guest rooms, which are motor-inn modern and surprisingly spacious, with all the amenities you'd expect from a Strip hotel.

Riviera Hotel and Casino
2901 Las Vegas Boulevard South; tel: 734-5110 or 800-634-6753; fax: 794-9451; www.rivierahotel.com; $$; bus: Deuce; map p.136 B2/C3

One of the older Strip resorts, the Riviera is best viewed as a historic lodging, Vegas-style. It was the largest casino resort hotel in the world when it was built some 50 years ago, and for decades it was considered the finest hotel on the Strip. Though renovated, the rooms have a certain quaintness. Most tower rooms offer views of the pool or mountains. Like other 1950s and 1960s-era hotels along the Strip, its rates offer great value for budget-conscious visitors.

Sahara Hotel and Casino
2535 Las Vegas Boulevard South; tel: 737-2111 or 888-696

Prices for a standard double room not including breakfast:
$ $35–60 weekdays
$90–140 weekends
$$ $60–100 weekdays
$140–250 weekends
$$$ more than $100 weekdays
more than $250 weekends
$$$$ The sky's the limit

Venetian

3355 Las Vegas Boulevard
South; tel: 414-1000 or 877-
883-6423; fax 414-1100;
www.venetian.com; $$$$;
monorail: Harrah's/Imperial
Palace; bus: Deuce; map
p.138 B4/C4

The breathtaking Venetian is
reigning monarch among the
Vegas destination resorts
that strive to re-create great
cities of the world. All guest
accommodations are suites,
the smallest of them being
650sq ft. Done in elegant
Old-World style, they have
canopied beds and sunken
living rooms, with a minimum of two TVs and three
phones, as well as in-room
fax/ copier/printer units and
other business amenities
that suggest this as an ideal
place for conventioneers
with unlimited expense
accounts.

Wynn Las Vegas

3131 Las Vegas Boulevard
South, tel: 770-7100 or 888-
320-9996; www.wynnlas-
vegas.com; $$$$; bus: Deuce;
map p.136 B1/B2

The flagship property of
international hotel tycoon
Steve Wynn, who built and
sold the Mirage and then the
Bellagio; this is the only

Above: though the Stratosphere towers over its competitors,
rooms are only located in its shorter buildings.

casino resort in the world to
have received a Mobil 5-Star
rating and a AAA 5-Diamond
rating. Guest rooms, the
smallest of which are a generous 640sq ft, are deco-
rated in warm tan and
sienna, with original paintings on the walls, and all feature pillow-top mattresses,
sofas, desks, and dining
tables, as well as flat-screen
LCD high-definition televi-
sions. Suites come in a variety of individually decorated
configurations (Steve Wynn
himself lives in one of them),
and most have views of the
Strip or the hotel golf course.
Rates are startling.

Beyond the Strip

There are many properties
offering rooms and suites,
gaming and other entertainment at lower rates than the
huge hotels and mega-
resorts. Perimeter hotels in
the greater Las Vegas area
are popular with locals and
visitors who want to enjoy
what the resorts have to
offer without having to deal
with the traffic and crowds
on the Strip. Some are
upscale and most have similar amenities offered by the
Strip resorts.

Alexis Park

375 East Harmon Avenue; tel:
796-3330 or 800-582-2228; fax:
796-4334; www.alexispark.com;
$$$; map p.139 D4

A Mediterranean villa on 20
acres of beautifully land-
scaped grounds, this resort
offers volumes beyond the
typical Vegas hotel. Styled
with classy European ele-
gance, all rooms are suites,
with 10 distinct floor plans
and different decor through-
out. A lack of gaming means

Below: Wynn Las Vegas has set new standards for luxury
shopping and dining on the Strip.

Above: exotic room themes dominate some of Vegas's more imaginative hotels.

the place is quiet, but the Alexis is directly across from the Hard Rock Hotel and Casino *(see p.27)* if you are in the mood to hit the tables.

Arizona Charlie's Hotel and Casino
740 South Decatur Boulevard; tel: 258-5200 or 800-342-2695; fax: 258-5192; www.arizona charlies.com; $–$$$; bus: 103

The original Arizona Charlie's (there is another on the way to Boulder City), located about a mile west of the Strip and about 11 miles from the airport, has attractive rooms in earth tone hues with Native American motifs. The premium-rate rooms have flowers, large overstuffed chairs and armoires containing televisions. Hotel amenities include a wedding chapel, swimming pool, airport shuttle, five restaurants, and a buffet.

Artisan
1501 West Sahara Avenue; tel: 214-4000 or 800-554-4092; fax: 733-1571; www.theartisan hotel.com; $$$; bus: 204; map p.136 A3

This small (64-room), elegant European-style boutique hotel has richly appointed rooms and suites in light-and-dark brown hues. Walls are hung with oil paintings and full-length mirrors, and brass sculptures and fittings round out the decor. The lower-rate rooms are on the cozy side, and the suites – including one that has its own billiards table – are amazingly spacious. On the premises are a café and lounge as well as a swimming pool.
SEE ALSO BARS AND CAFÉS P.35

Atrium Suites Hotel
4255 South Paradise Road; tel: 369-4400 or 800-330-7728; fax: 369-3770; $$$; bus: 108; map p.139 D4

East of the Strip, this non-gaming, all-suites hotel is 3 miles from the airport. Guest suites are all alike except that the bedrooms offer a choice of one king or two double beds. The living rooms have armchairs, dining tables and chairs, coffee tables and sofas that fold out into extra beds. Room amenities include refrigerators and wet bars. Exercise facilities, business services and meeting rooms, pool, airport shuttle, concierge desk, restaurant, room service, cable TV, and data port.

Carriage House
105 East Harmon Avenue; tel: 798-1020 or 800-221-2301; fax: 798-1020; www.carriage-house lasvegas.com; $$$; map p.139 D3

This condo suite hotel, one block from the Strip near the MGM Grand, has no casino, but it does have in-room movies, pool, whirlpool, sports court, airport shuttle, concierge desk, restaurant, room service, and cable TV. Fully equipped kitchens are a big plus.

Clarion Hotel– Emerald Springs
325 East Flamingo Road; tel: 732-9100 or 800-732-7889; fax: 731-9784; www.clarionlas vegas.com; $$; bus: 202; map p.139 D2

This attractive non-gaming hotel has soft-hued standard

Below: most casino resorts have sizeable shopping and eating areas within easy reach of your room.

rooms and suites feature typical motor home amenities such as refrigerators, hair dryers and voice mail. The TVs have pay-per-view movies and Nintendo. Hotel features include exercise facilities, business services, a pool, airport shuttle, restaurant and room service. The location is good – 3 miles from the airport and only three blocks from the Strip.

Convention Center Marriott Suites

325 Convention Center Drive; tel: 650-2000 or 800-228-9290; fax: 650-9466; www.marriott. com; $$$; monorail: Las Vegas Hilton, bus: 108; map p.136 C2

This all-suite hotel 3 miles from the airport is designed for conventioneers, with meeting rooms of all sizes for breakout sessions. Guest suites are light and airy, with business extras like voice mail and wireless Internet access. The hotel has exercise facilities, business services, a swimming pool, and restaurant.

SEE ALSO CONFERENCE SURVIVAL P.62–3

Embassy Suites Convention Center

3600 Paradise Road; tel: 893-8000 or 800-362-2779; fax: 893-0378; www.eslvcc.com; $$$; bus: 108; map p.137 D1

Located just three blocks from the Convention Center, this non-gaming, all-suites venue has a restaurant, room service, shopping, exercise facilities and pool.

Gold Coast Hotel and Casino

4000 West Flamingo Road; tel: 367-7111 or 800-331-5334; fax: 367-8575; www.goldcoast casino.com; $$; bus 202; map p.138 A3

The centerpieces of the guest rooms at the Gold Coast are 32-inch LED TVs with in-room movies. The rooms, with their subdued decor and picture windows, have all standard amenities, and there is a bowling center, three lounges, a dance hall, and a theatre on the premises.

Greek Isles Hotel and Casino

305 Convention Center Drive; tel: 952-8000 or 800-633-1777; fax: 952-8100; www.greek islesvegas.com; $$; bus: 108; map p.136 C2

This business-oriented hotel is characterized by its Greek decor, with a fountain in the lobby and an indoor "sidewalk" taverna. Showroom and comedy lounge, wedding chapel, exercise facilities, business services, pool, airport shuttle, and restaurant. Rooms are spacious, with blackout drapes. Suites and "mini-suites" have views of the mountains or the Strip.

Hard Rock Hotel

4455 Paradise Road; tel: 693-5000 or 800-HRD-ROCK; fax: 693-5010; www.hardrockhotel. com; $$; bus: 108, 711; map p.139 D4

The ultramodern rooms and suites have wide-screen plasma TVs and Bose CD systems. Otherwise, the furnishings are minimal enough so that even the rowdiest of rock bands would have a hard time trashing them.

Below: straight through the golden axes for the Hard Rock Hotel.

Hooters Casino Hotel

115 East Tropicana Avenue; tel: 739-9000 or 866-584-6687; fax: 736-1120; www. hooterscasinohotel.com; $$; monorail: MGM Grand, bus: 201; map p.139 D2

Formerly the Hotel San Remo, this small hotel a block off the Strip, dwarfed by the neighboring Tropicana Hotel, features Florida-casual decor, with narrow rooms that have potted palms and king-size beds with tropical print bedspreads. The elaborate swimming pool area rocks with reggae and island music. The hotel seems to be entirely staffed by young women in bikinis and sarongs. Affordable rates and a party atmosphere make this a students' favorite.

King Albert Motel

185 Albert Avenue; tel: 732-1555 or 800-553-7753; $; map p.139 C1

Low rates and a dog-friendly policy are the main reasons to consider this mom-and-pop motel about a mile from the Strip. Some rooms have kitchenettes, and there is a pool and a laundromat.

Las Vegas Hilton

3000 Paradise Road; tel: 732-

Above: off the Strip, competition is fierce amongst smaller motels.

5111 or 888-732-7117; fax: 794-3611; www.lvhilton.com; $$$; monorail: Las Vegas Hilton, bus: 108; map p.137 C3

The most luxurious of the conventioneer-oriented hotels clustered around the huge Las Vegas Convention Center, the Hilton has been popular ever since it opened more than 30 years ago. The newly renovated rooms have all the classic amenities you would expect, including king-size beds, large bedroom closets and marble-tiled bathrooms. Pricier rooms have plasma TVs and views of the Strip. Within the hotel are a swimming pool, Jacuzzis, a spa, tennis courts and a video arcade that has extreme sports simulators.

Orleans Hotel and Casino
4500 West Tropicana Avenue;

Splurge for a suite in the Rio's Masquerade Tower and you get a panoramic 180-degree view of the city.

tel: 365-7111 or 800-675-3267; fax: 365-7500; www.orleans casino.com; $$–$$$; bus: 201; map p.138 A1

The guest rooms here are among the city's largest— from 450sq ft for standard "deluxe" rooms to as much as 2,500sq ft for the largest suites – and can be an excellent bargain. They are lavishly appointed, with decor in brass, antiques, and lace. All have separate sitting areas and views of either the Strip or the mountains. Valet service and 24-hour room service round out a full house of conventional amenities. On the premises are no less than 14 restaurants, cafés, and fast-food outlets, as well as a large casino, a spa, a showroom, bowling alleys, and an arena where the Las Vegas Wranglers pro hockey team plays.

Palms Casino Resort
4321 West Flamingo Road; tel: 942-7777 or 866-942-7770; fax 942-7001; www.palms.com; $$$; bus 202; map p.138 A2

This towering casino hotel has two unique claims to fame – an on-premises recording studio (guests who reserve studio time can record from any room in the hotel) and the world's last remaining Playboy Club. Guest rooms range from minimally appointed "deluxe" rooms to large, colorful, lavishly furnished penthouse suites with some of the best Strip views in town.

Renaissance Las Vegas
3400 Paradise Road; tel: 784-5700 or 800-750-0980; fax 735-3130; www.renaissance-las vegas.com; $$$$; monorail: Las Vegas Hilton, bus: 108; map p.137 C2

This new hotel next to the Las Vegas Convention Center

has colorful rooms – many of them accented in lime green and pumpkin orange – with spacious, fully equipped work areas and flat-screen LCD TVs in every room.

Rio All-Suites Hotel and Casino
3700 West Flamingo Road; tel: 252-7777 or 866-746-7671; fax: 252-8909; www.riolas vegas.com; $$–$$$$; bus: 202; map p.138 A3

Good value off the Strip, this huge, illuminated all-suite casino hotel has large, spacious rooms and the best buffet in town. Each suite has at least 600sq ft of space and a 32-in TV. Furnishings are a mix of Old-World and ultra-modern styles.

St Tropez All Suite Hotel
455 East Harmon Avenue; tel: 369-5400 or 800-666-5400; fax: 369-8901; www. sttropez lasvegas.com; $$–$$$$; map p.139 C3

Palms and pines shade the park-like grounds surrounding the St Tropez, with its large free-form swimming pool and low-rise Mediterranean-style buildings. Rooms are decorated in the palest of earth tones for a light, cheery feel. Rooms with whirlpool tubs are available. The small (150-room) hotel has no casino on

Right: one of the cheapest rooms (well, beds) in town.

Prices for a standard double
room not including breakfast:
$ $35–60 weekdays
$90–140 weekends
$$ $60–100 weekdays
$140–250 weekends
$$$ more than $100 weekdays
more than $250 weekends
$$$$ The sky's the limit

the premises, but gaming
enthusiasts can cross the
street to the Hard Rock Hotel
(see p.27). Hotel features
include a restaurant and a fitness center. Pets are
accepted, and there is parking for motor homes.

Sam's Town Hotel and Casino
5111 Boulder Highway; tel: 456-
7777 or 634-6371; fax: 454-
8017; www.samstown.com;
$–$$$; bus 107

The rustic Wild West and
Native American decor may
sound kitschy, but the rooms
here are quiet, comfortable,
and attractive. The real treat
is the nine-story atrium over
an indoor park, complete
with live trees, running water,
and footpaths.

Silverton Hotel and Casino
3333 Blue Diamond Road;
tel: 263-7777 or 800-588-7711;
fax: 896-5635; www.silverton
casino.com; $–$$

Near the airport, this West-
ern-themed "lodge" features
faux wood-beam ceilings, pillow-top beds, and rustic dark
wood furnishings. Some
suites even have hunting trophies on the walls. There's a
swimming pool, several
restaurants and a buffet as
well as room service, a cocktail lounge, and a showroom.

Sin City Hostel
1208 Las Vegas Boulevard
South; tel: 868-0222; fax 384-
1490; www.sincityhostel.com;
$; bus: Deuce; map p.134 B2

This friendly, recently refurbished former IYH hostel

Above: most hotels have a pool of some description to provide
guests with relief from the intense desert heat.

offers the cheapest beds in
town, in both six-bed co-ed
dorm rooms and very basic
private rooms. Facilities
include a communal kitchen
and shared baths, as well as
a TV room with DVD player.

Sunset Station
1301 West Sunset Road; tel:
547-7777 or 888-786-7389; fax:
547-7744; www.sunsetstation.
com; $$

The Mediterranean interior
of the Sunset Station is
stunning. Amenities include
a 13-screen movie theater
and KidsQuest indoor play
area, making this a sure-fire
family winner.

SEE ALSO MOVIES P.94–5

Downtown

Binion's Horseshoe Hotel and Casino
128 East Fremont Street; tel:
382-1600 or 800-237-6537; fax:
382-5750; www.binions.com; $;
map p.134 B3

Following a recent interior
renovation, the guest rooms
are clean and modern,
though there are no frills.
There's a rooftop pool, seven
restaurants, a buffet, room
service, and cable TV.

California Hotel
12 East Ogden Avenue; tel: 385-
1222 or 800-634-6505; fax:
388-2610; www.thecal.com; $;
map p.134 B4

Despite its name, the rooms
at this hotel are decorated in
Hawaiian style, with tropical
pastel hues, rattan furniture,
and white plantation shutters.
The hotel has a rooftop
swimming pool, a concierge
desk, three restaurants, and
room service, as well as in-
room first-run movies.

El Cortez Hotel and Casino
600 East Fremont Street; tel:
385-5200 or 800-634-6703; fax:
385-1554; www.elcortezhotel
casino. com; $; map p.134 B3

29

Above: the theme Downtown portrays is a bygone era.

The most pleasant guest accommodations at this vintage hotel are in the 14-story tower, where suites are bright and nicely furnished with French Provincial influences, but the fine older rooms seem stuck in time somewhere in the mid-20th century.

Fitzgeralds Casino and Hotel

301 Fremont Street; tel: 388-2400 or 800-724-5825; fax: 388-2478; www.fitzgeraldslas vegas.com; $; map p.134 B3
Many rooms offer nice views of the city and mountains within comfortable surroundings. Accommodations are of the Holiday Inn variety. Attractive views of the Fremont Street Experience can also be enjoyed in this (mostly) low-roller haven.

Four Queens Casino and Hotel

202 East Fremont Street; tel: 385-4011 or 800-634-6045; fax: 387-5185; www.fourqueens. com; $; map p.134 B3
The pleasant, affordable rooms have Southwestern earth-tone decor, and all feature 32-inch high-definition flat-panel TVs and wireless Internet access.

Fremont Hotel and Casino

200 East Fremont Street; tel: 385-3232 or 800-634-6460; fax: 385-6229; www.fremont casino. com; $; map p.134 B3
Daily fresh flowers enliven the Fremont's guest rooms, which are decorated in soft, relaxing tones. Guests can use the rooftop pool at the Fremont's sister hotel, the California (see p.29).

Golden Gate Hotel and Casino

1 Fremont Street; tel: 385-1906 or 800-426-1906; fax: 393-9681; www.goldengatecasino. net; $; map p.134 B3
This charming old hotel was established in 1906. It had Vegas's first telephone and electric sign. Today, its small, period-style rooms, with plaster walls and mahogany doors, hark back to another era.

Golden Nugget

129 East Fremont Street; tel: 385-7111 or 800-846-5336; fax: 386-8362; www.goldennugget. com; $$; map p.134 B3
The 1946 Golden Nugget is the jewel of Downtown; metropolitan elegance supersedes the surrounding glitz. Guests enter a gilded lobby full of marble and crystal. The misted pool area is landscaped with palms. Rooms, decorated in rich brown and beige with wood-paneled or fabric walls, fine furnishings, and marble baths with separate vanity areas, are luxurious enough to have earned a top AAA rating.

Main Street Station Brewery and Hotel

200 North Main Street; tel: 387-1896 or 800-713-8933; fax: 386-4466; www.mainstreet casino.com; $; map p.134 B4
Main Street Station's Victorian theme does not carry over into the recently refurbished guest rooms, which are spacious, quiet, and simply decorated.

Plaza Hotel and Casino

1 Main Street; tel: 386-2110 or 800-634-6575; fax: 382-8281;

Main Street Station is Las Vegas's best-kept secret, as the Victorian-styled casino is filled with antiques. The lobby even has Buffalo Bill Cody's railroad car, and there's a piece of the Berlin wall in the men's room.

Prices for a standard double room not including breakfast:
$ $35–60 weekdays
$90–140 weekends
$$ $60–100 weekdays
$140–250 weekends
$$$ more than $100 weekdays
more than $250 weekends
$$$$ The sky's the limit

www.plazahotelcasino.com; $; map p.134 B4

A few steps from the Greyhound station. Rooms are clean and functional, though many are small, and all have cable TVs. There are exercise facilities, a rooftop swimming pool, a wedding chapel, and three restaurants.

Vegas Club Casino Hotel
18 East Fremont Street; tel: 385-1664 or 800-634-6532; fax: 387-6071; www.vegasclub casino.net; $; map p.134 B4

Pretty in pink, an odd decor choice for a sports-themed hotel, the Vegas Club's rooms come in a variety of sizes. All are spacious, with sofas or love seats and cable TVs. Guests have the use of the rooftop pool at the nearby Plaza Hotel *(see left)*.

MOTELS
Crest Budget Motel
207 North Sixth Street; tel: 382-5642; $; map p.134 B4

The best that can be said for this vintage apartment motel is that it is close to the downtown casinos, allows pets, and costs less than staying in the local youth hostel. Amenities include complementary coffee and breakfast, cable TV, and microwave ovens.

Downtowner Motel
129 North Eighth Street; tel: 384-1441 or 800-777-2566; $; map p.134 C4

This large motel offers plain, somewhat run-down rooms with kitchenettes, but at least

it offers free donuts and coffee in the morning.

Mount Charleston
Mount Charleston Lodge
1200 Old Park Road, 872-5408 or 800-955-1314; www.mtcharlestonlodge.com; $$$–$$$$; map p.14

This rustic lodge in Humboldt-Toiyabe National Forest's Kyle Canyon offers the only accommodations on Mount Charleston. Nestled among ponderosa pine and aspen trees, its rooms are in individual rough-hewn A-frame log cabins, each with a fireplace, king-size beds, a separate living room, and a private deck. Some also have VCRs or DVDs, microwaves, and refrigerators. Views are spectacular, wildlife abounds, and the excitement of the Las Vegas Strip is only 35 minutes away.

SEE ALSO RED ROCK CANYON AND MOUNT CHARLESTON P.14–5

Boulder City
Boulder Dam Hotel
1305 Arizona Street; tel: 293-3510; fax: 293-3093; www.boulder damhotel.com; $$; map p.16

This quaint, historic and centrally located 22-room bed-and-breakfast has a restaurant that is considered

Boulder City's best, as well as room service, a gift shop, and exercise facilities.

SEE ALSO LAKE MEAD, VALLEY OF FIRE AND HOOVER DAM P.17; MUSEUMS AND GALLERIES P.102

Hacienda Hotel and Casino
US Highway 93; tel: 293-5000 or 800-245-6380; fax: 293-5608; www.haciendaonline.com; $$; map p.16

Accommodations at this outlying casino resort run the gamut from very simple "economy rooms" to spacious, luxury-lake view rooms and suites. The hotel has three restaurants and a buffet, a 24-hour store, a swimming pool, Jacuzzis, and helicopter tours of Lake Mead and Hoover Dam.

North of the City
Suncoast
9090 Alta Drive; tel: 636-7111 or 877-677-7111; fax 636-7288; www.suncoastcasino.com; $

This casino hotel in the Vegas suburb of Summerlin offers exceptionally spacious rooms with floor-to-ceiling picture windows. Good value and low prices. The hotel has a bowling alley, movie theater complex, and 500-seat showroom with dance floor.

SEE ALSO MOVIES P.95

Below: some executive suites make a comfortable home away from home.

31

Bars and Cafés

Las Vegas has ranked as the apex of the US bar scene for more than half a century. Though yesteryear's casino lounge crooners may be mostly a memory, replaced by techno DJs, hip-hoppers, and old-time rockers, the range of bars and clubs in the big hotels and beyond includes everything from ultra-sophisticated dance venues to raunchy country-and-western saloons, aquarium bars to Irish pubs. Famous-name club franchises from NYC, Hollywood, and South Beach have also established trendy Vegas outposts. Here is a definitive cross-section of the best places to see, be seen, scream and shout, or just mellow out.

Southern Strip

Bar at Times Square
New York New York, 3790 Las Vegas Boulevard South; tel: 740-6969; Mon–Wed 10am–2am, Thur and Sun til 3am, Fri and Sat til 4am; bus: Deuce; map p.139 C2

This polished-wood New York-style pub features high-energy dueling pianos that spew everything from Elton John and Billy Joel hits to Barry Manilow covers. It is always New Year's Eve at this not-at-all-mellow piano bar packed to the rafters with folk waiting for the ball to drop.

Café Bellagio
Bellagio Casino, 3600 Las Vegas Boulevard South, tel: 693-7223; 24 hours; monorail: Bally's/Paris Las Vegas, bus: Deuce; map p.138 B3

Located in Bellagio's ever-changing Conservatory, this gleaming café has a light and airy atmosphere with a gorgeous pool and botanical garden views.

SEE ALSO RESTAURANTS P.109

Caramel Bellagio
Bellagio Casino; 3600 Las Vegas Boulevard South; tel:

Above: casino cocktail bars create exotic drinks.

693-8300; daily 5pm–4am; monorail: Bally's/Paris Las Vegas, bus: Deuce; map p.138 B3

Leather couches and blown glass decor set the mood for pricy martinis and music that ranges from vintage Sinatra to hip-hop in this sleek watering hole with a view of the casino floor. Reservations required; dress code.

Cleopatra's Barge
Caesars Palace, 3570 Las Vegas Boulevard South; tel: 731-7845; daily 6pm–3am; monorail: Flamingo/Caesars Palace, bus: Deuce; map p.138 B3/B4

The usually packed dance floor, a replica of the boat that carried the queen of Egypt on the Nile in ancient times, floats in a pool just deep enough to rock gently. The music is slow-dancing classic pop.

Coyote Ugly
New York-New York, 3790 Las Vegas Boulevard South; tel: 212-8804; daily 6pm–3am; cover after 9pm; bus: Deuce; map p.139 C2

Hot-looking women in skin-tight blue jeans dance on the bar and whoop it up, ensuring a nonstop loud party atmosphere. There are no chairs or stools, only standing room, and only beers and straight shots are served. Decor includes a "Bra Wall of Fame" where women patrons can leave their undergarments for posterity.

Non-drinkers need not feel left out of Las Vegas's something-for-everybody club scene. Most bars and lounges now offer highly caffeinated "energy drinks," and a few even sell hits of pure oxygen.

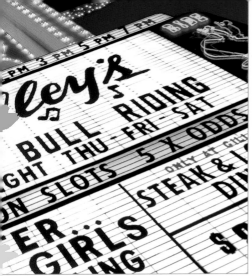

Left: Gilley's motto: "cold beer, dirty girls."

730-7777; daily 11am–2am, food til 10pm; snacks til late; bus: Deuce; map p.138 C2
Good meals, great brews, and music from 9pm nightly in the first microbrewery in a Las Vegas resort. The casual atmosphere tends to attract a noisy, but fun-loving crowd.

Napoleon's Champagne Bar
Paris Las Vegas; 3655 Las Vegas Boulevard South; tel: 946-7000; Sun–Thur 4pm–2am, Fri–Sat til 3am; monorail: Bally's/Paris Las Vegas, bus: Deuce; map p.138 C3
Though Las Vegas's controversial ban on smoking in public places (except casinos) pulled the rug out from under the Paris resort's renowned cigar and pipe lounge, the elegant club continues to serve fine cognac and single-malt scotch as well as more than 100 champagnes and sparkling wines.

Below: probably not the pot of Goldschlager she had hoped for.

Dublin Up
O'Sheas Casino; 3555 Las Vegas Boulevard South; tel: 697-2711; 24 hours; monorail: Flamingo/Caesars Palace; bus: Deuce; map p.139 B4/C4
Remove the glitz and the glamour from The Strip and this is what it boils down to: shots poured in your mouth by a vertically challenged bartender *(see picture right)* and an 18-hour happy hour. Still, the lack of pretention is refreshing.

Harley Davidson Café
3725 Las Vegas Boulevard South; tel: 740-4555; www.harley-davidsoncafe.com; Sun–Thur 11am–11pm, Fri–Sat til midnight; monorail: MGM Grand, bus: Deuce; map p.139 C2
Hard to miss with its seven-ton giant replica of a Harley hog protruding above the entrance, this fun eatery serves 50s drive-in fare – cheeseburgers, fries, malts – amid Route 66 memorabilia and vintage customized bikes.

Jimmy Buffet's Margaritaville
Flamingo, 3555 Las Vegas Boulevard South; tel: 733-3302; www.margaritavillelasvegas.com; Sun–Thur 11am–2am, Fri–Sat til 2.30am; monorail: Flamingo/Caesars Palace, bus: Deuce; map p.138 B4/D4
You can't miss the parrot-head music spilling out onto the Strip from this self-consciously laid-back saloon appropriately located in the Flamingo hotel. Jamaican jerk, Cuban sandwiches, and house-brand tequila are served under a full-size plane hung from the ceiling.

Mix
THE hotel at Mandalay Bay, 3950 Las Vegas Boulevard South; tel: 632-9500; daily from 5pm, cover after 10pm; bus: Deuce; map p.139 C1/D1
Sixty-four stories above the Strip's neon spectacle, the colored lighting illuminates the futuristic white-and-black interior of this ultra-elegant penthouse restaurant and lounge. No dress code, though the disco lounge is packed with beautiful people dressed to the nines.

Monte Carlo Pub & Brewery
Monte Carlo Casino; 3770 Las Vegas Boulevard South; tel:

33

Above: Ra nightclub at the Luxor has a state-of-the-art light and sound system.

Piano Bar
Harrah's Casino, 3475 Las Vegas Boulevard South; tel: 369-5000; Mon–Fri 4pm–2am, Sat and Sun 9am–3am; monorail: Harrah's/ Imperial Palace, bus: Deuce; map p.138 B4

Though this bar just off the casino floor, with its day-at-the-beach decor, is no longer known as La Playa, the new incarnation still features duelling pianos and nightly karaoke – your chance to be a Vegas lounge singer, aided by boat drinks in exotic glasses.

Ra
Luxor, 3900 Las Vegas Boulevard South; tel: 262-4400; www.ralv.com; Wed–Sat 10.30pm–dawn; bus: Deuce; map p.139 C1

An enormous club full of pretty young things dancing the night away and a sushi bar for the more sophisticated.

Red Square
Mandalay Bay; 3950 Las Vegas Boulevard South; tel: 632-7407; Sun–Thur 5pm–11pm, Fri–Sat til midnight; bus: Deuce; map p.139 C1/D1

Unique and unforgettable, this Russian-themed club features a statue of Lenin decapitated during the fall of the USSR and more than 100 varieties of vodka served on an ice bar in a freezer vault

(fur coats and hats provided). Playboy calls it "the best bar scene in America."

Rumjungle
Mandalay Bay, 3950 Las Vegas Boulevard South; tel: 632-5300; Sun, Tue and Wed 11pm–2am, Fri–Sat and Mon til 4am, Thur til 3am; bus: Deuce; map p.139 C1/D1

Priced to keep the riffraff out – $25 cover, $40 for an all-night restroom pass, plus an extra charge to sit at a table – the newly refurbished Rumjungle boasts waterfalls, walls of fire and the biggest bar in town, plus hot Caribbean dance music.

Shadow Bar
Caesars Palace; 3750 Las Vegas Boulevard South; tel: 731-7110; Mon–Thur 4pm–2am, Fri–Sat 2pm–3am, Sun 2pm–2am; monorail: Flamingo/ Caesars Palace, bus: Deuce; map p.138 B3/B4

You can sit at the curvaceous purple neon bar and stare for hours at naked (well, body-stockinged) women dancers silhouetted behind, hence the name of this club, which caters to a rather upscale casino crowd.

Northern Strip

Dino's
1516 Las Vegas Boulevard South; tel: 382-3894,

www.dinoslv.com; 24 hours; bus: Deuce; map p.134 B1

Decorated with neon beer signs, big-screen TVs and ceiling murals of boxers, this neighborhood-style bar, managed by the same family for three generations, has been a local favorite since 1960.

Dolphin Bar
The Mirage; 3400 Las Vegas Boulevard South; tel: 791-7111; seasonal hours; monorail: Harrah's/Imperial Palace, bus: Deuce, map p.138 B4

Tropical gardens bloom, lofty palms sway and waterfalls spill into manmade creeks that run through this lush poolside bar. There's mellow piano music after dark. Swimsuits okay. Open only during swimming pool season.

Gilly's
New Frontier; 3120 Las Vegas Boulevard South; tel: 794-8434; www.gilleyslv.com; daily from 4pm; bus: Deuce; map p.136 B1

The only country-and-western bar on the Strip is a Vegas version of the famed Houston-based Urban Cowboy club, and serious swing dancers come here to strut their stuff. Free dance lessons, mud wrestling, and midnight bikini bull riding.

Horse-a-Round Bar
Circus Circus, 2880 Las Vegas Boulevard South, tel: 734-0410; 24 hours; bus: Deuce; map p.136 B2
This small, carousel-style revolving bar, a Vegas classic frequented by Johnny Depp in *Fear and Loathing in Las Vegas*, commands a great view of the casino floor below and aerial circus acts overhead from its location off the mezzanine-level midway.

Kokomo's Lounge
The Mirage; 3400 Las Vegas Boulevard South; tel: 791-7111; 24 hours; monorail: Harrah's/Imperial Palace, bus: Deuce; map p.138 B4
Located outside the Mirage's flagship restaurant, Kokomo's Lounge is surrounded by a well designed tropical rainforest that includes a waterfall.

Peppermill's
Fireside Lounge
2985 Las Vegas Boulevard, tel: 735-7635; 24 hours; bus: Deuce; map p.136 B2
A longtime Vegas classic, this dark, mirrored bar with its friendly waitresses, loveseat booth and a blazing fireplace set in the center of

Above: gourmet bites are available, but most people at Kokomo's Lounge are splashing cash for a pre-meal drink.

a fountain is so intimate that many couples come here just to cuddle and kiss.

V Bar
Venetian; 3355 Las Vegas Boulevard South; tel: 414-3200; daily 5pm–4am; monorail: Harrah's/Imperial Palace, bus: Deuce; map p.138 B4/C4
The claim to fame here is a great selection of the world's finest liquors, served neat or in original specialty cocktails. The minimalist decor focuses attention on the inviting rich leather-upholstered conversation pits. Postmodern jazz gives way to reggae later, and the crowd is just too hip.

Beyond the Strip

Artisan Lounge
Artisan Hotel; 1501 West Sahara Avenue, tel: 214-4000; 24 hours; map p.136 A3
This comfortable bar, its dimly lit leather sofas and dark wood walls, accented with lots of paintings and sculptures, is peacefully tucked away in a non-gambling boutique hotel. It is among the most laid back spots in Las Vegas – until weekend nights at 9pm, when a DJ starts playing hot Latin dance music.

SEE ALSO ACCOMMODATIONS P.26

Champagnes Café
3557 South Maryland Parkway, tel: 737-1699; 24 hours; bus: 109; map p.137 E2
One of the last old-time neighborhood bars in town, Champagnes has Frank and Dino songs on the jukebox, slots that still clatter coins and low-priced drinks, including champagne for less than a beer in any Strip hotel lounge.

Crown and Anchor Pub
1350 East Tropicana Avenue; tel: 739-8676; 24 hours; $20 cover to watch football matches; bus: 711 & 201; map p.10
Fish and chips, more than 70 draft beers from around the world, and UK soccer on the telly make this, the grandfather of all Las Vegas's many English and Irish pubs, one of the most authentic "international" bars in town. There's also live music on Saturdays.

Dispensary Lounge
2451 East Tropicana Avenue; tel: 458-6343; 24 hours; bus: 201, 710, 711
Dim lights, barely heard background music, a beige color scheme, oversized plaid-upholstered chairs, and waitresses in demure leotards and tights, plus the perpetual lulling trickle of a 10-ft

Below: fighting rum luck at Rumjungle.

Above: fantastic German beers and Bavarian cuisine are the Hofbräuhaus's main attraction.

water wheel, make this a perfectly relaxing hideaway.

Ghostbar

The Palms; 4321 West Flamingo; tel: 942-7777; http://ghostbarlas-vegas.com; daily 8pm–late; reservations recommended; bus: 202; map p.138 A2

A stylish crowd frequents this postmodern indoor-outdoor lounge with a panoramic city view. Soft purple and aqua lighting set the mood for techno dance music. A transparent terrace lets you look straight down into the swimming pool 55 stories below.

Hofbräuhaus

4510 Paradise Road; tel: 853-3227; www.hofbrauhausvegas.com; daily 11am–late; bus: 108, 711; map p.139 E4

This faithful reproduction of Munich's famous four-century-old brewery and beer garden is under the same ownership. It serves imported beers made according to traditions passed down from the original founder, the Duke of Bavaria, in a lively Oktoberfest setting with live German music.

Hookah Lounge

Tiffany Square, 4147 South Maryland Parkway; tel: 731-6030, www.hookahlounge.com; Mon–Thur 5pm–1am, Fri–Sat 5pm–3am; bus: 109; map p.137 E1

Despite Las Vegas's ban on tobacco smoking in public places, this quiet, dimly lit lounge decorated with fine Mediterranean art keeps its tabletop water pipes bubbling with relaxing herb- and sugar cane-based substances.

Ipanema Bar

Rio; 3700 West Flamingo Road; tel: 777-6869; 24 hours; bus: 202; map p.138 A3

Set off the center of the main pit in the Rio casino, the "I-Bar" features projected images of nature with low-key mood music, changing to erotic imagery as the evening goes on. Women bartenders double as go-go dancers in flesh-colored body stockings.

Tilted Kilt

Rio; 3700 West Flamingo Road; tel: 777-2463; www.tiltedkiltnv.com; Mon–Fri 4pm–2am, Sat–Sun noon–2am; bus 202; map p.138 A3

Waitresses scantily clad in tartan plaid are the most authentic thing about this "Scottish Pub" in the Rio resort (with two other identical Las Vegas locations, see website). It features pool tables, plasma TVs and an unexceptional bar menu of Buffalo hot wings, pizzas, clam sandwiches, and the like.

Viva Las Vegas

Hard Rock Casino; 4455 Paradise Road; tel: 800-HRD-ROCK; 24 hours; bus: 711, 108; map p.139 D4

Unfortunately, the Hard Rock does not offer a bar to live up to its heady reputation. This is its best effort, and it at least serves decent cocktails.

Voodoo Lounge

Rio; 3700 West Flamingo Road; tel: 252-7777; daily 24 hours; bus: 202; map p.138 A3

Atop a 50-story hotel tower, this chic dance club features go-go dancers on Plexiglas platforms and great indoor and outdoor city views. The house specialty is a bubbling, smoking concoction of five rums and three liqueurs known as a "Witch Doctor."

Wine Cellar and Tasting Room

Rio; 3700 West Flamingo Road; tel: 777-7962; Sun–Thur 3–11pm, Fri–Sat 3pm–midnight; bus 202; map p.138 A3

This wine bar and retail store boasts the largest selection of fine wines in the United States, with 300 labels served by the glass and 120,000 bottles for sale, ranging in price from $3 to $200,000. You pay for the wines you try; cheese and crackers are free.

Downtown

Beauty Bar

517 Fremont Street; tel: 598-1965; www.beautybar.com; Sun–Tue 9pm–2am, Wed & Thur 5pm–2am, Fri 5pm–4am, Sat 9pm–4am; map p.134 B3

Just when you thought that you had seen everything weird in Las Vegas, here is a trendy club disguised as a 1950s beauty parlor. Vintage hair-dryer chairs and happy-hour manicure demonstrations set the stage for pumping DJ techno and 80s retro glam dance music.

Dave's Aloha Bar

California Casino; 12 East Ogden Avenue; tel: 800-634-6505; 24 hours; map p.134 B4

Just beside the sportsbook and with a couple of slot machines for the more obsessed, you would be forgiven for thinking you had not left the casino. Hardly the place to unwind when you are not gambling.

Ice House Lounge

650 South Main Street; tel: 315-2570; www.icehouse-lounge. com; 24 hours; map p.134 B2

With its Art Deco interior, 1960s furniture and real ice

Above: the California has two casual, but quite basic, places to have a drink.

bar, this reincarnation of the old plant that used to supply ice for all of Las Vegas in the days before home refrigeration is a cool spot for relaxing and watching sports on more than a dozen big plasma TVs.

Triple 7 Brewpub

Main Street Station Casino; 200 North Main Street; tel: 385-7111; daily 11am–7am; map p.134 B4

Among copper-clad brewing pots and antique fixtures, choose between five kinds of burger, gourmet pizzas, barbecue ribs, or pale-ale battered shrimp. There is also an oyster-and-sushi bar, but the

real attraction here is the beer. Connoisseurs rank this as the best microbrewery in Las Vegas.

West of Vegas

J.C. Wooloughan

Rampart Casino; 221 North Rampart Boulevard; tel: 869-7725; daily Sun–Thur 11am–1am, Fri–Sat 11am–2am

Among the most authentic of the Irish pubs that have been opening all over town recently, the interior was built in Ireland and pieced together in Las Vegas. A variety of Irish whiskys and beers are served to the accompaniment of a live Irish band or televised soccer games.

South of Vegas

Mermaid Lounge

Silverton Casino, 3333 Blue Diamond Road; tel: 263-7777; Sun–Thur 10am–3am, 24 hours Fri and Sat; map p.14

The centerpiece of this Poseidon-themed casino bar is the largest aquarium in Las Vegas, a 117,000-gallon tank containing thousands of jellyfish, stingrays, and brightly coloured tropical fish as well as tons of living coral cared for by staff marine biologists. The specialty drinks served here have nautical names.

Below: Viva Las Vegas – the Hard Rock's best drinking den – is filled with memorabilia.

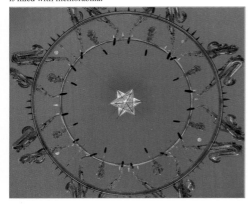

Casinos

Casinos gave Las Vegas its start, first as a saloon town catering to cowboys from area ranches and workers on the Boulder (Hoover) Dam project. When gambling was legalized in Nevada in the 1930s, the city boomed as a mob stronghold as notorious characters such as Bugsy Siegel and Meyer Lansky realized that casinos could be the ultimate money-laundering vehicle. Today the gangsters of yore are gone, and so are most of the cowboys, but games of chance still provide a huge cash flow that supports the Strip's spectacularly over-the-top high life and low life.

Southern Strip

Bally's

3645 Las Vegas Boulevard South; tel: 739-4111 or 800-634-3434; www.ballyslv.com; monorail: Bally's/Paris Las Vegas, bus: Deuce; map p.138–139 C3/C4

Originally built by the world's leading slot machine manufacturer, Bally's has eschewed transformation over the years. Despite the $14-million futuristic light-and-water show out front, Bally's is an exercise in classic Vegas style.

The approach to Bally's is dramatic, via 200ft long moving walkways surrounded by cascading water, lighted pylons, and giant palm trees. Every 20 minutes the entry area erupts with a sound-

Plants and flowers are distributed lavishly throughout the Bellagio's Italianate decor. Nowhere is the display more abundant than under the 50ft high glass ceiling of the Conservatory and botanical garden. The hotel employs 150 gardening staff alone.

Above: before showgirls there were the Dice Girls, El Rancho Las Vegas's pioneering temptations.

and-water show involving a wave machine and blow-hole fountains. Water is very much in favor here. In the multimillion dollar (adult-only) show **Dan Arden's Jubilee!**, which pays tribute to the classic showgirl experience, a replica of the Titanic sinks on stage every night.

In an effort to attract players willing to wager hundreds of thousands of dollars on a single hand ("whales" in

gaming parlance), Bally's has doubled the size of its baccarat room. It also has a highly rated spa for big-spenders to enjoy.

The hotel's Big Kitchen Buffet is also one of the best on the Strip with its Sterling Brunch on Sunday, which includes caviar, lobster, crab legs and prime cut steaks, a further step up in class.

SEE ALSO LIVE ENTERTAINMENT P.88

Bellagio

3600 Las Vegas Boulevard South; tel: 693-7111 or 888-987-6667; www.bellagioresort.com; monorail: Bally's/Paris Las Vegas, bus: Deuce; map p.138 B3

One of the most lavish resorts in Vegas, the Tuscan-themed Bellagio cost more than $1.5 billion to build, requires $2.5 million a day to break even and has almost 9,000 employees.

Approaching from Bally's on the bridge over the Strip, visitors are greeted by operatic arias soaring over the lake, where hundreds of fountains dance to music (ranging from Pavarotti to Gene Kelly), all perfectly programmed to coordinate

Left: casinos tag and number their dice for security purposes.

Casinos play an enormous role in Vegas's travel industry. Here we focus on their atmosphere, history and gaming facilities. For Accommodations see p.20–31, the best in live entertainment is reviewed on p.80–9, while places to eat and drink are reviewed in Bars and Cafés *(see p.32–7)* and Restaurants *(see p.106–19)*

with jets as high as 240ft, fading to clouds of mist in quieter interludes. It is a wonderful spectacle but can get repetitive if staying at one of the classy rooms directly above. The water theme also extends to Bellagio's sensuous Cirque du Soleil Show, **O**.

From the Bellagio bridge, entrance to the resort is along a retail arcade, the **Via Bellagio**, which includes Tiffany, Chanel, Gucci, Armani, Prada, and Hermes.

By the bank of reception desks inside is a wonderfully refreshing garden below an original, iridescent work of glass flowers by the famed artist Dale Chihuly *(see picture p.21)*. Surrounding the lake is an imitation of a village on Lake Como in Italy.

The water for Bellagio's spectacular fountains, all 1.5 million gallons of it, emanates from an aquifer via the resort's exclusive treatment plant. This water also fills the less elaborate lagoons in front of the Mirage and Treasure Island.

Pathways lead to **Café Bellagio**, a 24-hour dining room, and to the Aqua restaurant, with Rauschenberg paintings. To one side of the lounge a pianist plays at the Petrossian caviar bar. This is only one of 17 different eating places in Bellagio, including a sister to New York's **Le Cirque**, and **Picasso**, with furniture and carpet designed by Claude Picasso, son of Pablo, and papa's paintings on the walls. Bellagio's showcases even more artists at its Gallery of Fine Art.

Amidst all this, it may be easy to forget that you have come here to gamble. Bellagio's well rated games compete with Binions downtown *(see p.54)* for the custom of serious gamblers. The casino features a wide range of table games, including Caribbean stud, Big Six, and three-card poker, as well as high-stakes baccarat.

Many Bellagio guests play the off-site Shadow Creek golf course, lined with 21,000 fragrant pine trees from California and Arizona, along with Vegas high rollers who do not mind the $1,000 greens fee (limo transportation, golf cart, and caddie included). Guests can also play the new Primm Valley Golf Course. Both courses are known for the

Below: Bellagio's 1,000-ft lake has around 1,000 water expressions and more than 4,000 individually programmed white lights.

beauty of their rolling terrain and waterfalls, designed by architect Tom Fazio.

SEE ALSO BARS AND CAFÉS P.32; LIVE ENTERTAINMENT P.83; MUSEUMS AND GALLERIES P.96; RESTAURANTS P.108, 109; SHOPPING P.123

Bill's Las Vegas

3595 Las Vegas Boulevard South; tel: 737-2100 or 866-245-5745; www.billslasvegas.com; monorail: Flamingo/Caesars Palace; bus: Deuce; map p.138 C4

Known until recently as the Barbary Coast, this venerable Strip casino was traded to Harrah's for the now-defunct Stardust and renamed for the hotel group's CEO, Bill Harrah. Its eclectic decor features chandeliers with big white globes, Art-Deco glass signs, and waitresses who wear red garters over black-net stockings. Along with its decorative windows in the Victorian Room is what it claims is the world's largest Tiffany-style stained-glass mural. Some tables are set aside for pai gow, a form of poker adapted from an Asian dominoes game, and there is a poker machine played with gold coins that pays $250,000 for a royal flush, or a mere free drink for two pairs.

Table games still dominate, though there are slots. This traditional feel attracts a large number of locals, as do the casino's fine restaurants.

Besides the Victorian Room, there is dining in the Steakhouse at Bill's.

Caesars Palace

3570 Las Vegas Boulevard South; tel: 731-7110 or 800-634-6661; www.caesars.com; monorail: Flamingo/Caesars Palace, bus: Deuce; map p.138 B3/B4

Classic and provocative, Caesars Palace has been a Sin City icon for more than 40 years. Its Roman Empire motif made it the first major international-themed resort in Vegas. The fabulous and venerable façade dominates the

Above: drinks are often complementary to guests playing games.

western side of this portion of the Strip with 50-ft cypresses imported from Italy, and a trio of eye-catching fountains spraying columns of water 35ft into the air.

The approach is dominated by four gold-leaf horses and a charioteer, the fine "Quadriga" statue. The casino's entrance doors are flanked by more replicas of classical statues, including a Venus de Milo. Most famous of all, an 18ft high David dominates the Appian Way inside the casino. Carved from the same Carrara marble as the Michelangelo original but twice the height, the replica weighs 9 tons. The theme continues on the gaming floor, where drinks waitresses wear togas.

The 5-acre Garden of the Gods, named after the Baths of Caracalla frequented by ancient Rome's elite, has three pools and two whirlpool spas, the whole complex landscaped with sweeping lawns, graceful fountains, and classically inspired statu-

Left: It should be no surprise that Caesars Palace has been the setting for more than a dozen movies and over 80 television shows.

ary. A sign at the entrance reads, "European-style topless bathing is permitted at Caesars' pools. We prefer that this is restricted to the Venus pool area." As with most hotel casinos, the pool is for the hotel guests only.

Caesars' 4,000-seat Colosseum is designed to recall the ancient Roman one, and was built specifically to showcase the talents of Canadian singer **Céline Dion**. The singer agreed a $45 million contract to give five shows a week. Caesars also has a long record of hosting concerts by some of the world's top performing artists. Elvis appeared here regularly, and today **Elton John** draws unprecedented crowds during runs of "The Red Piano" show.

Dion's contract is due to expire in 2008 and Bette Midler has already been lined up to be her replacement.

Caesars also has a long association with sports, having been the first hotel in Las Vegas with satellite equipment to relay live sporting events. They even employed former world heavyweight champion Joe Louis as their greeter up to his death in 1981. The former champ is remembered with a 7-ft marble statue standing at the entrance to the Race & Sports Book.

More than 160 major boxing contests, starting with the bout with Larry Holmes that

Above: the Forum Shops, like most of Caesars Palace, is filled with faux statuary and the ceiling provides a dramatic backdrop for consistently changing weather systems.

ended Muhammad Ali's ring career in 1980, and other championship events have been staged at the hotel.

The classy arcade known as the Forum Shops features Dior, Versace, Gucci, Bulgari, Ferragamo, and others, and is always crowded.

Approaching the entrance from the rotunda, with its circular aquarium, the arcade is filled with Aqua-Massage tanks, while Japanese slot machines allow you to box and dance with partners on screen.

When it comes to gambling, there are not many places where the limits are set so generously high, and its sports book is one of the finest in Vegas. It is also, one of the most enjoyable places to watch a big sporting event, even if you don't have any money riding on it. There is also a $500 slot machine with a $1million dollar jackpot.
SEE ALSO LIVE ENTERTAINMENT P.86; SHOPPING P.120

Casino Royale
3411 Las Vegas Boulevard South; tel: 731-3500 or 800-854-7666; www.casinoroyale.com; mono-rail: Harrah's/Imperial Palace, bus: Deuce; map p.138 B4

Like many of Vegas's smaller casinos, the Royale does its best to attract gamblers by setting low minimums and reducing the house's edge. There is even a 25¢ roulette table, which is a great way to learn. As for restaurants, three chains top the list: Denny's, Subway, and Outback Steakhouse.

Excalibur
3850 Las Vegas Boulevard South; tel: 597-7777 or 877-750-5464; www.excalibur.com; bus: Deuce; map p.139 C1/C2

The multicolored spires of the Excalibur look just like a DisneyWorld castle, and it is Disney's target market (the affluent family) that the casino caters to.

Sports books date back to Bugsy Siegel's innovative use of the Trans-America Wire Service, which had a monopoly on relaying horse-race information in the US directly from the race track. No bookie could operate without this information, so Siegel could charge what he liked.

Outside Caesars Palace stands one of Vegas's most unusual, un-Roman monuments: a 4-ton Brahman statue. It has become a site of pilgrimage for superstitious gamblers who leave flowers and other gifts for it and give it a little rub in hope that it will bring them luck.

Alighting from the monorail, visitors are greeted by a sign setting the tone: "Welcome to the medieval time of your life." Across the moat and drawbridge – where Merlin battles a fire-breathing dragon every hour nightly – the resort itself is filled with heraldic motifs, plastic knights bearing battle-axes, Sir Galahad's Prime Rib House, and giggling couples being photographed with their heads in stocks.

Through the endless corridors populated only by huge lamps, the first thing to reach is the Sherwood Forest Café, and then the casino itself. Inside, it is as impressive as its exterior, assuming you have a liking for faux olde England.

When this family-style resort was built in the early

> The Excalibur is one of the best places on the Strip to learn to play poker. Every morning, half-hour sessions of "Kitchen Table Poker" are held. These games are run without money and they teach you the games' various rules. You then play for real with a $10 bankroll.

1990s, it was the world's largest hotel-casino. Some floors are given over to family-friendly non-gambling entertainment, such as the Renaissance Faire on the second floor. Performers in medieval garb play period arrangements on mandolin, flute, and harp, to accompany puppets, mimes, and magicians. Performances are from 10am on the Court Jester's Stage at Medieval Village. Costumed figures

and strolling minstrels roam the area to provide entertainment.

Fantasy Faire holds two motion simulator theaters. The Magic Motion Machines lure visitors into hydraulically activated seats for a rolling ride in either a runaway train or an outer-space demolition derby directed by Hollywood's George Lucas.

The casino's tables cater to low rollers.
SEE ALSO CHILDREN P.56

Flamingo Las Vegas
3555 Las Vegas Boulevard South; tel: 733-3111 or 800-732-2111; www.flamingolv.com; monorail: Flamingo/ Caesars Palace; bus: Deuce; map p.138 B4/C4
The Flamingo of today is a far cry from the carpet joint of Bugsy Siegel's day that started gangland Vegas on its way. Almost the last traces of the mobster elite disappeared in 1995 when his bulletproof casino office with its elaborate escape routes was bulldozed.

It may be known for its garish pink neon sign, but the casino's 15-acre garden, with more plastic flamingos and real penguins, is one of the most charming sights on the Strip, especially at night. There are pools, waterfalls, a lagoon, and a turtle observation bridge, plus a wildlife habitat, with koi, swans, ducks, and – of course – flamingos. The garden is free to the public most days, to hotel guests only at night.

Harrah's
3475 Las Vegas Boulevard South; tel: 369-5000 or 800-HARRAHS; www.harrahs.com; monorail: Harrah's/Imperial Palace; bus: Deuce; map p.138 B4
Carnaval-themed Harrah's La Playa Lounge, with its multicolored palm trees, illuminated rocks, and 3-D mural,

Below: the Flamingo was the first casino on the Strip to use a neon sign.

Above: the Imperial Palace is the only casino with "Dealertainers," who double as celebrity impersonators doing everyone from Dolly Parton to Alice Cooper.

evokes "a day at the beach," the fantasy enhanced by tropical drinks in exotic glasses. There's an outdoor pool and an entertainment plaza, Carnaval Court, with added blackjack tables and stage performers. There is also a bar where bartenders are selected for their skills in singing, dancing, juggling glassware, and breathing fire.

Harrah's vast 87,000-sq ft casino caters to low and high rollers.

Imperial Palace
3535 Las Vegas Boulevard South; tel: 731-3311 or 800-634-6411; www.imperial palace.com; monorail:

While most casinos have toned down the noise by replacing coin-operated slot machines with those that pay out via tickets you cash in, the Bally Pro slot machines at Harrah's are advertised as having noisy stainless-steel trays, to make the payoffs even more exciting. The trays are even designed to prevent coin cups being placed in them, which would modestly deaden the sound.

Harrah's/Imperial Palace, bus: Deuce; map p.138 B4/C4
The Imperial Palace opened in 1979 with an Oriental theme, the roof covered in blue tiles from Japan. Inside are carved dragons, giant wind-chime chandeliers, and the Geisha and Ginza bars.

Until his death in 2003, owner Ralph Engelstad was the only sole proprietor of a major Vegas casino, earning himself an untold fortune; currently the premises are being operated by representatives of the Engelstad family trust. Engelstad was acclaimed for his friendly policies toward disabled people, who form 13 percent of the 2,600 employees here.

Gamblers should be on the alert for the sometimes short-lived promotions like the Imperial Palace's "New Member Mania." Under this plan, enrollees could qualify for a variety of freebies ranging from room vouchers to car-rental days, concert tickets, spa passes, free meals, and even airline credit vouchers.

The Imperial's owner was renowned for his antique cars, which are now on show as the **Imperial Palace Auto Collection**.

Wayne Newton was once in the Guinness Book of Records as the world's highest-paid entertainer and, as "Mr. Las Vegas," played 25,000 shows at the now-defunct Stardust before leaving to entertain USO troops. In 2005, he starred in a TV show auditioning hopefuls for his "Las Vegas Extravaganza." He now appears regularly at the Flamingo, where he first performed in Las Vegas.

SEE ALSO MUSEUMS AND GALLERIES P.103

Luxor
3900 Las Vegas Boulevard South; tel: 262-4000 or 800-288-1000; www.luxor.com; bus: Deuce; map p.139 C1
The huge atrium of the Luxor is lined with reproductions from the Luxor and Karnak temples in Egypt, including portraits of Tutankhamen and Nefertiti, simulated archeological digs, talking camels, and a recreation of Tutankamen's tomb with replicas of its contents when unearthed in 1922.

The 30-story, black-glass-paneled pyramid's atrium is said to be spacious enough to park nine Boeing 747s, and the beam of light from its sum-

Below: some of Harrah's blackjack tables have a $25 minimum, but plenty of cheaper options are available, including one of the best slot clubs in the city.

mit shines 10 miles into the sky, running up an electricity bill of $1 million per year.

On the fourth floor, reached by elevators from the lobby, are video arcades, a 3-D IMAX theater, and video karaoke machines.

Elegant stone walkways lead to the Giza Galleria where, in the Cairo Bazaar, artisans and vendors offer themed wares such as perfume, papyrus art, carved statuary, and small leather items imported from Egypt.

The Luxor's Sports Book area has individual television monitors for each seat, making it easy to bet in comfort.

Mandalay Bay
3950 Las Vegas Boulevard South; tel: 632-7777 or 877-632-7800; www.mandalaybay.com; bus: Deuce; map p.139 C1/D1

Elegant Mandalay Bay is a luxurious, tropically themed resort on a lagoon that is aimed at hip young things. It has its own rum distillery and a pool with a sandy beach swept by waves from a giant machine that can generate 6-ft breakers for body surfing. Visitors can see the pool through windows near the entrance to **Shark Reef**, but only guests are allowed to swim.

The Mandalay Bay also has a fine gift shop, selling

upscale crafts and clothes from around the world.

The property includes a 12,000-seat Events Center that hosts sports and special events all year long and competes with Caesars Palace to be the main boxing venue.

The restaurants and clubs here are superb, one of the best collections in Vegas.
SEE ALSO CHILDREN P.58

MGM Grand
3799 Las Vegas Boulevard South; tel: 891-7777 or 877-880-0880; www.mgmgrand.com; monorail: MGM Grand, bus: Deuce; map p.139 C3/D2

The MGM Grand's entrance is flanked by a 45ft high lion, which is claimed to be the largest bronze statue in the US. This is the second lion on door duty here. The first

was thought by Asian gamblers (of whom there are many) to bring bad luck, as guests' entry to the casino was through the lion's open mouth. The doorway was promptly removed.

On the casino floor, visitors walking through the glass entrance to the **Lion Habitat** find lions sleeping over their heads or beneath their feet. The 450-lb beasts frolic with their trainer among waterfalls in a rocky African Savannah enclosure.

MGM's casino is the biggest in town and significantly has 3,500 slots. Its sports book is impressive too, and the poker room is one of the city's finest. Pit minimums are usually $25, but can be lower during the week. The special events area seats 17,157 and has a reputation as a world-class venue for superstar concerts

Below: the monorail connects the casinos along the eastern side of the Southern Strip.

and world championship sports events.

SEE ALSO CHILDREN P.58

Monte Carlo

3770 Las Vegas Boulevard South; tel: 730-7777 or 888-529-4828; www.montecarlo.com; bus: Deuce; map p.138 C2

From the outside Monte Carlo seems low-key by Vegas standards, with arched domes, marble floors, ornate fountains, and gas-lit promenades; it is modeled after Monaco's Place du Casino.

Inside it features its own brewpub, whose giant copper tanks share space with restaurants and old-fashioned gas lamps on its period-style Street of Dreams.

Lance Burton, a longtime Vegas headliner, has been starring in his eponymously named theater at Monte Carlo since 1996.

SEE ALSO LIVE ENTERTAINMENT P.85

New York New York

3790 Las Vegas Boulevard South; tel: 740-6969 or 866-815-4365; www.nynyhotelcasino.com; bus: Deuce; map p.139 C2

Visitors flock to here not just to gamble but also to admire the meticulously recreated New York skyline, which includes the Chrysler and Century buildings, with recreations of the Brooklyn Bridge, the Empire State Building, and the Statue of Liberty overlooking the Strip.

Inside, New York's neighborhoods are remarkably recreated and attract more tourists than the gambling. The large gaming area modeled on Central Park is surrounded by Park Avenue and adjoins Times Square, which offers perhaps the city's best selection of fast food. Visitors can ride the **Manhattan Express** or a Coney Island-style roller coaster, and stroll along a prettily graffiti-covered

> The Monte Carlo stands on the site of the legendary Dunes Hotel, famous during the Rat Pack days of the 1950s, when high-profile partygoers like Frank Sinatra, Dean Martin, and Sammy Davis, Jr performed in Vegas clubs and chased girls behind the scenes.

Lower East Side street of stores and eateries.

New York New York spiced up the resort's image by staging the only R-rated Cirque du Soleil show on the Strip, called **Zumanity**, and taking its cue from an adult-oriented accent. The casino does make concessions for kids too, with the Coney Island Emporium, a collection of old-time midway style games.

Minimums are not low in New York New York, but they have an excellent range of slots. In homage to Chinatown there is a Dragon Pit where Asian games of chance are played and *dim sum* is served with green tea, *saké,* and Asian beers. There are also high-limit rooms with $100-minimum, $5,000-maximum blackjack tables and $500 slots.

SEE ALSO CHILDREN P.59; LIVE ENTERTAINMENT P.83

Paris Las Vegas

3655 Las Vegas Boulevard South; tel: 946-7000 or 888-266-5687; www.parislasvegas.com; monorail: Bally's/Paris Las Vegas, bus: Deuce; map p.138 C3

Las Vegas's second "city" after New York New York *(see above)*, this hotel casino is modeled on the 800-year-old Parisian Hotel de Ville, the Paris City Hall. It is distinguished by one of the city's more prominent landmarks, a 50-story replica of the Eiffel Tower, thrusting through the roof of the casino and rising 540ft in the air, accompanied by a neon copy of the Montgolfier balloon.

A half-size scale model of the original, the tower offers panoramic views of the city from its 11th-story piano bar, one of eight restaurants at the casino specializing in regional French cuisine from Alsace, Burgundy, and Lorraine.

Even Bastille Day is recreated every July 14 at the two-thirds scale Arc de Triomphe in solidarity with ceremonies at the Parisian Arc.

The 85,000-sq ft casino houses an attractive fountain and a plethora of signs like "Le Salon des Tables," "Les Toilettes," "La Réception,"

Below: slot machines, not gaming tables, dominate the floor space of all the casinos on the Strip or Downtown.

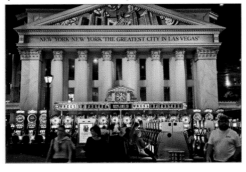

C

Above: the colossal legs of Paris Las Vegas's Eiffel Tower are solidly planted inside the casino.

"Le Bell Captain" and "Les Artistes Steak House."

A romantic, lamp-lit bridge straddles the casino high above the room but access is available only to those with a ticket to climb the tower.

Replicas represent various Parisian districts. Fronted at the Strip by the massive Academie National de Musique, Paris Las Vegas's other re-creations include the Champs Elysées, the Louvre, the Paris Opéra, and the Palace of Versailles.

The Notre Dame de Paris show at the Theater Paris Las Vegas plays most days. Stores offer ultra-chic Parisian fashion, and the casino has 2,200 slots. There are no live poker tables, but it is the only place offering a genuine French roulette table (in addition to a different layout to the betting area, the wheel itself has only one zero, thus lowering the house's edge).

Planet Hollywood Casino
3667 Las Vegas Boulevard South; tel: 785-5555 or 877-333-9474; www.planethollywoodresort.com; monorail: Bally's/Paris Las Vegas, bus: Deuce; map p.138–139 C3
Recently taken over by Starwood Resorts and Planet

Hollywood, the former Aladdin is in the process of a long, slow makeover, aimed at ultimately eliminating its Arabian Nights theme to avoid any anti-Islamic animosity in view of recent world events. In 2006 it unveiled its chic, ultramodern, LA-style lobby, where eight dazzling chandeliers made of more than half a million crystals reflect the black-polished granite floors and color-changing LED lights, and a complete renovation of the casino floor has been completed. The exterior façade is being replaced, and by the end of 2007 the transition should be complete, with new restaurants and shows and a new name and style for the atmospheric Desert Passage shopping mall.

Buffs bemoan the passing of the old Aladdin, yet another longtime landmark lost to progress. The place has had a checkered past ever since it began life as the Tally-Ho in 1963 and was owned by members of organized crime until the early 70s. To some, though, the site is still best known as the venue of Elvis's marriage to Priscilla in 1967 *(see picture p.77).*

Tropicana
3801 Las Vegas Boulevard South; tel: 739-2222 or 800-634-4000; www.tropicanalv.com; monorail: MGM Grand, bus: Deuce; map p.139 C2/D2
The Tropicana sports a kind of funky, old-fashioned charm, promoting its Caribbean theme with flamingos, macaws, and toucans. A wooden bridge overlooking a waterfall offers a romantic backdrop to the many weddings that are conducted here. Labyrinths of corridors lead from the flower-filled garden to the casino. An island fronts the hotel and is home to two 35ft tall sculptures of Aku Aku gods and a Polynesian house nestling in tropical landscaping; it gives nightly laser shows that are highly regarded.

The casino's main attraction is the long-running **Folies Bergère** show, with its cast of exotic showgirls.

For outside visitors there is little unique about the Tropicana's gaming, but for hotel guests there are swim-up blackjack tables.

Rumours abound that the 50-year-old hotel is about to undergo a multi-billlion dollar renovation.
SEE ALSO LIVE ENTERTAINMENT P.88–9

Northern Strip

Circus Circus
2880 Las Vegas Boulevard South; tel: 734-0410 or 800-444-2472; www.circuscircus.com; bus: Deuce; map p.136 B2

With free circus acts and a midway lined by carnival concessions, ample opportunities for inexpensive food, a vast family amusement park, bargain deals for hotel rooms, and 5,100 parking spaces, Circus Circus has packed in the crowds since 1968. It is probably the most successful of the low end, family-orientated casinos in Vegas, and hence the least desirable for those without children or interested in doing some serious gambling.

Crowds jam the midway attractions as acrobats, jugglers, aerialists, trapeze artists, and clowns perform from 11am till midnight in the world's largest permanent circus. Performances start every half an hour.

Miniature camels race along plastic tracks, children's faces are painted by a clown, and an endless line of hopefuls try to win prizes by bringing a big rubber mallet down heavily enough to propel a rubber chicken into a cooking pot.

Above: during the day, the Mirage's dramatic erupting volcano resembles a peaceful jungle waterfall.

Behind the Casino, the **Adventuredome** claims to be the country's largest indoor theme park and features the only double-loop and double-corkscrew roller coaster in the world. Admission is free, but rides are individually priced; or you can purchase a daily wrist band.
SEE ALSO CHILDREN PP.56, 59

Mirage
3400 Las Vegas Boulevard South; tel: 791-7111 or 800-374-9000; www.mirage.com; bus: Deuce; map p.138 B4

In 1989, when it opened, the Mirage certainly was different. From the erupting volcano just off the sidewalk to the white tigers' glass-enclosed habitat, to the arcade of smart stores underground, it drew huge crowds of curious spectators right from the beginning.

The spectacular appeal of the royal tigers and their magician owners, Siegfried & Roy, was enough to fill the 1,500-seat show room 480 times a year. But Siegfried & Roy have not performed since October 4, 2003, when Roy was attacked and dragged off stage by one of his tigers. Roy is never expected to fully recover, and the show is now permanently closed. The

Left: bargain basement, but a big hit with families.

statue on the Mirage's premises of Siegfried, Roy, and one of the animals has become a place of pilgrimage for devoted fans, who for months after the attack draped the brass figures with flowers.

Nevertheless, Siegfried & Roy's white tigers are safe and well in the **White Tiger Habitat**, and the **Secret Garden** displays even more wild animals, this time in semi-tropical splendor.

Sharks and exotic sea life swim in a 20,000-gallon tank behind the Mirage's registration desk, inside a glass-enclosed atrium 90 ft high and filled with lush gardens, palm trees, and tropical foliage.

The Dolphin Habitat, which houses 10 Atlantic bottle-nose dolphins in 2.5-million gallon saltwater tanks, has been visited by half-a-million schoolchildren since it opened in 1990. As for the Volcano, it erupts 128,000 recirculated gallons of water a minute down its sides, a phenomenon powered by a natural-gas pipeline.

When it comes to gambling, the Mirage's baccarat

> Circus Circus has an RV park called "Circusland" with its own pool, laundromat, and general store.

47

Above: New Frontier attracts a younger crowd with some of the lowest room rates on the Strip.

tables, with their steep $100 minimum, are some of the finest in the city.
SEE ALSO CHILDREN P.58

New Frontier

3120 Las Vegas Boulevard South; tel: 794-8200 or 800-421-7806; www.frontierlv.com; bus: Deuce; map p.136 B1

The New Frontier's atrium is an indoor garden with fountains, pools, and waterfalls. It is also the longest-established hotel on the Strip, and has a venerable history. Not only was it the place where Kirk Kerkorian – the city's richest man – began his Vegas career with junkets on his fledgling airline, but it was also the venue where Liberace, and later Elvis, first played in Vegas.

Old-fashioned one-armed bandit slot machines with pistol-arms you can pull stand as a greeting in the doorway, and Micky Gilly's clone of his now-defunct Texas nightclub, Gilly's, scaled-down but with a bucking mechanical bull, packs in the punters every evening.
SEE ALSO BARS AND CAFÉS P.34

Riviera

2901 Las Vegas Boulevard South; tel: 734-5110 or 800-634-6753; www.rivierahotel.com; bus: Deuce; map p.136 B2/C3

The Riviera, styled on the luxury resorts of the Cote d'Azur, opened with Liberace in 1955 but has shifted from big name headliners to more broad-based, but equally camp stage shows. The latest version is a rather tawdry skin show called **Crazy Girls**. It used to push the boundaries for Vegas but now seems rather dated.

Piecemeal expansion has not helped by creating a confusing layout, but the fast-food court just off the sidewalk is a convenient and inexpensive place to eat. There are half a dozen other restaurants, including a hot-dog counter in Nickel Town, where lower limit machines and tables are kept.

Among the stores is one selling pearls right from the oyster; a magic tricks shop; and one representing Pahrump Valley Vineyards, the state's only commercial winery. The hotel, with its

> The Sahara was one of the first casinos to display video poker machines on which a pair of phantom hands on screen "deal" the cards.

Olympic-size swimming pool, was the setting for Martin Scorsese's 1995 film *Casino*.
SEE ALSO LIVE ENTERTAINMENT P.87–8; MOVIES 93–4

Sahara

2535 Las Vegas Boulevard South; tel: 737-2111 or 888-696-2121; www.saharavegas.com; monorail: Sahara, bus: Deuce; map p.136 B3/B4

When the Sahara opened in 1952, one could have been forgiven for thinking it was being sensitive to its surroundings. After all it was based on a desert, featured real camels and had a North African theme. It also quickly became a haunt of the Rat Pack. Now the Sahara is entered via a dramatic, neon-lit rotunda with a motif of neon camels and a **NASCAR Café** that features racing on giant projection screens with Surround Sound.

There is a **NASCAR Cyber Speedway** at the rear, where visitors can choose a type of car and course to take on a virtual-reality adventure.

Below: eight pairs of bare bronze buttocks, shiny from being caressed by thousands of passers-by, mark the theater entrance to the Riviera's Crazy Girls nightshow.

Above: why take a chance in a high-roller suite: Slots A Fun guarantees free coffee… and donuts.

"Speed-The-Ride," a roller coaster, lasts only 45 seconds, but riders are propelled from zero to 35mph in two seconds, in a loop skyward and then back down.

"The Rat Pack is Back," a sign proclaims, promoting a show that captures some of the ambiance of the old days when Sinatra, Dean Martin, and Sammy Davis, Jr hung out here. Nowadays, the Sahara is cornering the market on memories from "Motor City," also known as Motown. A mainstay act in its Congo Room are members of The Drifters, The Platters and The Coasters, who croon, sing and swing their way through a 90-minute show that borrows heavily from their "blasts of the past." The performers seem to have as good a time as their (mainly middle-aged) audiences.

The Casbar Lounge also features live music and is free, with no drinks minimum.

The casino features a wide range of table games such as war, Texas Hold-em bonus poker, no-bust blackjack and Spanish 21, all with affordable minimums.

Watch this space, the Sahara was sold in May 2007 and changes are likely.
SEE ALSO CHILDREN P.59–60; LIVE ENTERTAINMENT P.81; RESTAURANTS P.113

Slots A Fun
2800 Las Vegas Boulevard South, tel: 734-0410; bus: Deuce; map p.136 B2
Next door to Circus Circus, Slots-A-Fun is the closest thing to a boozy bowling alley that you'll find on the Strip. It offers free beer to all players and has penny slots, but as they only take dollar bills, you get to play 100 pennies at a time. There's a glass case near the door exhibiting Polaroid photos of earlier winners and usually somebody handing out free ticket booklets and offering a free pull (sorry Brits, it's only valid on a slot machine). In some casinos you can find machines that take $500 tokens, but not in Slots-A-Fun, where high rollers simply do not exist.

Stratosphere Tower
2000 Las Vegas Boulevard South; tel: 380-7777 or 800-998-6937; www.stratosphere-hotel.com; bus: Deuce; map p.136 B4
Speedy elevators whisk visitors to the top of the Stratosphere Tower in an ear-popping 30 seconds – to a height of 1,149ft, where on a clear day California and Arizona are visible. The deck is also a nightspot for visitors, who relish the finest view of the world's best display of neon.

The resort has a showroom, pool, and spa, and a choice of restaurants including the Around the World Buffet, the **Top of the World** revolving restaurant with the best view on – and of – the Strip, and a 1950s diner. Romantically inclined visitors can get married near the top of the tower.

The gaming room is well thought of, with loose slots, low-limit table games, mini-

---

For thrill seekers, the Stratosphere is a must, with the highest rides in the world. You already start 1,200ft in the air on the High Roller roller coaster. The Big Shot is a kind of reversed bungee jump, and the extreme X Scream ride *(right)* is only for the truly brave!

Piazza San Marco in which jugglers, singers, and dancers seem to be continually performing. The square is the culmination of the **Grand Canal Shoppes**, which begins with a colorful, awe-inspiring frescoed ceiling and segues into the bluest skies ever seen.
SEE ALSO MUSEUMS AND GALLERIES P.97–8, 102–3; PAMPERING P.104–5; SHOPPING P.121

Wynn Las Vegas
3131 Las Vegas Boulevard South; tel: 770-7100 or 888-320-9966; www.wynnlasvegas.com; bus: Deuce; map p.136 B1/B2
The resort, accessible via a new walkway crossing above the Strip, has an artificial mountain covered in pine trees that forms a natural barrier between the Strip and the casino; a coursing fall of water, and a lake spanning 3 acres. There's also a 50-story tower with 2,716 rooms, a 120,000-sq ft casino, and two showrooms, plus a well-watered championship golf course, the only one on the Strip, for the exclusive use of the resort's guests.

The new casino is a suitably stylish venue for Wynn's impressive collection of art, which hangs in the **Wynn Art Collection**. The shopping, too, is in the upscale mode, with Chanel, Cartier, Gaultier, and Manolo Blahnik lining the **Wynn Esplanade**.
SEE ALSO MUSEUMS AND GALLERIES P.98; SHOPPING P.123

Beyond the Strip

Arizona Charlie's
740 South Decatur Boulevard; tel: 258-5200 or 800-342-2695; www.arizonacharlies.com; bus: 103

bacarrat, a single-zero roulette wheel and some of the best odds on The Strip.
SEE ALSO RESTAURANTS P.113–4; WEDDINGS P.131–2

TI – Treasure Island
3300 Las Vegas Boulevard South; tel: 894-7111 or 800-944-7444; www.treasureisland.com; bus: Deuce; map p.136 B1
Treasure Island is month-by-month shedding its family image, rebranding itself as "TI" and targeting the adult-only market. TI's showroom hosts **Cirque du Soleil's Mystère**. Outside, a vast lagoon is the spectacular scene of the Sirens of TI – a stand-off between a group of tempting sirens and a band of pirates.

Inside, the casinos identity seems to fluctuate between cheesy pirates and sophisticated youth. Betting limits start low, but quickly rise as the sun sets.
SEE ALSO LIVE ENTERTAINMENT P.83

Venetian
3355 Las Vegas Boulevard South; tel: 414-1000 or 877-883-6423; www.venetian.com; monorail: Harrah's/Imperial Palace; bus: Deuce; map p.138 B4/C4
Vegas's third, and most accomplished, artificial city, the Venetian was designed to be the world's largest hotel and convention complex under one roof. The restaurants are served by top chefs, the luxurious 65,000-sq ft spa and fitness club is operated by the renowned **Canyon Ranch**, the **Guggenheim-Hermitage Museum** is one of the city's finest, **Madame Tussaud's** one of the city's most popular, and the complex has enough marble-and-stone flooring to cover a dozen football fields. It adjoins a pool deck modeled after a Venetian garden.

Along with the Doges Palace and Rialto Bridge, the resort sports a scaled-down

> Viewed from the Strip, the lavish Venetian really does look like Venice, from the Campanile Bell Tower roaring above the Grand Canal to the *gondolieri* in striped shirts. Adding to the realism, thousands of pigeons fly out and swirl around at least twice a day.

Located just off-Strip in a quiet neighborhood near a local shopping mall, this small hotel with its Pacific Northwest theme has a casino with a limited number of table games and more than 1,400 slots, as well as Vegas's only 24-hour bingo parlor. The Naughty Ladies Saloon offers nightly entertainment ranging from karaoke to live big-band classics.

Gold Coast
4000 West Flamingo; tel: 367-7111 or 800-331-5334; www.goldcoastcasino.com; bus 202; map p.138 A3
One of the earliest hotels to open west of the Strip, Dixieland jazz has long been a mainstay in the lounge, and there's a 70-lane bowling center with its own snack bar, bingo, karaoke lounge, movie theater and video arcade.

Anyone wishing to learn the intricacies of that liveliest of table games – craps – should roll out of bed and into the casino on a Friday, Saturday, or Sunday morning for a free lesson.

The true casino draw is in the huge number of video poker machines and its generous slot club, both attract mainly locals, and their mini-baccarat tables with low minimums ($10) for those who would like to learn the game. At the other end of the gaming spectrum, the Gold Coast has the only million-dollar keno game in Vegas. A free shuttle runs to the com-

pany's sister hotel, the Orleans *(see p.52).*

Greek Isles Casino
305 Convention Center Drive; tel: 952-8000 or 800-633-1777; www.greekislesvegas.com; bus: 108; map p.136 C2
The Greek Isles Casino has the blue-and-white decor of a typical Greek village and Cyrillic-style signs for the bar and restaurant. The Greek Isles was formerly owned by the financially troubled Debbie Reynolds casino, then briefly owned by the WWF (World Wrestling Foundation).

The casino is slot and machine only, but does have an interesting electronic roulette machine and a long mural running along the outside wall depicting a prototypical fishing village.

Hard Rock Hotel and Casino
4455 Paradise Road; tel: 693-5000 or 800-HRD-ROCK; www.hardrockhotel.com; bus: 108, 711; map p.139 D4
Located about three blocks east of the Strip, the Hard Rock Hotel is a magnet to rock fans and Vegas's young, beautiful party elite, with its lively vibes, guitar-shaped chandeliers, and glass cases

filled with the ephemera of rock aristocracy. These include a large Rolling Stones display with a couple of "Keef's" guitars and one of Mick's leopard-skin jackets. Though there is no continuing show, top-name rock acts like Cheap Trick, Guns N' Roses, Kid Rock, and Crosby, Stills and Nash perform in the hotel's theater, **The Joint**, with its 25ft tall speakers.

It has 657 rooms, the **Rock Spa**, and a huge Beach Club. Restaurants include the **Pink Taco**, a version of the Japanese restaurant **Nobu**, and a steak house said to be reminiscent of 1950s Las Vegas. But a sad piece of rock history was made here; the day before a US tour was to commence, John Entwistle, bass player of The Who, died on June 27, 2002.
SEE ALSO LIVE ENTERTAINMENT P.87; PAMPERING P.104–17; RESTAURANTS P.118

Hooters Casino Hotel
115 East Tropicana Avenue; tel: 739-9000 or 866-584-6687; www.hooterscasinohotel.com; monorail: MGM Grand, bus: 201; map p.139 D2
There is some sense of relief when you walk into Hooters,

Below: TI – Treasure Island has abandoned its child-friendly pirates and now features the more saucy Sirens of TI.

Above: oysters and other seafood are shipped in daily from west coast fisheries.

as at last you know Vegas has gone as low as it can go. It's the only casino in Vegas that would wager it all on a decent pair. For those familiar with Hooters' theme, what constitutes that pair will come as no surprise; for others, well, let's just say it isn't a couple of barn owls. Surprisingly, this is one of Vegas's brighter and more relaxed casinos. But with such an adolescent "theme," expect it to pull in the overtly keen college crowd and sad businessmen who should know better.

Las Vegas Hilton
3000 Paradise Road; tel: 732-5111 or 888-732-7117; www.lvhilton.com; monorail: Las Vegas Hilton, bus: 108; map p.137 C3
The Las Vegas Hilton is a hotel familiar to high rollers who enjoy its opulent, marble-floored penthouse apartments. Its proximity to the convention center makes it popular with the less high rollers too.

It has introduced a million-dollar blackjack tournament, where the $1,000 entry fee includes a three-night stay at the hotel (how generous of them). There are 13 restaurants, a pool, a spa, a spacious casino, and **Star Trek:**

The Experience. The Hilton also has a showroom where Elvis Presley famously performed 800 times. There are no permanent shows, but headliners from old standbys such as Barry Manilow, Tony Bennett, and Johnny Mathis to the likes of Heart and ZZ Top perform concerts here.
SEE ALSO MUSEUMS AND GALLERIES P.103

Orleans
4500 West Tropicana Avenue; tel: 365-7111 or 800-675-3267; www.orleanscasino.com; bus: 201; map p.138 A1
The casino's New Orleans-style attractions include the French Quarter, Garden District, and Mardi Gras – all with pre-hurricane detail left intact. The casino is more akin to a warehouse than the Big Easy, but the 50-ft ceiling does well to irradicate the typical claustrophobic casino atmosphere. A 72-lane bowling center and 12-screen movie theater attract locals. Cajun and Mexican cuisines are available.

Showroom tickets at the Orleans are inexpensive compared with Strip hotels, a bargain to see headliners like Frankie Valli, Frankie Avalon, Neil Sedaka, Chubby Checker,

Little Richard, Glen Campbell, and The Moody Blues.

The poker room is one of the best in town with the Bad Beat Jackpot awarded to high losing hands. It can be worth tens of thousands of dollars.

Palace Station
2411 West Sahara Avenue; tel: 367-2411 or 800-634-3101; www.palacestation.com; bus: 204; map p.136 B2
Reasonably priced, newly renovated rooms and a dramatic glass elevator are among the most attractive features of this hotel. Though it stands only nine stories high – small by Vegas standards – it is the tallest structure around its west side neighborhood. Slots are king in the casino, which also has blackjack, pai gow, baccarat, and craps tables. There is also a poker room, a bingo hall, and a race and sports book.

Palms
4321 West Flamingo Road; tel: 942-7777 or 866-942-7770; www.palms.com; bus 202; map p.138 A2
Designed by the celebrated architect Jon Jerde with an understated Polynesian theme, the 42-story hotel is decorated in soft color schemes of beige and taupe and has exterior lighting that can be seen from many miles away.

The five bars include the stylish 55th-floor **Ghostbar**, accessed by high-speed elevators, with panoramic views of the city's skyline and an open-air deck in whose floor

Pamper yourself in novel style. Near the Palms Casino Resort's swimming pool, which is "the color of sapphires and amethysts," is a spa offering "fruity body slushes" in a yummy choice of amaretto sour, margarita, or piña colada.

is inset a plexiglass window. Apparently guests find it exciting to jump up and down on this, despite the fact that there is nothing below it but 54 stories of space.

Fiber optic-lit drink rails rim the bar both here and in the steak house, Nine, where it encircles the champagne and caviar bar. The night-club, called Rain in the Desert, has a color-changing wall of water and an elaborate electronic system that produces fog, haze, fireballs, and dancing fountains.
SEE ALSO BARS AND CAFÉS P.36

Rio
3700 West Flamingo Road; tel: 252-7777 or 866-746-7671; www.riolasvegas.com; bus: 202; map p.138 A3
West of the freeway is the ostentatiously lit Rio, an all-suite hotel. The smallest of the more than 2,500 suites are 600sq ft and the largest almost three times that size, featuring wrap-around windows and great views. The hotel promotes a Latin American aura with its Samba Theater, Copacobana Showroom, **VooDoo Lounge**, and **Ipanema Bar**. Catch the panoramic view from the Rio's VooDoo Lounge on the 52nd

floor. The tropical lagoon, complete with waterfalls, has four pools, five whirlpool spas, and a sandy beach.

The spectacular 12-minute show **Masquerade in the Sky**, which takes place four times every afternoon and evening except Tuesday and Wednesday, is performed above spectators' heads as a procession of gaily decorated floats moves around a 950-ft track. Exotically dressed performers sing from a balloon, and from vehicles decked out as gondolas or riverboats.

The Rio is one of the properties owned by Harrah's, and a free shuttle runs between the two casinos every 15 minutes until midnight (until 1am on weekends). Guests can also use the Rio Secco Golf Club, which is located 15 miles from the resort.
SEE ALSO BARS AND CAFÉS P.36; CHILDREN P.60

Terrible's
4100 Paradise Road; tel: 800-640-9777; bus 108; map p.10
Owned by the Terrible Herbst gas station chain, Terrible's has something of a truck-stop feel. The only restaurants are a run-of-the-mill café and a decent all-you-can-eat buffet. The casino's

For a fee, guests of the casino can join Rio's elaborate parade – this prospect seems particularly popular with young children – and leave with a photograph. All of this takes place in the lively Masquerade Village, complete with eating, shopping, and gaming facilities.

emphasis is on video poker, but there are also tables, roulette, double-deck blackjack, and 3x, 4x, and 5x odds craps. The best feature is the large free-form swimming pool surrounded by palms. And yes, you can fill your car up with gasoline there.

Wild Wild West
3330 West Tropicana Avenue; tel: 800-634-3488; www.wwwesthotelcasino.com; bus 201; map p.10
And speaking of truck stops, the main claims to fame at the Wild Wild West are easy access from the interstate and a 15-acre truck plaza. The no-frills rooms are small, motellike – and cheap. The cramped casino has a mere 240 slot machines and a sports book. If you believe the old road-trip adage that the best eateries are the ones

Below: both the Palms and the Las Vegas Hilton have state-of-the-art sports book facilities.

Left: after the glitz of the Strip, Downtown feels pretty down to earth.

now one of the last places with penny slots. A man once won $76,000 playing them, but don't hold your breath. They are undoubtedly a reflection of Gaughan's attention to the less affluent corner of the market. The affordable guest rooms are some of the nicest in the downtown area. No pool.

Fitzgerald's
301 East Fremont Street; tel: 388-2400 or 800-274-5825; www.fitzgeraldslasvegas.com; map p.134 B3

Next door to the Four Queens *(see below)* is Fitzgerald's, which has 200 slot machines in its Nickel Zone. It claims that it has paid out over a billion nickels. Fitzgerald's will give you a free O'Lucky Bucks card to improve your gambling chances and offers trinkets like key chains, beanie animals, autographed sports memorabilia, and free meals. Displaying shamrocks everywhere, Fitzgerald's is so Irish in theme that it has instituted a "Halfway to St Patrick's Day" celebration in mid-September with green beer and Irish stew.

Four Queens
202 East Fremont Street; tel: 385-4011 or 800-634-6045; www.fourqueens.com; map p.134 B3

The Fremont Casino's past points a finger at just how easy it used to be to stand out in Las Vegas. When it opened it was not only one of the city's only high-rise buildings, but it was the first to feature wall-to-wall carpet in its gaming area. Other casino floors were covered in dust.

with the most semi-trucks outside, this is the place for you, with its $1.99 breakfasts and monster buffalo burgers.

Downtown

Binion's
128 East Fremont Street; tel: 382-1600 or 800-237-6537; www.binions.com; map p.134 B3

Benny Binion arrived in the 1940s, a colorful Texas gambler with a trademark buffalo-hide overcoat and a big, white cowboy hat. He took over the Eldorado Club, renamed it Binion's and began a remarkable 40-year career that endeared him to his customers. He was almost always accessible to the public, sitting at a corner table wearing a cowboy shirt with gold coins for buttons and no tie.

Binion died in 1989, and a statue of him on horseback sits at Ogden Avenue and Casino Center Boulevard.

Binion's offers late-night gamblers a New York steak dinner for around $5 (10pm–5:45am) and is more gambler-friendly than most casinos. Almost everywhere

on the planet, casinos charge a 5 percent commission on winning baccarat bank bets, but Binion's only charges 4 percent. Also, while the norm is eight-deck blackjack games dealt from a plastic shoe, at Binions it is mostly a hand-held single deck, favored by players who think they have mastered the fiendishly difficult art of card-counting.

California
12 East Ogden Avenue; tel: 385-1222 or 800-634-3484; www.thecal.com; map p.134 B4

One block from the Las Vegas Club is Sam Boyd's California, promoting what it calls "an aloha spirit," derived from Boyd's five years working in Hawaiian bingo parlors.

The hotel's arcade stores sell foods, souvenirs and clothes from the 49th state.

El Cortez
600 East Fremont Street; tel: 385-5200 or 800-634-6703; www.elcortezhotelcasino.com; map p.134 B3

Beyond Neonopolis is Jackie Gaughan's 308-room El Cortez Hotel & Casino, the oldest standing casino in Las Vegas, built in the 1940s and

Downtown's older casinos have always had a battle to woo the punters from the Strip, so they give free food to almost three quarters of them. In contrast, the Strip casinos give nearly half their customers free drinks, which is a slightly better ratio than Downtown.

The Four Queens Casino claims that some of its slots have a 97.4 percent payback, which is better than the Downtown average of 95.6 percent. Whether or not it is justified, the Four Queens describes itself as "the jackpot capital of the world."

The Queens promotes both, "the world's largest blackjack table" and "the world's largest slot machine," which can be played by six people at a time. Magnolia's Veranda offers views of the casino as you eat, and **Hugo's Cellar** has had good reviews from food critics. The Queens is one of the few casinos that invites visitors to take photos, though not of people, and no video is allowed.
SEE ALSO RESTAURANTS P.119

Fremont Hotel & Casino
200 East Fremont Street; tel: 385-3232 or 800-634-6460; www.fremontcasino.com; map p.134 B3
Completing the neon quadrant of hotels, the Fremont Hotel and Casino claims that with 450 seats in its garden buffet, diners do not get stuck in the usual long lineups. The hotel has three other restaurants, including a Tony Roma's and 24-hour Lanai Express. If you hit $100 on the slots, there is a free T-shirt.

Golden Nugget
129 East Fremont Street, tel: 385-7111 or 800-846-5336; www.goldennugget.com; map p.134 B3
There are four glittering, pulsating casinos at the main intersection of Fremont Street and Casino Center Boulevard, but the Golden Nugget stands out against the neon crassness of its neighbors, with its classy white exterior trimmed with soft golden lights.

The Golden Nugget has retained the Victorian style that it displayed when it first opened as a saloon more than 50 years ago, an era when horses could still be seen on the streets. Crystal chandeliers reflect off polished brass and marble in the lobby. Brass and granite squares shine from the surrounding sidewalk. Its **buffet** always has long lines, especially for champagne brunch on Sundays. An outdoor pool sits in landscaped gardens with tall palms, the terrace is lined with alabaster swans and bronze sculptures of fish. In the Spa Suite Tower, the Grand Court is modeled on a room in the Frick Museum of New York. On display in the casino is the world's biggest gold nugget, weighing a staggering 59.84lb, and called the Hand of Faith.

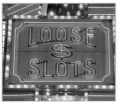

Above: Downtown's slots have a higher payout than those on the Strip.

Plaza
1 Main Street; tel: 386-2110 or 800-634-6575; www.plaza-hotelcasino.com; map p.134 B3
Towering at the top end of Fremont Street, the neon-lit, 1,000-room Plaza was the first downtown casino to install cashless slots. There are eight daily sessions of bingo upstairs, and free music in the Omaha Lounge. Behind the Plaza are the railroad tracks that started it all, currently used only by freight trains.

Vegas Club
18 East Fremont Street; tel: 385-1664 or 800-634-6532; www.vegasclubcasino.net; map p.134 B3
Pitching itself as the city's only sports-themed casino is the Las Vegas Club, decorated with framed pictures of sports heroes, medals, and trophies. Old posters abound near the sports book.

Below: the world's largest golden nugget is on display inside the Golden Nugget.

Children

N ot so long ago, when Native American casinos and lotteries were proliferating throughout the United States and threatening to dilute Las Vegas's appeal, resort owners made an attempt to transform Las Vegas into a family destination. It didn't really work, and after a few years they went back to promoting a "sin city" image, though a more PG-rated one. Today, virtually every large resort offers activities and attractions to keep kids occupied, so that parents can slip away for a few hours of gambling or shopping. Minors under age 21 are not allowed on the casino floor, even with their parents.

Accommodations

Circus Circus

2880 Las Vegas Boulevard South; tel: 734-0410 or 800-444-2472; www.circuscircus.com; bus: Deuce; map p.136 B2/B3

The biggest hotel in Vegas when it was built 40 years ago, this towering complex is fronted by a magenta-and-white casino lobby built in the shape of a circus tent with a neon portico. It is still the fifth-largest hotel in the world. It has always worked hard to maintain its status as the most kid-friendly resort in town – successfully, as evidenced by the myriad children romping everywhere except the casino floor.

Circus Circus was the first Strip hotel to start appealing to children by offering midway (sideshows) and circus acts to entertain them while the parents gambled. Of course, it turned out that the adults enjoyed the acrobats and the midway almost as much as their kids did, and both are crowded for most of the day, as are the video games and county-fair-style games. Children stay free when accompanied by their parents, and the circus acts, midway, and candy and toy stores, as well as the best amusement park around, offer endless enticements for the younger set.
SEE ALSO ACCOMMODATIONS P.23

Excalibur

3850 Las Vegas Boulevard South; tel: 597-7777 or 877-750-5464; www.excalibur.com; bus: Deuce; map p.139 C1/C2

Like Circus Circus, this 4,000-room medieval castle, with its glowing red and blue turrets, moat, strolling costumed entertainers, and jousting tournament dinner show complete with dragons, is a place you probably wouldn't stay without kids.
SEE ALSO ACCOMMODATIONS P.21

Green Valley Ranch Resort

2300 Paseo Verde Parkway, tel: 617-7777 or 866-617-1777; bus 111; map p.16

At first this South American-themed luxury spa resort in Henderson, 10 minutes by freeway from the Strip and the airport, might seem like an overly ritzy pick for a family vacation. But in fact, its well-equipped video game room and 10-screen movie theater offer plenty to keep

Below: never let your kids out of your sight at Circus Circus, or you'll lose them in the crowd instantly.

Left: Circus Circus's Adventuredome has several thrill rides and tamer options for the younger children.

zebra, gazelle, rhino, hippo, baboon, and cheetah, all cohabiting peacefully at the neutral zone of the waterhole.

A large room is filled with life-like lions, bison, leopard, antelope, musk ox, ibex, peacock, ostrich, geese, vultures, and flamingos. The shimmering blue walls of the next room are like a rippling ocean in which striped baby sharks swim in an open tank. Other fish swim in a separate aquarium, all compatible and "of the same size so no fish considers another a possible dinner." The sharks are fed at 2pm on Monday, Wednesday, and Saturday.

Two huge, sleepy pythons named Bonnie and Clyde sprawl behind glass. They are from Burma and are said to have "highly developed heat sensors for detecting warmblooded animals." Pythons naturally grow to a length of 24ft and can devour animals as big as leopards. With a digestion like that, it is not surprising that one good meal might last these canny reptiles several months.

Leaflets are offered to parents with questions and suggestions to stimulate interest among younger visitors. In the Young Scientists Center there

kids occupied while parents enjoy more sophisticated pursuits. Children stay free with parents. The location is close to the entrance to Lake Mead National Recreation Area, with its beaches, boating, and Native american rock art. A Whole Foods natural grocery store on the premises makes it easy to avoid pricey restaurants and still feed your kids healthy food.

SEE ALSO LAKE MEAD, VALLEY OF FIRE, AND HOOVER DAM P.16–7

Family Dining

Plaza Food Court
Fashion Show Mall, 3200 Las Vegas Boulevard South; tel: 733-1020; bus: Deuce; map p.136 B1
Every large Las Vegas resort hotel has an abundance of fast-food places, but for family dining the easy way none can compare to the 11,000-sq ft food court at this upscale outlet mall, where kids can indulge their eating whims at carry-out places serving quickie cuisine of many different nations, from pizza and sushi to Mongolian stir fry. There's plenty of seating in the central table area.

Museums

Howard W. Cannon Aviation Museum
McCarran Airport; tel: 366-1522; 24 hours; free; map p.139 E2
Named after the band leader turned senator who helped establish Nellis Air Force Base, this tells the story of aviation in southern Nevada. It also makes a handy diversion at the airport when your little one gets tired of waiting for the flight home.

Las Vegas Natural History Museum
900 Las Vegas Boulevard North; tel: 384-3466; daily 9am–4pm; bus: 113, MAX; map p.12
The museum's hallway proclaims it to be "a walk through time in which each foot represents a million years." The animated dinosaur reproductions move convincingly, and a huge T-Rex growls impressively when a button is pressed.

Interactive exhibits include an African Rainforest feature where spectators can create a thunderstorm against a backdrop of Mount Kilimanjaro and dioramas bring to life in Vegas a savannah packed with

> At the child-friendly Excalibur castle, the main attractions for youngsters include Merlin's Arcade, featuring larger-than-life-size Shrek figures, a Sponge Bob Squarepants "4-D" ride and an array of video games that are more exciting than the casino's slots. Children under the age of 12 stay free with their parents.

Above: The Las Vegas Natural History Museum has several exhibitions explaining the life of dinosaurs.

are hands-on exhibits challenging children to identify familiar aromas and teaching them about different tastes.

Lied Discovery Children's Museum
833 Las Vegas Boulevard North; tel: 382-3445; Mon–Sat 10am–5pm, Sun 1–5pm; bus: 113, MAX; map p.12

There is plenty to engage the attention of adults as well as kids here. (Note a common mistake: the name of the museum is pronounced "leed," not "lied.")

If you ever wondered what a million pennies ($10,000) looks like, here's an exhibit to show you. Also in the make-believe post office, young, would-be customers can sort, weigh, and mail packages.

Irresistible to all ages, the Discovery Grocery Store makes shopping a game, and there's a musical pathway where you can play a tune by jumping on panels. You can put your head in a tube stretching up several floors and talk to hear the echo.

Heavy boots can be donned for Planet Walking to experience the difference in gravity. What weighs 80lbs on earth would weigh 95lbs on Saturn, Uranus, or Neptune, 188lbs on Jupiter, and 2,232lbs on the Sun. The Language Map lights up, speaks,

and shows the location where a particular language is spoken. The new Virtual Gestures lets kids stand in front of a green screen and play in video soccer, hockey, basketball, and volleyball games.

Animals

Lion Habitat
MGM Grand, 3799 Las Vegas Boulevard South, tel: 891-1111; daily 11am–10pm; free; monorail: MGM Grand, bus: Deuce; map p.139 C2/D2

Here the 450-lb beasts frolic with their trainer among waterfalls in a rocky African Savannah enclosure. Metro, Goldie, and Louis B, three of the resident pride, are said to be descendants of the MGM signature lion whose yawn-like roar was the company's movie logo.

Secret Garden and Dolphin Habitat
Mirage, 3400 Las Vegas Boulevard South; tel: 791-7111 or 800-627-6667; summer daily 10am–7pm, winter 11am–5.30pm weekdays and from 10am on weekends; bus: Deuce; map p.138 B4

Past azure pools where dolphins swim are 40 rare or endangered species, including Siegfried & Roy's Royal white tigers and white lions.

Sharks and exotic sea life swim in a 20,000-gallon tank

behind the Mirage's registration desk, within a glass-enclosed atrium 90ft high and filled with lush gardens, palm trees, and tropical foliage.

The Dolphin Habitat houses 10 Atlantic bottlenose dolphins in 2.5-million gallon saltwater tanks. Since the habitat is designed to show the dolphins in a natural state, they are not taught to perform tricks, but these intelligent mammals often come up with stunts of their own.
SEE ALSO CASINOS P.47–8

Shark Reef
Mandalay Bay, 3950 Las Vegas Boulevard South; tel: 632-7777; bus: Deuce; map p.139 C1/D1

An open 90,000-sq ft aquarium holds 2,000 marine animals. Installed soon after the hotel opened, its sunken temples, statues, old stone stairways, and shipwreck rest in 1½ million gallons of water filled with strange fish of all shapes and sizes.

The exhibit contains a dozen species of shark, ranging from a baby Port Jackson shark, only 10in long, to a 12ft long nurse shark which, in its coral-reef habitat, sucks its prey out of holes in the rocks.

Below: Lied Discovery Children's Museum is highly interactive, and entertaining for younger children.

The Shark Reef aquarium exhibit points out that despite their fearsome reputation, millions of sharks are killed every year by humans for every human that is killed by a shark. Some species of shark are even being threatened with extinction due to over-fishing and through accidentally becoming entangled in nets.

Southern Nevada Zoological-Botanical Park

1775 North Rancho; tel: 647-4685; daily 9am–5pm; entrance charge; bus: 106

This small zoo provides a home for more than 200 animal and plant species in only 3 acres. Among the denizens are such rarities as an Indochinese tiger, a pair of catlike predators from Madagascar called fossas, and an international collection of alligators, rattlesnakes, and other reptiles, as well as the last family of Barbary apes in the US and the largest collection of swamp wallabies in North America. Kids can feed the goats and watch Canadian river otters frolic.

Thrill Rides and Arcades

Adventuredome

Circus Circus, 2880 Las Vegas Boulevard South; tel: 794-3939; open daily, hours vary; free, but rides priced individually; all-day passes available; bus: Deuce; map p.136 B2

The Canyon Blaster, the only double-loop, double corkscrew roller coaster in the United States, is the centerpiece of America's largest indoor amusement park. A recent addition, the Sling Shot, shoots riders up to the ceiling at 4Gs and then "gently" freefalls down

again at -1G. An all-day pass costs from $15–$23, depending on the height of the ticket-holder.

Gameworks

Showcase Mall, 3769 Las Vegas Boulevard South; tel: 432-4263; www.gameworks.com; Sun–Thur 10am–midnight, Fri and Sat until 1am; free, games priced individually; monorail: MGM Grand, bus: Deuce; map p.139 C2

Kids will love this video playground created by Steven Spielberg. A joint venture between DreamWorks, Sega Enterprises, and Universal Studios. Games run the gamut from old-time pinball machines to full-motion rides like Power Sleds, a Japanese-based game where several racers are pitted against each other on the same icy course. Youngsters can also try virtual versions of skiing, horse racing, and skateboarding and do mock battle in jet fighter and tank simulators. No need for cash either; patrons buy a Smart Card from which rides, attractions, food, and drink are debited.

Las Vegas Mini Grand Prix

1401 North Rainbow Boulevard; tel: 259-7000; www.lvmgp.com; Sun–Thur 10am–10pm, Fri and Sat until 11pm; entrance charge; bus: 101

This is the West's only banked-oval stock car track. Along with the go-karts and kiddie karts, the 7-acre facility provides Grand Prix cars for big drivers too. There is also a video game arcade, slides, and a small roller coaster to keep boisterous youngsters occupied while waiting for a car.

Manhattan Express

New York New York, 3970 Las Vegas Boulevard South; tel: 740-6969; Sun–Thur 11am–11pm, Fri–Sat 10.30am–midnight; entrance charge; bus: Deuce; map p.139 C2

The original Strip resort roller coaster careens at speeds up to 67mph along the hotel roofline and above replicas of skyscrapers, New York Harbor, and the Statue of Liberty. The 3-minute ride features two drops of more than 100ft, a unique 180-degree heartline twist and dive, and a 540-degree spiral.

NASCAR Cyber Speedway

Sahara, 2535 Las Vegas Boulevard South, tel: 737-2111; daily from 10am; entrance charge; monorail: Sahara, bus: Deuce; map p.136 B3/B4

Visitors can choose among life-size NASCAR race cars and take a virtual-reality adventure, roaring around the

Below: the Dolphin Habitat has been visited by half-a-million schoolchildren since it opened in 1990.

Left: at last, face painting tries to broaden its market audience.

from vehicles decked out as gondolas or riverboats, recreating some of the world's great celebrations. For a fee, casino guests can join the parade – especially enticing to children – and leave with a photograph.
SEE ALSO CASINOS P.53

Las Vegas Motor Speedway track or hurtling along the Strip at breakneck speed as the vehicle shakes and sways up and down and side to side as a fast-moving racetrack is projected onto a 20-ft wraparound screen. Though Speed – The Ride lasts only 45 seconds, riders are propelled from zero to 35mph in 2 seconds and can reach simulated speeds of up to 220mph.

Stratosphere Tower
2000 Las Vegas Boulevard South; tel: 380-7777 or 800-998-6937; bus: Deuce; map p.136 B4
In a town where scary roller coaster rides are the norm, the Stratosphere – the eighth-tallest building in the world – goes one step further in pandering to the primal fear of falling. X Scream, installs riders in a very open eight-passenger roller coaster-type car and plunges them over the edge of the observation deck at a speed of 30mph, to hang and rock 900ft above the ground before being lifted back to safety. Sixteen dollars might seem like a lot for a one-minute ride, but it includes admission to the tower, a $10 value in itself. Other rides on the tower include the Big Shot, a bungee slingshot ride, and Insanity, a centrifuge ride that lets you spin face-down over the city far

below. Kids must be at least 54 inches tall to ride on it.
SEE ALSO CASINOS P.49–50

Masquerade in the Sky
Rio, 3700 West Flamingo Road, tel: 777-7777; free; bus: 202; map p.138 A3
The spectacular, mildly sexy, 12-minute show takes place seven times every afternoon and evening above the heads of spectators in the Rio's Masquerade Village mall. A procession of gaily decorated floats moves steadily around a 950-ft track and exotically dressed performers sing and wave from a balloon and

Shopping

M&M's World
3785 Las Vegas Boulevard South; tel: 736-7611; Sun–Thur 9am–11pm, Fri–Sat 9am–midnight; monorail: MGM Grand, bus: Deuce; map p.139 C2
The world's largest factory outlet candy store includes not only tons of confectionary but also spectacular exhibits such as a 3-D theater, a full-size replica of the NASCAR race car sponsored by M&Ms, and an wall cov-

Right: taking the plunge at the Adventuredome.

In Floyd Lamb State Park, fascinating guided carriage tours take visitors to the remains of one of the Las Vegas area's earliest ranches and an archeological dig where archaic Native American relics and fossils of prehistoric mammals, many of which are in the Las Vegas Natural History Museum *(see p.57–8)*, have been discovered.

ered with M&Ms in every color of the rainbow, including many you can not buy at supermarkets. There are candy-themed gift products galore, from T-shirts to cocktail glasses.

Build a Bear Workshop
Planet Hollywood, 3663 Las Vegas Boulevard South; tel: 836-0899; www.buildabear. com; Sun–Thur 10am–11pm, Fri–Sat 10am–midnight; monorail: Bally's/Paris Las Vegas, bus: Deuce; map p.138–139 C3; **Fashion Show Mall**, 3200 Las Vegas Boulevard South, Space 2530; tel: 388-2574; Mon–Sat 10am–9pm, Sun 11am–7pm; bus: Deuce; map p.136 B1
Kids can select and customize their own furry friends at this assembly-line store in the Aladdin's Desert Passage mall, picking a skin, stuffing it with cotton and choosing a wardrobe to create a baseball player bear, a biker bear, or any of a hundred other possibilities. Each bear comes with its own birth certificate and a bar code to identify its owner if it becomes lost.

FAO Schwarz
Forum Shops at Caesars Palace, 3500 Las Vegas Boulevard South; tel: 796-6500, www.fao.com; Sun–Thur 10am–11pm, Fri–Sat 10am–midnight; monorail: Flamingo/Caesars Palace, bus: Deuce; map p.138 B3/B4

Amid the high-fashion boutiques of Caesars' Forum Shops, you will find this upscale toy store—a new branch of the oldest toy store in the world (*c.* 1862)—where you can shop for robots, toy bunnies, and playthings exclusive to the store's Vegas location, such as a Sydney Chase doll dressed as a showgirl.

Toys of Yesteryear
2028 East Charleston Boulevard; tel: 598-4030; bus: 206; map p.135 D3
Old-fashioned wind-up toys, electric train sets, and vintage dolls from the mid-20th century are the stock-in-trade at this unusual antiques shop for kids adjacent to the Antique Square Shopping Center.

Supplies and Furniture Rental

Baby's Away
1760 Nuevo Rd, Henderson; tel: 458-1019; www.babysaway.com
This baby-and-child equipment center rents strollers, car seats, cribs, beach gear, and a multitude of other products, from backpacks to kids' DVDs.

Parks

Sunset Park
2681 East Sunset Road (at Eastern Avenue); bus: 212, 110; map p.10
Near the airport, this park surrounding a natural spring-fed lake with a manmade island has picnic areas with children's playgrounds and a winding, paved hiking and biking trail. Several times a year it is the site of the Age of Chivalry Renaissance Festival, known locally as the "Ren Fair."

Floyd Lamb State Park
Tule Springs Road, off US 95 north of Las Vegas; tel: 486-5413
Named for a prominent United States senator from

Nevada, this large park north-east of the city has natural desert areas and grassy lawns where peacocks stroll free, as well as some pleasant picnic areas and four small trout fishing lakes.

Theater

Rainbow Company
Youth Theatre
821 Las Vegas Boulevard North; tel: 229-6553;
This award-winning theater company, a Las Vegas institution for more than 30 years, presents five quality plays a year, featuring an audition-picked cast of 40 kids age 12 and up. Children and teens also work on set construction, lighting and all aspects of theater production.

Ron Lucas
Desert Passage, 3667 Las Vegas Boulevard South; tel: 785-5555; shows Sat–Thur 3pm, dusk Fri; monorail: Bally's/Paris Las Vegas, bus: Deuce; map p.139 C3
Known as "The Man Who Can Make Anything Talk," Lucas puts on an afternoon ventriloquism act just for kids, co-starring a panoply of puppets.

Below: unique souvenirs are available at specialty toy stores located throughout the Strip.

Conference Survival

W hat happens in Vegas stays in Vegas, they say. But what if you do not want to leave anything in Vegas? While they are a necessity for most businesses, conventions can be crazy under the best of circumstances. Throw in casino gambling, free drinks, topless showgirls, and assorted other opportunities for bad behavior, and it is no wonder that more than a few executive reputations are ruined here every year. Here is what you need to know to have a successful business experience in Las Vegas.

Convention Venues

Las Vegas Convention Center

3150 Paradise Road; tel: 892-0711; www.lvcva.com; monorail: Las Vegas Convention Center, bus: 108; map p.137 C3/D2

Owned and operated by the Las Vegas Convention and Visitors' Authority, the convention center is one of the largest in the US. It's not only the size of the convention center that lets Vegas host the largest industry events in the country. The number of hotel rooms available to business visitors—presently 137,600 guest rooms and suites, predicted to rise to 171,000 by 2010—lets the city accommodate large numbers of visitors.

Conference Centers

Besides the convention center, many Strip hotels have their own conference facilities, used for smaller conventions and as breakout venues for big convention center events. Among the largest are Paris Las Vegas, Mandalay Bay, MGM Grand and New York New York.

Some hotel conference venues are far outside the city and beyond the reach of bright lights and other distractions. Notable among these is the Ritz-Carlton, at Lake Las Vegas east of Henderson, and Green Valley Ranch Resort. There are even very small conference centers designed to accommodate executive gatherings of 12 to 20. A notable example is the Hotel at Mount Charleston.
SEE ALSO ACCOMMODATIONS P.20–31; CHILDREN P.56

Non-gaming hotels

Hotels adjacent to the Las Vegas Convention Center are set up with business travelers

Size matters: only McCormick Hall in Chicago is slightly bigger than the Las Vegas Convention Center, but that will no longer hold true after Las Vegas completes its pending $737 million, 500,000-sq ft expansion, now being built across Desert Inn Road from the main 3.2-million-sq ft facility.

in mind. This sometimes means eschewing the usual centrally located casino in favor of more traditional recreation facilities such as quiet, dimly lit lounges. The Las Vegas Hilton does have a casino, but other neighboring hotels such as the Convention Center Courtyard by Marriott and the Convention Center Marriott Suites do not.

Away from the convention center are a growing number of hotels that have no casinos. Their hospitality is represented by other amenities instead. Tops in this genre are the Alexis Hotel, the first major nongambling resort in Las Vegas and the elegant little Artisan Hotel. Another, more self-consciously businesslike option is the Amerisuites near the airport.
SEE ALSO ACCOMMODATIONS P.20–31

Business Lunches and Dinners

Eating in the Las Vegas Convention Center, like any big convention center, generally involves long lines, high prices and variable food.

Left: a quick break by the pool, before the next meeting begins.

ing and leaving it at some strip hotel with free, unlimited parking. Transportation between Strip hotels and the convention center is easy. You could take bus 108 or call a taxi, but there's nothing like riding to the exhibit hall on the sleek, fast Las Vegas Monorail.
SEE ALSO TRANSPORTATION P.126–9

Should You Take the Spouse and Kids?

In US corporate culture, taking the spouse to a convention can be considered poor form. Vegas conventions are a special case, though. If you leave your spouse home, he or she could imagine you are guilty of all sorts of peccadillos. We recommend you take your spouse or "significant other" along. That way, while you're working the exhibit hall, he or she can be having a good time on the Strip. If you can manage it, leave the kids at home. Not that they would not want to come too, but your spouse will be free to have more fun if they don't: like expensive shopping or "girls'/boys' night out" shows. Just keep reminding yourself, "What happens in Vegas stays in Vegas."

Lunch possibilities are virtually unlimited, but rarely quick, along the Strip. The best lunch bet in the convention center area is the Paradise Café in the Las Vegas Hilton. Or, for a memorably goofy alternative, try the Hilton's Star Trek-themed Quark's Bar and Restaurant. For a business dinner Vegas-style, check out a local favorite like **Battista's Hole in the Wall** or **The Tillerman**. Benihana Village in the Las Vegas Hilton is unbeatable for convenience and ambience. Another unforgettable dining experience is dinner at the revolving **Top of the World** restaurant, 800ft up on the Stratosphere Tower.
SEE ALSO RESTAURANTS P.113, 116, 117

Relaxing After a Hard Day

Peace and quiet are not characteristic of most Vegas bars. If you want a traditional club-like atmosphere, complete with leather chairs and dark wood walls, the place to go is

the **Artisan Lounge** in the Artisan Hotel. Another peaceful little bar is the **Dispensary Lounge** on East Tropicana Avenue. For a unique experience that makes for barroom bonding, share a waterpipe at the low-key **Hookah Lounge**.
SEE ALSO BARS AND CAFÉS P.35–6

Convention Center Transportation

Although convention center exhibitors will usually need a rental car to transport props and promotional materials, parking during large conventions can be enough of a challenge to warrant foregoing a rental, or at least park-

Right: golfing amidst the beautiful, desert surroundings.

Environment

With its showy lighting and water displays, few people think of Vegas as a "green" city. But in reality, the collision of rapid population growth with the limits of scarce water and power resources is forcing the city to the forefront of alternative energy development, even as it brings new conflicts with rural areas that depend on underground water for ranching and farming. The desert around Vegas, despite its sparsity, is a finely balanced and beautiful ecosystem. If you leave the city behind, some of America's finest landscapes, including the cool heights of Mount Charleston and the inviting Lake Mead, are within easy reach.

The Cost of Energy

In 2004, one of the biggest resorts on the Strip had to close for a night, leaving thousands of guests to check in elsewhere. Bellagio was hit hard after a main

power line failed, and although by the next day normal relations were restored, the incident was yet another example of Sin City's almost crippling dependency on power.

Energy problems in the desert are now a constant worry. Three years prior to this incident, Vegas's natural gas prices rose and many casinos began to impose small "per room per day" energy surcharges. Since the turn of the millennium, electricity charges to businesses have risen by 65 per cent. A casino hotel on the Strip can use up as much energy as 10,000 private homes, and rising electricity bills have

> As of the last decade, there were 15,000 miles of neon on the Strip. The Rio's 125ft high marquee *(left)*, voted the city's best neon sign, uses 12,930ft of neon tubing and over 5,000 lightbulbs. Wasteful as some people consider it to be, the glare and glitter of this fantasy city in the desert is sacred to the casinos.

come as a shock to the neon-happy resorts.

At the MGM Grand and other hotels, the 750 watts of light in many rooms has been reduced to 500. Motion sensors turn off lights in empty offices. The current generation of slots are designed to consume 25 percent less electricity than their predecessors.

Seeing power bills rise so steeply, Bally's, Paris Las Vegas, and Caesars Palace adopted more energy-efficient lighting, and Fitzgerald's casino shuts off exterior spotlights at 2am. The Las Vegas Hilton also cut back its hours of floodlighting. At Caesars, "smart thermostat" systems have been installed.

The city's convention center was luckily between shows when Nevada Power asked customers to "shed load." Lights in the building are now being replaced with low-energy bulbs.

GENERATING POWER

Unfortunately, almost all the electricity generated at Hoover Dam goes to South-

Left: beautiful Red Rock Canyon *(see p.14)* is only a short drive from the Strip.

way of life. Natural springs and seeps that feed water-holes where livestock can drink will dry up if the aquifer levels fall by just 2ft.

Yucca Mountain

Almost 60 years ago, the first atomic bombs were tested at Yucca Flat, and the Federal government's occupation of this area finally led to Yucca Mountain being selected as a repository for 77,000 tons of radioactive waste. This will be stored in supposedly "safe" canisters in concrete-lined chambers. Nobody knows just how safe this will be, as the mountain's interior is not as waterproof as had previously been thought. If nuclear waste is transported by truck from facilities throughout the US, news of a "nuclear accident" on southern Nevada's highways could devastate Vegas's tourist economy.

Although the US Congress and Department of Energy authorized the opening of the Yucca Mountain Repository more than 20 years ago, state government and public opposition have prevented its opening, and the earliest projected date is now 2017.

SEE ALSO RED ROCK CANYON AND MOUNT CHARLESTON P.14–5

ern California. When the dam was built, the local government estimated that the town would never grow to more than 5,000 population, and only that much power was allocated to Las Vegas. The electricity that lights the neon extravaganza on the Strip comes from a coal-burning power plant north of the city, which is now being forced to look at more creative ways to meet its electricity needs.

According to the Geothermal Energy Association, 29 geothermal power projects now under development in Nevada will produce roughly 25 percent of the state's total power needs within three to five years. The power company is also investing in solar electrical systems.

Some Vegas subdivision developers are now building only "zero energy homes," which generate their own solar electricity.

The Thirst for Water

With a mere 4in of rainfall per year, Las Vegas is the driest metropolitan area in the US. Local water officials consider the conspicuous water consumption at some resorts – golf courses, dancing fountains, scenic canals and grand-scale pool complexes – to be vital to the city's economy. At the same time, residents face one of the country's most aggressive water conservation programs. The Southern Nevada Water Authority even pays homeowners to uproot their grass lawns and xeriscape with natural desert plants.

GOING UNDERGROUND

Yet officials acknowledge that water conservation alone cannot sustain the city's growth rate. The favored solution is to buy up water rights in a chain of underground water basins in sparsely populated Lincoln and White Pine counties to the north. The move is controversial. Some landowners are happy to take Las Vegas up on its top-dollar offer for their water rights. But many farmers and ranchers see the water grab as a threat to their

In earlier times, Lake Mead was seen as an almost unlimited water supply because all water used would otherwise be lost to evaporation from the lake's surface. But as its water was diverted to supply California and Arizona the water level has begun to fall so much that towns consumed during the lake's creation have re-emerged.

Essentials

One out of eight visitors to Las Vegas comes from another country, making a total of nearly 10 million foreign tourists a year a number surpassed in America only by New York and Washington, DC. For these travelers, we furnish the following information. It is helpful when coming to the US from another part of the world to know, at a minimum, what various denominations of US money are worth in your home currency, what Fahrenheit temperatures translate into in Celsius degrees and how to convert miles per hour to kilometers per hour.

Embassies and Consulates

There are no official international consulates in Las Vegas. In most cases, the consulate with Las Vegas jurisdiction is 300 miles away in Los Angeles, California.

Australia
Consulate, Century Plaza Towers, 19th Floor, 2049 Century Park East, Los Angeles, CA 90067; tel: 310-229-4800

Canada
Consulate General, 550 South Hope Street, 9th Floor, Los Angeles, CA 90071; tel: 213-346-2700

South Africa
Wilshire Boulevard, Suite 600, Los Angeles, CA 90048; tel: 323-651-0902

United Kingdom
Consulate-General, 11766 Wilshire Boulevard, Suite 400, Los Angeles, CA 90025; tel: 310-477-3322

Emergency Numbers

All emergencies: 911.
Metropolitan Police Department
400 Stewart Ave, tel: 795-3111 (non-emergency) or 229-3111.

Health

INSURANCE
Health care is very expensive in the US. Always take out comprehensive travel insurance in case of emergencies.

Hospitals

Desert Springs Hospital Medical Center
2075 East Flamingo Road; tel: 733-8800; bus: 203; map p.10
Lake Mead Hospital and Medical Center
1409 East Lake Mead Boulevard, North Las Vegas; tel: 649-7711

Below: pharmacies are often open 24 hours.

Sunrise Hospital and Medical Center
3186 South Maryland Parkway; tel: 731-8080; bus: 109; map p.137 E3
University Medical Center
1800 West Charleston Boulevard; tel: 383-2000; bus: 206; map p.134 A1
Valley Hospital
620 Shadow Lane; tel: 388-4000; map p.134 A1

Internet Access

The kind of Internet cafés where you can rent a computer terminal by the hour to check your e-mail are rare in the US. If you need to access the Internet while traveling here, it is essential to bring your own laptop. Most hotels and motels offer wireless Internet access. Many cafés have free wireless access, as does McCarren International Airport. The best place to find a public computer is the Las Vegas Library (833 North Las Vegas Boulevard, tel: 507-3500).

Money

CURRENCY
US Dollars ($) are divided into 100 cents. Bills come in

Left: the most important sign in Las Vegas.

Imperial to Metric Conversion	
ft–m	3.3=1
miles–km	0.62=1
acres–ha	2.47=1
lbs–kg	2.2=1
°F–°C	32°=0° (subtract 30, divide by 2)

Las Vegas Visitor Information Center
3150 Paradise Road; tel: 892-7573; daily 8am–5pm; map p.137 C2

Las Vegas Chamber of Commerce
3720 Howard Hughes Parkway; tel: 735-1616, fax: 735-2011.

$500, $100, $50, $20, $10, $5 and $1 denominations. Coins include 50¢ (half-dollar), 25¢ (quarter), 10¢ (dime), 5¢ (nickel) and 1¢ (penny) values; and there is a slot machine for each variety.

CREDIT CARDS AND ATMS

Credit cards are accepted almost everywhere, although not all cards at all places. They can also be used to withdraw money at ATMs.

TAX

Shoppers in Clark County pay 8.25 percent in taxes for all non-food items and for food items purchased already prepared such as in a restaurant.

> Package deals and favorable exchange rates for travelers from Europe make a trip to the US very affordable for the time being, and you should have little trouble exchanging money in Vegas. Most casinos' cashier desks will readily exchange foreign currency without charging commission.

Mail

Postal authorities are available to respond to questions or concerns 24hrs a day, seven days a week by calling 800-275-8777. There are branches of the post office throughout the Las Vegas Valley, but the main post office is located at 101 East Sunset Road.

Telephones

The country code for the US is 1; the area code for Clark County (where Las Vegas is located) is 702. While in the Vegas area, calls to the metropolitan vicinity require only the seven-digit number. International calls require 011 + (country code) + (city code) + (number).

Britain +44, Ireland +353, Australia +61, New Zealand +64, and South Africa +27.

Tourist Information

There are tourist offices throughout Clark County. Access via the Internet at www.lasvegas24hours.com, the website of the Las Vegas Convention and Visitors Authority (LVCVA).

Visas and Passports

All international travelers—including US citizens—must have passports to enter the US. Citizens of Canada and Mexico do not need visas, but do require passports. Citizens of most western European nations, as well as Australia, New Zealand, and Japan, can stay for up to 90 days without a visa, so long as they have a valid passport and a return air ticket. Others entering the US might need visas. Since 9/11, it is a good idea to always carry proof of identity wherever you go.

CUSTOMS

Adult visitors staying longer than 72 hours may bring along the following items duty free: 1 liter of wine or liquor; 100 cigars (non-Cuban), or 3lbs of tobacco, or 200 cigarettes; and gifts valued under $100.

Absolutely no food (even in cans) or plants of any type are permissible. Visitors may also arrive and depart with up to $10,000 currency without declaration.

Food and Drink

Dining in Las Vegas has been transformed. The wall-to-wall all-you-can-eat buffets have been sidelined, the celebrity chefs have moved in, and the standards and the stakes (steaks) have been raised all round. Although the high-ticket gastrodomes may not be perfect for every meal, they have definitely raised the culinary game. Unfortunately the days of cheap buffets are gone as well. Prices in most eateries have nearly caught up with their New York, LA, and San Francisco cousins, but so too has the food and the service. In fact, eating may be the only "genuine" experience available on the Strip.

Left: the legendary Vegas buffet still survives and has been smartened up for modern tastes.

Cuisines of the World

With the arrival of Wolfgang Puck's Spago in 1992, the city began a slow but sure ascent from the depths of continental cuisine into the modern world of the nouvelle, haute, California, Pan Asian, and Pacific Rim. Since then, more "name" chefs have brought their operations to Vegas, among them Emeril Lagasse and Jean-Louis Palladin.

Acting in concert with these arrivals was the hotels' newfound willingness to relinquish ownership and management of some of their dining spaces to experienced restaurateurs. The improvement of the dining experience led to an across-the-board renewal.

Today, some of the city's – and even the country's – best restaurants are within hotel-casinos, such as Picasso at Bellagio, Zeffirino at the Venetian, the Daniel Boulud Brasserie at Wynn Las Vegas, and Aureole at Mandalay Bay.

Bountiful Buffets

Despite these changes to the culinary landscape, buffets can still be a hit-and-miss affair, with many offering similar selections of prime rib, starchy vegetables, limp salads, and boring desserts. Others offer a wide array of cuisine – Mexican, Italian, American heartland – plus all the seconds, thirds, and fourths you can gulp down.

The tantalizing buffets of lore – where the food is imaginatively selected and the prices low – do exist, but may require some searching out.

The Rio's Carnival World Buffet is a cut above, as is Main Street Station's Garden Court Buffet. But it and The Buffet at the Gold Nugget are no longer rock-bottom cheap. Sunday champagne brunches were once the best of the buffets. Today, most are simply a more expensive version of the standard breakfast-lunch offerings. Bally's Sterling Brunch is a notable exception. Replete with ice sculptures and fresh flowers, it is a spread fit for a king, but also the most expensive.

Themed Affairs

Theme restaurants have proliferated in Vegas. Local versions of the Hard Rock Café and the Harley Davidson Café pull the same surpris-

> Food in Las Vegas always comes in colossal amounts: 21 tons of smoked salmon and 2,700oz of caviar are consumed in Caesars Palace's various restaurants every year, as well as 336,000 of the aptly named Caesar salads.

Left: showy displays and (imported) fresh ingredients are the key features of today's casino cuisine.

With the largest selection of wines in Vegas, this modern store (the "design" consists of pure white curved walls) serves 1.5-oz portions for you to see, swirl, smell, and sip.

Gee's Oriental Market
4109 West Sahara Avenue; tel: 362-5287; daily 10am–6pm; bus: 204
Sells hard-to-find ingredients for cooking authentic Thai or Chinese food. They also sell hot foods to go.

International Marketplace
5000 South Decatur Boulevard; tel: 456-7762; daily 10am–6pm; bus: 103; map p.10
This vast store sells an astonishing array of foods, with departments arranged by continent. You can get Brazilian candies, Japanese soft drinks, and Dutch soups.

Krispy Kreme
Excalibur, 3850 Las Vegas Boulevard South; 24 hours; bus: Deuce; map p.139 C1/C2
When you crave a donut, this is the place to get them while they are warm.

Whole Foods
8855 West Charleston Boulevard; tel: 254-8655; daily 7am–10pm; bus: 206
The local outlet of this nationwide natural foods chain offers organic produce, food supplements, wine, and beer. It has a large selection of ready-to-eat foods as well as a salad bar and a hot food and soup bar.

ingly brisk business that they do around the globe.

And then there are the international themed restaurants, from the imposing Hofbrauhaus, to a Parisian (indoor) sidewalk café, to a rainforest eatery complete with thunderstorms.

Home-grown Talent

When the population of Vegas sky-rocketed in the middle of the last decade, locally-owned dining also experienced a boom, and many ethnic and specialty restaurants have opened.

One of the traditional areas of any major tourist city – a so-called restaurant row – has evolved piecemeal along Paradise Road, adding to the options. Here, diners can choose from a plethora of major restaurants, locally-owned eateries, plus some small tasty ethnic cafés.

Chinatown, near Spring Mountain Road, is another good place to check out, offering excellent cuisine that

includes Filipino and Vietnamese as well as the more traditional Chinese.

Local Stores

Ethel M Chocolates
2 Cactus Drive, Henderson; tel: 433-2500; Sat–Sun 8.30am–7pm; map p.16
Ethel M was Ethel Mars, the wife of Frank Mars, who founded Mars Inc., makers of M&Ms and Snickers. This gourmet chocolatier, located by a cactus garden in Henderson, offers tantalizing gift boxes of candy, including liqueur-filled chocolates. Ethel M also has retail outlets in major Strip casino resorts.

55° Wine + Design
Mandalay Bay; 3950 Las Vegas Boulevard South; tastings every Fri at 3 and 6pm; bus: Deuce; map p139 C1/D1

DOUGHNUTS®

Right: not gourmet food, but better.

Gambling

There is only one sure-fire way to make money from a casino: buy one. If you play the slots, the tables, or the sports book in Las Vegas, do it to have fun. You may find Lady Luck and win a fortune at the tables. Then again, you may not (or you might win a fortune, then lose it all and more). The golden rule for happy gambling is to set a limit beforehand and not exceed it. If you can manage that, the other motto is to quit while you are ahead. Some serious players pre-calculate a stake range that will let them play through the night and stick to low bets until they hit a winning streak, then progressively raise their stakes.

Slot Machines

The century-long history of slot machines began with the original three-reel machine, which emerged from Charles Frey's San Francisco workshop in 1898. The German-born inventor pioneered many kinds of coin-operated gaming devices, most of which found a place in the gambling clubs of 'Frisco's Barbary Coast.

The basic design of "Liberty Bell," the granddaddy of all American slot machines, is still used today, although the simple trio of reels have evolved into microprocessor-controlled machines, with up to five spinning reels holding hundreds of symbols.

By the time Bugsy Siegel added slot machines to his Flamingo Hotel in the late 1940s, they had already spread across the US as a way to entertain the wives and girlfriends of high rollers. Soon they were making more revenue than table games.

The machines are pro-grammed for a jackpot rare enough to make a big pay-off, but still allow a tidy profit for the casino. Pay-outs are somewhere between 83 and 98 percent, and vary from one casino to another. The machines are inspected under seal by the state gaming commission to make sure payouts are within the legal range.

RANDOM LUCK

The phenomenal popularity of slot machines is doubt-less because they require no skill and the pace can be set by the player. The machines are driven by random gener-ators that make new selec-tions every 1,000th of a second, with no reference to what went before, so in real-ity the machines are never "ready to hit."

Many casinos have dis-pensed with the stainless steel trays that catch coins when you win, replacing them with a paper ticket that you must cash in. Harrah's and other casinos have kept the tradition allowing even little winners the joy of the sound of coins clinking in the tray.

Below: slot players are driven by the false illusion that a machine will be ready to pay off after a certain amount of play.

Left: the natural house edge for blackjack is around 3.5 percent, but a skilled player can reduce it to 1 percent or less, among the best odds in the casino.

nos, mostly downtown, play with a single deck, giving the player much better chances to predict the remaining cards. This may improve your odds of winning, but often single-deck games pay out at lower rates than multi-deck ones, tipping the balance back in favor of the casinos.

Poker

A tip from one professional poker player is this: sit down at the table and spot the sucker. If you haven't made them within five minutes, get up and leave. It's you.

The ability to read other players at the table can be as important in poker as getting the best cards. In the betting rounds, the players who think they have the strongest hand will try to lure money into the "pot." But players who believe they have weaker cards may bluff, to scare others out of the game. Poker is the only game where play is against other gamblers and not against the house. Instead, the house makes its living from a "rake"—usually around 5 percent—off the top of each pot.

Slot machines and video poker machines now generate about 85 percent of Nevada casinos' total take, with the nickel slots alone producing $1 billion annually. Slot machines take up 60 percent of casino floor space and generate more profits than all the other table games combined.

SMALL CHANGE
Another draw of slot machines are their small stakes. The El Cortez Hotel and Casino even offers penny slots. At the other end of the spectrum, the Four Queens downtown has the biggest machine in the world.

Bear in mind that the most you can win on a slot increases as you risk more coins. If you only stake the minimum, you will not be able to win the maximum advertised jackpot.

Card Schools

If you are inexperienced, there are several ways to overcome your lack of knowledge. The first is to read about the games. Another is to practice on the video versions of these games before moving to live table action. With minimum wagers as low as 5 cents and no other players waiting impatiently for you to make your next move, electronic gaming is an alternative that many novice gamblers never move beyond. The best option, though, is to take advantage of one of the free gaming lessons offered.

The following casinos offer gaming lessons. Excalibur, New York New York, Palace Station, Circus Circus, and Excalibur.

Blackjack

Originally known as "Twenty-One" or *vingt-et-un*, blackjack is a descendant from the French game of *chemin de fer*, as is *baccarat*. There are stories of the game having been played in casinos in France as far back as the early 1700s. It arrived in the US in the 1800s, and got its modern name from the frontier practice of paying out extra on a hand of an ace with the jack of spades.

The object is to get a hand of cards closer to 21 than the dealer. Cards take their numerical value, except for face cards 10, and aces, which the player can value as one or 11. The top hand, an ace with a 10 or a face card, makes 21: "blackjack."

Blackjack deals are usually from a six or eight-deck plastic "shoe." Some casi-

Above: payout can be a dizzying 35 to 1, but the 0 and 00 make roulette odds 37 to 1 against you predicting the correct number.

TEXAS HOLD 'EM

A common form of poker in Las Vegas is Texas Hold 'Em. Each player is dealt two cards, face down. Through progressive betting rounds, five "community cards" are dealt, face up. Each player then makes the highest five-card hand they can from the seven cards available.

Baccarat

Typically assumed to be a high-roller card game, baccarat is similar to blackjack, though it is played with stricter rules, higher limits and less player interaction. It is not for the faint of heart, as stakes can quickly mount to dizzying heights. The object of the game is to come as close as possible to nine; the only real skill involved is deciding whether to bet on the player or the bank. Most baccarat tables are located in quiet, sequestered sections of the casino. Lessons are highly recommended.

Craps

A crap game may look daunting, but is really fairly simple. It also offers good odds to players; the house edge on a simple "pass line" bet is only 1.4 percent. Bets are made for and against a dice roll, called "right" or "wrong" bets. The dice pass around the table. No one has to roll, but the thrower must bet on his own game.

At the first, or "come out" roll, a throw of 2, 3, or 12 is known as craps. This is a win for bets on the "don't pass" line, or wrong bets. The numbers 7 or 11 are automatic winners for "pass-line" right bets. Any other number rolled establishes the shooter's "point." The aim then is to roll the point again before hitting a 7. There are many other possible bets on a craps layout, but most of them –

such as field, big 6, big 8, hard way and hop bets – are "sucker bets" with horrendously bad odds.

Roulette

The wheel spins, the ball spins against it. The ball drops, and clatters. It bounces once, twice, and comes to rest in number 7. The dealer places the white marker next to your chip on the 7, and your $100 bet is joined by $3,500 in chips. Or not. If the ball falls on 0 or 00, all bets lose, save for those predicting that exact outcome. One to one payouts are offered by "red or black," "odd or even," or "first or last 18."

Keno

Keno is hugely popular as it is so simple to play, and a $50,000 payout is possible on a $1 bet. All you need do is pick some numbers on a ticket and wait. It's easy, and it's fun. It's also among the lowest player odds in the house, with a casino edge of 20 to 30 percent. If a runner returns with winnings, it is polite to tip.

Sports Books

In the sports book, players back their expertise in pre-

Below: the overall house edge for roulette is 5.26 percent, about the poorest table odds in town.

> Due to a mystery of Nevada gaming regulation, keno is not, technically, a lottery. Payouts must be collected immediately, before the next game starts, or they are forfeited. Take a place at the bar and call a keno runner over, pick your numbers and wait for the draw. Any number of tickets can be bought for each game, and there are endless combos to mark the numbers.

dicting sports events. Odds are offered on football, baseball, Indy car races, and championship boxing. But the main event in the book is horse racing, still the largest spectator sport in the US.

The sports book is the one (and only) place in a casino you are guaranteed to find a clock.

Books

Gamblers' Book Shop
630 South 11th Street; tel: 382-7555; map p.135 C2
There is hardly any aspect of gambling that this store does not have something about on its shelves, and when Brooklyn-born manager Howard Schwartz can not find anything on a subject he usually commissions somebody to write it.

Many of the titles were written by John Luckman, who in 1964 with his wife Edna founded the store. It now stocks more than a thousand titles, plus all the manila folders on everything from card tricks to slot-machine crooks.

About half of the store's sales derive from its extensive mailing list of 25,000 customers, whose demands are increasingly for computer games and videotapes.

TITLES

Burning the Tables in Las Vegas: Keys to Success in Blackjack and in Life, Ian Anderson. Huntington Press, 2003.

The Frugal Gambler, Jean Scott. Huntington Press 2005.

Knock-Out Blackjack: The Easiest Card-Counting System Ever Devised, Olaf Van-cura and Ken Fuchs. Huntington Press, 2006.

Comps

Comps can include just about anything: free rooms, shows, dining, or plays. The easiest route for their munificence is via slot clubs whose members – and that could include you – carry cards that rack up points each time they are used, irrespective of wins or losses.

The points, which can be exchanged for all kinds of favors, add up very fast, given the addictive way most people charge around Vegas, and what the casino gets out of it, of course, is that the cards keep you coming back.

You can also earn comps at table games by playing for a certain amount of time.

Glossary of Terms

Buy In
Amount of chips bought at the start of a gaming session.
Cage
The protected area from which the cashiers sell and buy chips.
Eye in the sky
Mirrors or concealed video cameras used to monitor table games (dealers and gamblers) to catch cheats.
Hand Pay
Winnings so large they are paid by a casino staff member. Tips are expected.
Pit boss
The person overseeing table games from behind a dealer.
Shoe
Small box on table from which poker cards are dealt.
Shooter
The player rolling the dice at a craps game.
Toke
A tip or gratuity usually given to casino employees by anyone who has hit a big win.
Whale or High Roller
A customer with the bankroll to bet large sums of money. Whales may arrive in Vegas by private jet courtesy of the casino, and be given complementary food and high-roller suites.

Below: because Las Vegas casinos collectively clear profits of about $17 million each day, they don't balk at giving away about $2 million a day in comps.

Gay and Lesbian

While Las Vegas may have a reputation as "Sin City" and has made a legend out of such figures as Liberace, the city itself is only quietly tolerant of its fairly large gay and lesbian community, in the same look-the-other-way manner in which many gay entertainers have been accepted. Many gay businesses, bars, and nightclubs are centered in the oddly named "Fruit Loop," around the intersection of Paradise Road and Naples Drive. For more information and a good source of listings, pick up *Q-Vegas* magazine, available at most major record and bookstores.

Helplines and Networking

Betty's Outrageous Adventures
PO Box 751472, Las Vegas, NV 89136; tel: 991-9929; e-mail: BOA_LV@usa.net; www.bettysout.com
Organizes social events for the lesbian community.

Gay and Lesbian Center
953 East Sahara Avenue, Suite B 25; tel: 733-9800; www.thecenterlv.com; Mon–Fri 11am–7pm, Sat 10am–3pm; map p.137 D4
Generally staffed seven days a week. The office provides a guide to local bars.

Human Rights Campaign
e-mail: HRC-LasVegas@cox.net; www.hrc.org
The Las Vegas chapter of the largest US civil rights organization working for LGBT equality holds monthly mixers and other events at various locations.

SNAPI (Southern Nevada Association of Pride, Inc.)
5015 West Sahara Avenue, Suite 125; tel: 615-9429; www.lasvegaspride.org
This volunteer group celebrates diversity with Las Vegas Pride Week in May.

Transgender Support & Advocacy Nevada
4343 North Rancho #234, Suite 8; tel: 392-2132
Provides group and individual counseling, medical referrals, and political advocacy for transgendered persons.

Bars, Cafés, and Clubs

Backdoor Lounge
1415 East Charleston Boulevard; tel: 385-2018; 24 hours; bus: 206; map p.135 D3
Open 24/7, this dance clubs features late-night (2am) entertainment, including Latin Seduction on Fridays.

Badlands Saloon
953 East Sahara Avenue; tel: 792-9262; 24 hours; bus: 204; map p.137 D4
An easygoing country-and-western neighborhood bar with a very friendly staff.

Buffalo
Paradise Plaza, 4640 Paradise Road; tel: 733-8355; 24 hours; bus: 108; map p.139 E3
This low-key local favorite has pool tables and video poker, with $5 beer busts on Tuesday and Friday evenings.

Charlie's Las Vegas
5012 South Arville Street #4; tel: 876-1844; www.charlieslasvegas.com; 24 hours; map p.10
Las Vegas's newest country-and-western men's nightclub has a saloon and dance hall motif, Monday and Thursday line dance lessons, and Sunday drag shows.

Eagle
3430 East Tropicana Avenue; tel: 458-8662; 24 hours; bus: 201
Home of the infamous Underwear Nights on Wednesday and Friday.

Flex Lounge
4371 West Charleston Boulevard; tel: 385-3539; 24 hours; bus: 206
This pool hall and dance club

It wasn't until 1993 that Nevada repealed the criminal statute against sodomy, which was defined to include all homosexual intercourse. Yet ten years later, the mayor of Las Vegas officially recognized the city's gay, lesbian, bisexual, and transgendered community by proclaiming Pride Day, an annual event that has now expanded to a full week of festivities in the "Fruit Loop," the arts district, and even on the Strip itself.

Left: Blue Moon Resort is the only resort in Las Vegas that caters exclusively to gay men.

A favorite with locals. Lots of community events, and friendly laid-back staff.

Suede
4640 South Paradise Road, Suite 4; tel: 791-3463; Tue–Fri 5pm–3am, Sat til 5am; bus: 108; map p.139 E3

This chic new night spot in the "Fruit Loop" has karaoke on Tuesday through Thursday, and female impersonators on Friday and Saturday.

Hotels

Blue Moon Resort
2651 Westwood Drive; tel: 361-9099 or 866-796-9194; www.bluemoonlasvegas.com; map p.136 A3

Las Vegas's only resort especially for gay men is a small place. It has just 45 spacious rooms and suites with Sealy pillow-top mattresses, refrigerators, and either wall-to-wall carpeting or Mexican tile. Facilities include a clothing-optional pool and sundeck, Jacuzzi grotto, steam room, fitness room, and movie room. Continental breakfast is included in the room rate. Day passes are available, too.

features male strippers Monday–Wednesday at midnight, ladies night female strippers on Thursday, and drag shows Tuesday and Friday.

FreeZone
610 East Naples Drive; tel: 733-6701; 24 hours; map p.139 E4

The most popular bar for women, but also a hit with men on boys' nights and weekends. Check out the "What a Drag" show.

Gipsy
605 Paradise Road; tel: 731-1919; Wed–Mon from 9pm; bus: 108; map p.138 E3

For years Gipsy has been the gay venue to beat: the most uninhibited and unpretentious dance club in town. So far no other has managed to match Gipsy's success.

Goodtimes Bar and Nightclub
1775 East Tropicana Avenue Suite 1; tel: 736-9494; 24 hours; bus: 201 map p.10

The gay bar located in Liberace Plaza features DJ dance music Friday and Saturday nights and "Las Vegas's Original Liquor Bust" on Monday nights 11pm to 4am, plus Friday tango lessons.

Krave
3663 Las Vegas Boulevard South; tel: 836-0830, www.kravelas vegas.com; Tue–Sun 11pm–6am; monorail: Bally's/Paris Las Vegas, bus: Deuce; map p.138 B2

The first and only diversity club on the Strip draws thousands of partygoers on weekends with the top dance club DJs in Vegas.

Las Vegas Lounge
900 Karen Avenue; tel: 737-9350; 24 hours; map p.137 C4

Las Vegas's only transgender bar has fantastic, splashy shows and a great crowd.

Snick's Place
1402 South 3rd Street; tel: 385-9298; 24 hours; bus: 108; map p.134 B1

Vegas's oldest gay bar has $5 Saturday beer busts and $6 liquor busts on Saturday nights, as well as package liquor sales and video poker, but the real claim to fame at this arts district bar is the outdoor mural celebrating the history of the city's LGBT community.

Spotlight Lounge
957 East Sahara Avenue; tel: 696-0202; 24 hours; bus: 204; map p.137 C4

Below: a matching ensemble.

History

BC 8,000	Paleolithic Native Americans hunted mammoths and other prehistoric beasts at the green desert oasis now called Las Vegas Valley.
AD 700	Early Pueblo Indians began developing the basketmakers' villages into Pueblo Grande de Nevada, the region's largest ancient settlement.
1150	Pueblo Grande de Nevada was abandoned. The reason remains a mystery.
1829	Rafael Rivera, a scout exploring the desert, discovered a spring and oasis and called it Vegas ("Meadows"). His find shortened the Spanish Trail trade route between Santa Fe, New Mexico, and Los Angeles, California, by 100 miles.
1844	American explorer John C. Fremont camped at Las Vegas Springs. Fremont Street would later be named after him.
1848	The Mexican War ended with the Treaty of Hidalgo, giving a vast area of the Southwest, including Las Vegas, to the United States.
1855	Mormon settlers from Salt Lake City built an adobe fort at Las Vegas and planted fruit trees.
1864	Following silver discoveries in the Carson City area, Nevada became a US state.
1890	Railroad developers picked the Las Vegas Valley as a site for a train station and town.
1905	Las Vegas was founded by Montana senator and railroad tycoon William Clark.
1906	The Golden Gate Hotel opened on Fremont Street – the first casino hotel in Las Vegas.
1910	A new law declared gambling illegal in Nevada. Underground casinos opened within three weeks.
1911	The city of Las Vegas was formally incorporated.
1931	Work began on Boulder Dam (now Hoover Dam). Vegas's population grew from 5,000 to 25,000 in one year. Gambling was legalized.
1941	With 63 rooms, El Rancho Vegas was the first casino hotel to open on the future Las Vegas Strip, across from the present-day Sahara.

AD 700: early rock art remains from the Pueblo Grande de Nevada.

1855: original Mormon settlers are remembered at the Old Mormon Fort.

1906: Golden Gate Hotel was the first Downtown casino hotel.

1931: work on the Hoover Dam begins.

1942	The Last Frontier opens, later to be called the Frontier and today the New Frontier.
1945	Benjamin "Bugsy" Seigel opened the Flamingo Hotel. Nevada levies the first gaming taxes, boosting the state's economy.
1951	Sinatra made his Vegas debut at the Desert Inn.
1955	The nine-story Stardust opened as the first high-rise hotel on the Strip. The Riviera opened, head-lining glam pianist Lee Liberace, the highest paid performer in Vegas history up to that time.
1959	The Nevada Gaming Commission was created.
1967	Nevada's legislature allowed publicly traded corporations to obtain gambling licenses, while banning organized crime figures from casino ownership.
1969	Making his musical comeback, Elvis Presley pre-miered at the International Hotel on the Strip.
1989	The Mirage opened as the most expensive hotel on the Strip, costing $630 million to build.
1993	The new MGM Grand Las Vegas opened. It is presently the world's largest hotel.
1996	The Sands was demolished to make way for the new Venetian, and the Hacienda was imploded to be replaced by the Mandalay Bay. The Monte Carlo and the Stratosphere Tower opened.
1998	The Bellagio opened, the most expensive Strip hotel to date ($1.7 billion).
2000	The Venetian opened.
2003	Caesars Palace opened the Colosseum Theater, the largest concert venue in Las Vegas, with Céline Dion as continuing headliner.
2004	The Desert Inn and its golf course were demol-ished, to be replaced by the Wynn Las Vegas.
2006	MGM Mirage broke ground on Project CityCenter, a $7 billion resort and condo development next to the Bellagio. The project is scheduled for comple-tion in 2010. Plans were unveiled for the World Jewelry Center, a 57-story office tower and jew-elry trade show space, in Downtown Vegas.
2007	The Palms opened its new Pearl stadium, surpassing Caesars' Colosseum as the city's largest concert venue.

1950s: the Rat Pack dominates the Strip's lounge scene.

1967: Elvis and Priscilla tie the knot at the Aladdin casino on the Strip.

2005: Wynn becomes the tallest tower in Las Vegas, for now...

2007: The Stardust is demolished to make room for the Echelon Resort, slated for completion in 2010.

The King, a Queen and Cowboys

Characters in Vegas's past are as made up as a showgirl's frock. Liberace, a master of "don't ask, don't tell" despite a wardrobe of rhinestones, first set the standard for glam. Elvis eschewed the tight slacks of his youth for white catsuits that inspired a spate of middle-aged impersonators. The tradition is very much alive in Vegas today, where Elton John tickets sell out before scalpers can horde them. Still, you can't help wondering if it all started with dusty young men in 10-gallon hats who just wanted to grab the bull by its horns.

Elvis

Elvis-A-Rama

For eight years, Elvis-A-Rama, the world's largest collection of Presley memorabilia, was also one of the hottest tickets in Vegas despite its seedy off-Strip location. Then, after a run of bad luck, it was sold on several times and closed down in 2006.

But Elvis fans have long memories, and are unlikely to let the King be run out of town so easily. Current majority shareholder Robert F.X. Sillerman has confirmed plans to open an Elvis museum and casino next door to the Harley Davidson Café on the Strip.

> The Liberace museum's brochure says that "though the Strip may sparkle and the neon may shine, nowhere in Las Vegas can be found a more dazzling spectacle...". Inside a black-diamond mink coat is lined with 40,000 Austrian rhinestones and a separate display exhibits the world's biggest rhinestone, weighing 50lb.

Impersonators

You are more likely to see Elvis in Vegas than Mickey Mouse in Disneyworld. Impersonators abound, as do Elvis Live shows.

Legends in Concert

Imperial Palace, 3535 Las Vegas Boulevard South; tel: 731-3311 or 800-634-6441; www.legends inconcert.com; shows Mon–Sat 7.30 and 10.30pm; monorail: Harrah's/Imperial Palace, bus: Deuce; map p.138 B4/C4

Legends has been running for 20 years and features utterly convincing impersonations of luminaries like Liberace, Madonna, Dolly Parton, and, of course, Elvis.

Musical History of the King

Sahara, 2535 Las Vegas Boulevard South; tel: 737-2515; Mon–Sat 9pm; monorail: Sahara, bus: Deuce; map p.136 B3/B4

Legends veteran Trent Carlini re-creates Elvis's career, from pelvis-shaking 50s idol to 70s Vegas headliner.

Fitzgerald's

301 Fremont Street; *(see p.54)* This budget hotel and casino not only presents an endless line-up of Elvis impersonators in its lounge, but features Elvis slot machines.

Liberace

Liberace Museum

1775 East Tropicana Avenue, tel: 798-5595; www.liberace.org; Mon–Sat 10am–5pm, Sun 1–4pm; entrance charge; a free shuttle bus runs from Strip casinos to the museum; bus: 201; map p.10

A roomful of outrageous items are on show here, such as the entertainer's piano-shaped 260-diamond ring and antiques, including an inlaid desk that belonged to Czar Nicholas II. There are dozens of pianos, pride of place given to a 1920 grand on which Gershwin composed, plus a hand-painted instrument that Chopin played.

Cowboy culture

Sandy Valley Ranch

The Ranch, HCR 37 Box 1158, Sandy Valley, NV 89019; tel: 255-7948; www.bossladyranch.com You can learn the ins and outs of roping steers, as well as taking part in barn

Left: the catsuit with more than nine lives.

www.bighornrodeo.com;
bus: 202
The Nevada Gay Rodeo Association sponsors this rough-and-tumble competition annually in September or October.

HORSEBACK RIDING
Bonnie Springs Old Nevada
1 Gunfighter Lane, Blue Diamond; tel: 875-4191; map p.14
Red Rock Riding Stables offers guided desert tours.
Silver State Old West Tours
Spring Mountain Ranch State Park; tel: 798-7788; map p.14
Scenic trailrides including sunset and sunrise tours, and Western BBQs.
Cowboy Trail Rides
800 North Rainbow, Suite 204; tel: 387-8778; fax: 248-9336; www.cowboytrailrides.com
Guided tours on horseback to Red Rock Canyon, Coyote Canyon, and Red Springs.

TOURS
Annie Bananie's Wild West Tours
Tel: 804-9755; www.anniebananie.com
Runs 6hr guided van tours to the Valley of Fire and Lake Mead.

dances, barbecues, and storytelling around moonlight campfires.
Spring Mountain Ranch
Blue Diamond Drive; tel: 875-4141; daily 10am–4pm; map p.14
Once the home of rich cattle-owner Vera Krupp, the sandstone cabin and blacksmith's shop were built in 1864 and can still be visited. Along with the Old Mormon Fort in downtown Vegas *(see p.100)*, they are the oldest buildings in the valley.
Vegas Vic
25 East Fremont Street; map p.134 B3
A familiar old-time icon, Vegas Vic was a 40ft tall neon cowboy who used to wave his arm and welcome visitors with a booming "Howdy, pardner" every 15 minutes. He was featured in many movies, including *Viva Las Vegas* (1964), and *Casino* (1995). He then fell on hard times: several feet were sawed off his hat and his waving arm was disabled. He's still standing, though. You just can not take a good man down!

SEE ALSO MUSEUMS AND GALLERIES P.103

RODEOS
National Finals Rodeo
Thomas & Mack Center, 4505 South Maryland Parkway; Tickets: 866-388-3267 or online at www.nfrexperience.com; bus 109; map p.139 E4
Every December, Las Vegas hosts the final event in the exciting ProRodeo Cowboys Association rodeo calendar. Broncos are ridden and steers broken in pursuit of the World Champ All-Around Cowboy title.
Big Horn Rodeo
Horseman's Park, 5800 East Flamingo; tel: 888-643-6472;

Below: in 1963 Liberace was diagnosed with uremic poisoning after inhaling carbon tetrachloride fumes from his costumes.

Live Entertainment

L as Vegas is the unrivalled capital of live entertainment, where headliner showroom acts surpass any after-dark entertainment to be found in New York, Chicago, or LA, not to mention Paris and London, in terms of sheer spectacle. In fact, virtually all stage effects used on Broadway today are developed first in Las Vegas's huge-budget venues. Besides the big productions and long-running headliner shows, Vegas is known for its abundance of "tribute" (impersonator) shows, magicians, and topless extravaganzas. These days, though, topless dancers are as likely to be men as women.

Tribute shows

American Superstars
Stratosphere Hotel and Casino, 2000 Las Vegas Boulevard South; tel: 380 7777; shows Sun–Tue 7pm 6.30 and Wed, Fri and Sat 8.30pm on ; dark Thur; (special rate for children age 5–12); bus: Deuce; map p.136 B4

Of the cavalcade of impersonator shows, this one is skewed heavily toward the modern era. Talented performers provide energetic renditions of Madonna, Ricky Martin, and Christina Aguilera, among others.

Barbra and Frank
Riviera, 2901 Las Vegas Boulevard South; tel: 734-5110; shows Tue–Sun 8.30pm, dark Mon; bus: Deuce; map p.136 B2

Separate performances are linked by video montages of the two very different superstars' early years to present the looks and voices of the couple who never were.

Danny Gans – The Man of Many Voices
Mirage Hotel and Casino, 7900 Las Vegas Boulevard South; tel: 791-7111; shows Sat–Sun, Tue–Thur 8pm, dark Mon and Fri; bus: Deuce; map p.138 B4

What started as a short-lived Vegas stint at the Stratosphere Tower has evolved into one of the most popular shows in town. Gans is an amazing impersonator and an energetic showman.

Gordie Brown
Venetian, 3555 Las Vegas Boulevard South; tel: 414-4500; shows Thur–Tue 7.30pm, dark Wed; monorail: Harrah's/Imperial Palace; bus: Deuce; map p.138 B4

Brown blends equal parts music and comedy in rapid-fire impressions of singers Garth Brooks, Willie Nelson, Elton John, Ozzie Osbourne, Bob Dylan, and others, as well as non-musical impersonations that include Clint Eastwood, Robert de Niro, and President Bush.

Legends In Concert
Imperial Palace Hotel and Casino, (see p.78).

A favorite of many return visitors, this impersonation show features greats from yesterday and today. Impersonators render uncanny performances of a stellar lineup that always includes Elvis and changes season by season to cover stars that presently include James Brown, Madonna, and The Temptations.

Left: a Britney Spears impersonator performs at American Superstars.

Left: over-the-top costumes and a bit of cheek dominate Vegas's live entertainment.

Led Zeppelin, Madonna, Crystal Method, and Lords of Acid, among others.

Forever Plaid
Gold Coast, 4000 West Flamingo Road; tel: 367-7111; shows Tue–Sat 7.30pm, Sun 3 and 7.30pm; bus 202; map p.138 A3
This "one last gig" musical tells the story of a fictitious harmony quartet wiped out in a car crash on their way to their debut performance on the Ed Sullivan Show.

Le Rêve
Wynn Las Vegas, 3131 Las Vegas Boulevard South; tel: 770-7100; shows Thur–Mon 7.30 and 10.30pm; dark Tue and Wed; bus: Deuce; map p.136 B1/C1
Subtitled "a Small Collection of Imperfect Dreams," this is a visually stunning journey into the world of sleep, set in and around a huge tank of water that serves as a stage. Note: visitors in the first three rows of the audience might get wet.

Phantom
Venetian, 3355 Las Vegas Boulevard South; tel: 414-1000; shows Mon and Fri 7pm, Tue and Thur 7 and 10pm, Sat 6 and

A Neil Diamond Tribute
Riviera, 2901 Las Vegas Boulevard South; tel: 734-5110; shows Sun–Thur 7pm, dark Fri; bus: Deuce; map p.136 B2
Even Neil Diamond's mother endorses Jay White's uncanny impersonation, which was born in the Legends in Concert show more than a decade ago and has been playing to packed houses ever since.

Platters–Drifters–Coasters
Sahara, 2535 Las Vegas Boulevard South; tel: 492-3690; shows nightly at 7.30pm; monorail: Sahara, bus: Deuce; map p.136 B3/B4
This nostalgia show brings back three great soul bands from the 1950s and early 1960s and includes performers with ties to the original groups.

The Rat Pack Is Back
Greek Isles, 305 Convention Center Drive; tel: 952-8000; shows Sat–Thur 6 and 8.15pm, dark Fri; bus: 108; map p.136 C2
Old-time Vegas superstars Frank Sinatra, Dean Martin, Sammy Davis, Jr, and Joey Bishop are sent back from

heaven to "do it one more time" in this corny musical homage that draws its humor from the contrast between yesterday's Strip and today's.

Performing arts

Blue Man Group
The Venetian, 3355 Las Vegas Boulevard South; tel: 987-2222; shows Sun, Mon, Wed, Thur 8pm; Tue, Fri, Sat 7 and 10pm ; monorail: Harrah's/Imperial Palace; bus: Deuce; map p.138 B4
This award-winning show features three bald and blue characters. The one-of-a-kind showroom experience is innovative, hilarious, and musically powerful.

Fashionistas
Empire Ballroom, 3765 Las Vegas Boulevard South; tel: 737-7376; shows Thur–Tue 9.30pm; dark Wed; bus: Deuce; map p.139 C2
Graceful and sexy, this gender-bending adults-only dance extravaganza has become the most popular erotic stage show on the Strip. The program features performances to the music of

Below: more than mime, the Blue Man Group has toured the world.

Above: a $40-million stage set recreates the Paris Opera House… in "Venice."

comedy, special effects, and of course showgirls – for a modest ticket price.

Cirque du Soleil

This French Canadian acrobatic company has so many shows going on simultaneously in different Vegas venues that it's a category in itself. Founded in 1984 in Montreal, Quebec, Cirque du Soleil now runs 13 shows simultaneously. Of their six permanent locations, five are in Las Vegas.

KÀ

MGM Grand, 3799 Las Vegas Boulevard South; tel: 891 7777; shows Tue–Sat 7.30 and 10.30pm, dark Sun and Mon; monorail: MGM Grand, bus: Deuce; map p.139 C2
Barbarian pirates, young lovers, shipwrecks, and pyrotechnics are all part of Cirque du Soleil's biggest spectacle yet, played out on a five-story-high stage with a floor that tips from horizontal to vertical.

The Beatles – LOVE

Mirage, 3400 Las Vegas Boulevard South; tel: 791-7111; shows Thur–Mon 7 and 10pm; dark Tue and Wed; bus: Deuce; map p.138 B4

Below: Cirque du Soleil's latest production is based on the Fab Four.

9pm, Sun 5 and 8pm; monorail: Harrah's/ Imperial Palace; bus: Deuce; map p.138 B4
Andrew Lloyd Webber's hit musical Phantom of the Opera has been resurrected Vegas-style, with astonishing new special effects and Webber himself supervised the paring of dialogue from the original production, keeping all songs intact, to transform the sometimes languorous musical into a fast-paced thrill-a-minute show. All lead roles are double-cast, using major stage and opera stars.

The Producers

Paris Las Vegas, 3655 Las Vegas Boulevard South; tel: 492-3960; shows Thur–Tue 8pm, dark Wed; monorail: Bally's/Paris Las Vegas, bus: Deuce; map p.138 C3
David Hasselhoff plays the lead in this revival of the hit Broadway comedy about a washed-up producer trying to lose investors' money by staging the biggest flop ever, "Springtime for Hitler."

Shag with a Twist

Plaza, 707 East Fremont Street; tel: 388-1400; shows Thur–Mon 7pm, dark Tue and Wed; map p.134 C3

Riding the wave of Vegas entertainment aimed at the baby-boom generation, this "cartoon come to life" comedy show brings the Sixties back to life with music, dance, comedy, and psychedelia that spills off the stage and into the audience.

Spamalot

Wynn, 3131 Las Vegas Boulevard South; tel: 770-7000; shows Sun, Mon, Wed 8pm; Tue, Fri, Sat 7 and 10pm; dark Thur; bus: Deuce; map p.136 B1/C1
Based on skits from Monty Python's Flying Circus, this comic extravaganza features lusty maidens, dancing divas, a killer rabbit, and the only legless knight on the Strip.

Viva Las Vegas

Stratosphere Tower Hotel and Casino, 2000 Las Vegas Boulevard South; tel: 380 7777; shows Mon–Sat 2 and 4pm, dark Sun; bus: Deuce; map p.136 B4
The longest-running daytime show on the Strip features GP-rated versions of everything that characterizes Vegas showroom entertainment – singing, dancing,

Conceived by the late George Harrison and Cirque director Guy La Liberté, this 1960s nostalgia show built around new digital remixes of original Beatles studio recordings uses acrobatics to recreate the psychedelic mood of the era.

Mystère

TI–Treasure Island, 3300 Las Vegas Boulevard South; tel: 894 7111; shows Wed–Sun 7.30 and 10.30pm, dark Mon and Tues; bus: Deuce; map p.136 B1

The internationally famed Cirque takes the circus to new levels of sophistication in an amazing state-of-the-art theater. No animals are used, just 72 performers of amazing physical and emotive skill and grace. A unique Las Vegas performance art experience.

O

Bellagio, 3600 Las Vegas Boulevard South; tel: 693-7111; shows Fri–Tue 7.30 and 11pm, dark Wed and Thur; monorail: Bally's/Paris Las Vegas, bus: Deuce; map p.138 B3

The acclaimed international troupe dazzles audiences in an aquatic environment that utilizes 1½ million gallons of water. Around 75 highly skilled acrobats – all scuba-certified – dive, swim, and perform trapeze and high-wire acts in a remarkable auditorium.

Zumanity

New York-New York, 3790 Las Vegas Boulevard South; tel: 740 6969; shows Tue–Sat 7.30 and 10.30pm dark Sun and Mon; bus: Deuce; map p.139 C2

In 2003, the owners of New York New York decided to spice up the resort's wholesome image by staging the third Cirque du Soleil show on the Strip. Called Zumanity, it takes its cue from the adult-oriented accent that is part of Vegas's post-2001 redefini-

Right: one of the key ingredients of Cirque du Soleil's Zumanity is human sexuality.

tion. Zumanity is, in fact, a circus of sexuality, from homoerotic to racy to kinky, offering G-strings, fetish wear, and nudity aplenty. The stage juts out suggestively into the audience, and there are scenes of naked people woven into the carpet.

Dinner shows

Hawaiian Luau

Imperial Palace, 3535 Las Vegas Boulevard South; tel: 732-5111; shows Tue, Thur, Sat 6.30pm, dark Mon, Wed, Fri, and Sun; monorail: Harrah's/Imperial Palace, bus: Deuce; map p.138 B4/C4

This Polynesian-flavored music and dance review, featuring Rozita Lee's Drums of the Islands, takes place under swaying palms beside the hotel swimming pool. Included are a tropical dinner buffet and all-you-can-drink mai tais and piña coladas.

The Sopranos' Last Supper

Empire Ballroom, 3765 Las Vegas Boulevard South; tel: 737-7376; shows Thur–Tue 6pm, dark Wed; bus: Deuce; map p.139 C2

The art of impersonation plumbs new depths with this audience participation dinner show that mimics TV characters, bringing the mob back to Vegas for one last blowout. After dinner, the audience is invited to dance in a conga line with Tony, Carmella, Dr Malfi and the gang to live performances of "That's Amore" and other Italian American hit songs of yesteryear.

Tony 'n' Tina's Wedding

Rio, 3700 West Flamingo Road; tel: 252-7777; shows nightly 7pm; bus: 202; map p.138 A3

The audience is asked to suspend reality and become guests at an Italian American wedding reception filled with dysfunctional relatives and family friends. You're welcome to dance.

Tournament of Kings

Excalibur, 3850 Las Vegas Boulevard South; tel: 597 7600; shows Wed–Mon 6 and 8.30pm,

83

dark Tue; bus: Deuce; map p.139 C1/C2

A classic dinner show and great fun for families: a re-creation of a medieval knights' jousting tournament.

Comedy

Carrot Top
Luxor, 3900 Las Vegas Boulevard South; tel: 262-4000; shows Sun–Mon, Wed–Fri 8pm, Sat 7 and 9pm, dark Tue; bus: Deuce; map p.139 C1

Dissed by critics as the worst headliner show on the Strip, the redheaded joke-ster with his trunk full of props still manages to pack in the crowds and keep them laughing.

Comedy Stop at the Trop
Tropicana, 3801 Las Vegas Boulevard South; tel: 739-2714; www.comedystop.com; shows nightly 8 and 10.30pm; mono-rail: MGM Grand, bus: Deuce; map p.139 C2/D2

Some of the best comedians in the country show what they've got at this adults-only club.

David Brenner
Westin Casuarina, 160 East Flamingo; tel: 836-5900; shows Fri–Wed 6.30pm, dark Thur; bus: 202; map p.138 C4

A perennial Las Vegas favorite who has also appeared on the Tonight Show more than 150 times, Brenner recently moved into his own dinner theater at the Westin Casuarina, a smallish spa hotel so new the eleva-tors were not running when this book went to press.

Improv Comedy Club
Harrah's, 3475 Las Vegas Boulevard South; tel: 369-5111 or 800-392-9002; Tue–Sun times vary; monorail: Harrah's/Imperial Palace, bus: Deuce; map p.138 B4

This comedy club features three comics nightly, includ-ing one headliner, usually a Tonight Show veteran.

Larry G. Jones
Fitzgerald's, 301 Fremont Street; tel: 388-2400; shows Thur–Mon 9pm, dark Tue and Wed; map p.134 B3

"The Man of 1002 Voices" revives the art of comic impersonation in this rapid-fire show, delivering more than an impression a minute as he mimics George W. Bush, Bill Clinton, and other ex-presidents, as well as Frank Sinatra, Ray Charles, Jack Nicolson, Johnny Cash, Cher, Jerry Lee Lewis, and Michael Jackson among others.

Louie Anderson: Larger than Life
Excalibur, 3850 Las Vegas Boulevard South; tel: 597-7777 or 800-937-7777; shows Sat–Thur 7pm, dark Fri; bus: Deuce; map p.137 C1/C2

Comic giant Anderson takes a break from his nice-guy TV persona to take pokes at gamblers, alcoholics, and the horrors of family life.

Riviera Comedy Club
Riviera, 2901 Las Vegas Boulevard South; tel: 794-9433; shows nightly 8.30 and 10.30pm; bus: Deuce; map p.136 B2

The original comedy show-case in Las Vegas presents top shock comedians, hyp-notists, ventriloquists, and headline comics.

Rita Rudner
Harrah's, 3475 Las Vegas Boulevard South; tel: 785-5555; shows Mon–Sat 8pm, dark Sun; monorail: Harrah's/Imperial Palace, bus: Deuce; map p.138 B4

This seemingly softspoken lady is now a master of ad lib, and has emerged as one of the most popular comics in Vegas with her witty satire about marriage, male-female relationships, and shopping.

Second City Las Vegas
Flamingo, 3555 Las Vegas Boulevard South; tel: 733-3111; shows Tue–Sun 8pm, dark Mon; monorail: Flamingo/Cae-sars Palace; bus: Deuce; map p.138 B4/C4

Second City has been a starting point for many US

Left: Rita Rudner began her career as a dancer before realising her comic potential.

Above: Penn and Teller add new style to the oldest of tricks.

comedy actors, writers, and directors, including Joan Rivers, Dan Aykroyd, John Candy, and John Belushi. Enjoy some of the finest improvisational comedians.

George Wallace
Flamingo, 3555 Las Vegas Boulevard South; tel: 733-3111; shows Tue–Sat 10pm, dark Sun and Mon; monorail: Flamingo/ Caesars Palace, bus: Deuce; map p.138 B4/C4

Wallace, who began his career as a gag writer for legendary comic Red Foxx, consistently ranks among the top funnymen in Vegas. He sometimes shares the stage with 1960s funk-rock group Sly and the Family Stone.

Magic

Las Vegas – where David Copperfield warehouses his enormous sets – has become the world's magic

Many short running shows sell out quickly, so while planning your Vegas getaway it's a good idea to check who will be in town using one of the several Las Vegas entertainment websites, such as www.todayinlv.com, www.vegas.com, or www.lasvegas-nv.com.

capital, not only because almost every magician aspires to play here, but because it can offer a certain stability for big shows.

The Amazing Jonathan
Sahara, 2535 Las Vegas Boulevard South; tel: 737-2111; shows Fri–Tue 10pm, dark Wed and Thur; monorail: Sahara, bus: Deuce; map p.136 B3/B4

Billed as "The Freddy Krueger of Comedy," this guy is so weird he even scares Penn and Teller. Sarcasm, sight gags, and special effects enhance his illusions. Under 18 admitted only with a parent or guardian.

Lance Burton– Master Magician
Monte Carlo, 3770 Las Vegas Boulevard South; tel: 730 7777; shows Tue–Sat 7 and 10pm; dark Sun and Mon; bus: Deuce; map p.138 C2

Lance Burton is a long-time Vegas headliner who has been starring in his eponymously named theater at the Monte Carlo since 1996. The amiable Burton's act includes ducks, Elvis the parakeet, and a seemingly endless flight of white doves.

Set in a wonderful environment—an impeccably gilded theater that somehow maintains intimacy—he pulls off extraordinary illusions with the assistance of a talented group of dancers.

Mac King
Harrah's, 3475 Las Vegas Boulevard South; tel: 785-5555; shows Tue–Sat 1, 2, 3 and 4pm; monorail: Harrah's/ Imperial Palace, bus: Deuce; map p.138 B4

Quirky, family-oriented and hilarious, King is best known for his trademark Amazing Goldfish Trick, where he catches live goldfish over the heads of the audience on a fishing line baited with Fig Newtons.

Penn and Teller
Rio, 3700 West Flamingo Road; tel: 252 7777; shows Wed– Mon 9pm, dark Tues; bus: 202; map p.138 A3

The dynamic magic duo entertain in their own theater in the Rio Hotel, performing new tricks, exposing how old ones are done, and generally being genial, though often in gross ways.

Rick Thomas
Orleans, 4500 West Tropicana Avenue; tel: 792-7111; shows daily 2, 4 and 7pm; bus: 201; map p.138 A1

Seigfried & Roy (see p.47) may be gone for good from the Las Vegas stage, but you can still see a live white Bengal tiger in Rick Thomas's act, along with beautiful dancers and exotic birds. Winner of the "Magician of the Year" award from the Academy of Magical Árts,

Thomas is ranked among the best family-oriented magicians in town.

Steve Wyrick Real Magic
Desert Passage, 3667 Las Vegas Boulevard South; tel: 785-5555; shows Sat–Thur 7 and 9pm, dark Fri; monorail: Bally's/Paris Las Vegas, bus: Deuce; map p.139 C3
The Aladdin lured Steve Wyrick away from the Sahara after a three-year run by building him his own entertainment complex in the Desert Passage mall. Now that the Aladdin is being transformed into the Planet Hollywood Hotel, the mall's future is in question, but Wyrick's theater seems here to stay. His prop-heavy act includes a "death crane" with whirling saw blades and a disappearing motorcycle.

Music
Headliners
The performers below are under contract for long-term runs at major resorts. Of course, hundreds of other top-name singers and bands have limited engagements in Las Vegas every year, in casino showrooms

Left: the House of Blues also hosts frequent jazz performances.

as well as at the big concert venues listed here.

To illustrate the range of concert performances you can expect, headliners scheduled for limited Vegas runs as this guide went to press included Jay Leno, Tony Bennett, Wayne Newton, the Beach Boys, Frankie Avalon, Bobby Rydell, Etta James, Prince, Damon Wayans, Glen Campbell, Neil Sedaka, George Thorogood and the Destroyers, and the Smothers Brothers.

Céline Dion
Caesars Palace, 3570 Las Vegas Boulevard South; tel: 731-7110; shows Wed–Sun 8.30pm, dark Mon and Tue; monorail: Flamingo/Caesars Palace, bus: Deuce; map p.138 B3/B4
Céline Dion began a $45 million four-year engagement in August of 2003, performing at least five shows a week in a purpose-built showroom at Caesars Palace. The 4,000-seat Colosseum was designed and built around her performances. She has opted out of extending her contract and will be replaced by Bette Midler in early 2008.

Barry Manilow
Las Vegas Hilton, 3000 South Paradise Road; tel: 732-5111;

Show guides are available in print publications like *Today in Las Vegas* or *Las Vegas Leisure Guide*, distributed in most Vegas resort hotels.

shows Wed–Sat 8pm, dark Sun–Tue; monorail: Las Vegas Hilton, bus: 108; map p.137 C3
The reigning king of the crooners had announced his retirement and was on his farewell tour when the Hilton offered him a permanent gig, complete with his own theater. His new show traces his career from its Brooklyn beginnings to the big time.

Elton John
Caesars Palace, 3570 Las Vegas Boulevard South; tel: 731-7110; shows Wed–Sun 8.30pm; monorail: Flamingo/Caesars Palace, bus: 108; map p.138 B3/B4
Since 2003, Elton John's show, The Red Piano, has been filling in for Céline Dion during hiatuses. Three decades of music and a production spectacle unrivalled this side of Cirque du Soleil have made this intermittent extravaganza the hottest ticket in Vegas. Shows sell out soon after dates are announced.

Concert venues
House of Blues
Mandalay Bay, 3950 Las Vegas Blvd South; tel: 632-7600; bus:

Right: if you want to see Elton John, you'll have to book in advance.

Deuce; map p.139 C1/D1
Nightly, live entertainment including high-class performers like the Blues Brothers, Sheryl Crow, and Bob Dylan. Book early for big stars.

The Joint
Hard Rock Hotel, 4475 Paradise Road; tel: 693-5000; bus: 108; map p.139 D4
Hard Rock's 8,000-sq. ft concert venue presents top performers like David Bowie, Green Day, Blues Traveller, Kid Rock, and Metallica on its state-of-the-art stage, while TV monitors and supersize screens bring audiences up close to the action. Satirist Bill Maher often appears on nights when no concert is booked.

Railhead Saloon
Boulder Station, 4111 Boulder Highway; tel: 432-7777; bus: 107
Country, classic rock, and blues greats like the Alan Parsons Project, John Lee Hooker, Jr and Magic Slim play this small venue, which looks like a standard casino lounge but charges hefty admissions for name acts.

Pearl
The Palms, 4321 West Flamingo Road; tel: 942-7777; bus: 202; map p.138 A2
With a construction price tag of more than $50 million, this impressive, enormous

venue opened in Spring 2007 as the largest concert hall and special-events facility in Vegas. It is hardwired to the Palms' recording studio so that bands performing here can cut live CDs and concert DVDs.

Showgirls and burlesque

Back in 1957, the Dunes introduced topless showgirls to the Strip with Minsky's Follies, thus inaugurating a showgirl style. Since 1959, the showgirl tradition has been maintained by 25,000 performances of the Folies Bergere at the Tropicana. Today, all but a few of the classic tits-and-glitz shows have faded into Las Vegas's seamy past, but a new adult entertainment phenomenon has arisen to replace them: the for-women-only male strippers review.

American Storm
Riviera, 2901 Las Vegas Boulevard South; tel: 734-5110; shows Tue–Sun 10.30pm, dark Mon; bus: Deuce; map p.136 B2
American history with male strippers? Only in Las Vegas would you find this adults-only bachelorette show, in which buff toy-boys peel off camouflage fatigues and tight American flag jeans to the beat of patriotically macho rock music.

Above: unlike a standard striptease, burlesque clubs are overtly over the top and sometimes filled with saucy humor.

An Evening at La Cage
Riviera, 2901 Las Vegas Boulevard South; tel: 734-5110; shows Wed–Mon 7.30pm, dark Tue; bus: Deuce; map p.136 B2
This curiously family-friendly drag queen show presents dead-on impersonations of standbys like Barbra Streisand, Judy Garland, and Bette Midler, along with Céline Dion and spoofs of Madonna and Michael Jackson.

Chippendales
Rio, 3700 West Flamingo Road; tel: 252 7777; shows Sun–Thur 8.30pm, Fri–Sat 8.30 and 10.30pm; bus: 202; map p.138 A3
One of the most popular shows in Las Vegas, this fantasy for the ladies begins in the Rio's Flirt Lounge, where chivalry reigns, and moves into the Chippendales Theater for an evening of tastefully sexy song and dance starring a dozen physically perfect men.

Crazy Girls
Riviera, 2901 Las Vegas Boulevard South; tel: 734-5110; shows Wed–Mon 9.30pm, dark Tue; bus: Deuce; map p.136 B2
The sexiest old-fashioned topless showgirl review still playing on the Strip, Crazy Girls evolved from a private

Below: a cheap sign for a peep show.

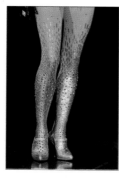

Formerly known as *La Femme*, this topless review uses elaborate light and shadow effects and a kaleidoscope of colorful lighting to tantalize the audience with a sensual collage of body parts. Adults only.

Don Arden's Jubilee!

Bally's, 3645 Las Vegas Boulevard South; tel: 739-4111; shows Sat–Thur 7.30 and 10.30pm , dark Friday; monorail: Bally's/Paris Las Vegas, bus: Deuce; map p.138 C3/C4

The sinking of the *Titanic*, this show's amazing signature special effect for more than 20 years, inspired the grandiose spectacles of modern Vegas production shows. Of course, Jubilee! also features dozens of topless and costumed showgirls, making this an event for adults only.

Men! The Show

Club Seven, 3724 Las Vegas Boulevard South; tel: 739-7744; shows Wed–Sun 9.30pm, dark Mon and Tue; bus: Deuce; map p.138 C3

This sexy "ladies' night out" review is a successor to Vegas's original male stripper show, Vegas Bad Boys, which premiered in 1987. With a whole new cast of championship bodybuilders and the same producers, Men! bounced around several casino hotel venues before finding a permanent home at Club Seven.

Fantasy

Luxor, 3900 Las Vegas Boulevard South; tel: 262-4400; shows Mon, Wed, Fri, Sun 10.30pm, Tue

8 and 10.30pm, Sat 11pm, dark Thur; bus: Deuce; map p.139 C1

Designed as entertainment for couples, this topless adults-only review features music, comedy, and spectacular choreography that focuses on secret sensual fantasies.

Folies Bergère

Tropicana, 3801 Las Vegas Boulevard South; tel: 739-2222; shows 7.30 and 10pm, dark Thur; monorail: MGM Grand, bus: Deuce; map p.139 C2/D2

With its origins in Paris in 1869, the show was brought to the Tropicana in 1959 by Lou Walters, father of ABC-TV's Barbara Walters, and has now given more than 25,000 performances. There are two shows: the "classic" show is at 10pm, while a show "suitable for children," i.e. no nudity and no drinks, begins at 7.30pm. A Folies performance with no bare breasts seems a strange concept, since nudity is what the show was founded on.

Visitors can also book an afternoon tour, which goes backstage through dressing rooms that are strewn with sequined costumes, wigs, false eyelashes, and feathered fans. Personal items, flowers, and photographs adorn the dressing tables

stag show in 1987 to its present rendition, attended mostly by couples. You will want to allow time to find the intimate 400-seat Crazy Girls theater in the depths of the Riviera, which has been turned into a labyrinth over the years. Once you are there you can not miss the eight pairs of bare bronze buttocks, shiny from being caressed by thousands of passers-by, at the theater entrance *(see picture p.48)*.

Crazy Horse Paris

MGM Grand, 3799 Las Vegas Boulevard South; tel: 891-7777; shows Wed–Mon 8 and 10.30pm, dark Tue; monorail: MGM Grand, bus: Deuce; map p.138 C2

Brothels are legal in Nevada by county option – but not in Las Vegas, where prostitution is illegal, though lap dances in strip clubs are not.

Right: an enormous champagne glass is a favored prop at Caesar's Pussycat Dolls Lounge.

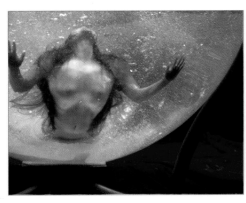

lined up in a row. Each dancer has at least half a dozen pairs of $150 shoes.

Along with their entertainment abilities, performers must have minimum height qualifications to work here — 5ft 3in for acrobats, 5ft 6in for dancers, 5ft 10in for showgirls — and the cast range in age from 18 to about 40.

Thunder from Down Under
Excalibur, 3850 Las Vegas Boulevard South; tel: 597-7777; shows Sun–Thur 9pm, Fri–Sat 9 and 11pm; bus: Deuce; map p.139 C1/C2

The mainly family-oriented Excalibur offers moms a break from the parental routine with this "girls' night out" review featuring ten Australian studmuffins. Adults only.

BURLESQUE CLUBS
Cheetah's
2112 Western Avenue; tel: 384–0074; 24 hours; map p.136 A4

This off-Strip strip club, a Vegas classic, was the location for the 1995 movie *Showgirls*. On-stage performers are mirrored on wide-

screen TVs, sports bar-style, throughout the club. Very expensive lap dances are available in the private, mirrored G-Spot Room.

Forty Deuce
Mandalay Bay, 3950 Las Vegas Boulevard South; tel: 632-9442; www.fortydeuce.com; shows nightly 10.30pm–dawn; bus: Deuce; map p.139 C1/D1

Showgirls put the "tease" back into the Strip in this retro-sexy club, dancing to sultry jazz and rock in front of a curtain of pearls at intervals through the night. The club's most infamous event is Silicone Sundays, a gathering of performers from the city's top "gentlemen's lounges," hosted by porn queen Jenna Jameson.

Pussycat Dolls Lounge
Caesars Palace, 3570 Las Vegas Boulevard South; tel: 731-7110; shows every 30 minutes from 10.30pm nightly; monorail: Flamingo/Caesars Palace, bus: Deuce; map p.138 B3/B4

Exotic dancers revive the glory days of the 1930s – to the beat of classic 1980s rock music – as they pop out of giant champagne glasses

Left: the number of strip clubs appealing to women is continually increasing.

and swing from the rafters in this uninhibited lounge act.

Spearmint Rhino
3344 Highland Drive; tel: 796-3600; 24 hours; map p.136 A1

Always packed, this classy, improbably elegant establishment is widely considered to be the city's best strip club, featuring the most beautiful topless showgirls anywhere. The 18,000-sq. ft club has four tipping stages and numerous private lap dance cabanas.

Topless Girls of Glitter Gulch
20 East Fremont Street; tel: 385-4774; daily 1pm–4am; map p.134 B3

This small strip club, a local landmark left over from the days when Fremont Street was sleazy, has become controversial due to the city's persistent attempts to shut it down as part of the downtown Fremont Street Experience facelift. Less raunchy than many more discreetly located strip clubs, it's a bona fide piece of Vegas history.

The Dunes, located where the Bellagio is today, presented Vegas's first topless showgirls in 1957.

Losing

Gamblers come to Las Vegas hoping to go home rich, but the glitz and glamour of the casinos, not to mention their electricity, has its price, and odds are you will go home with less cash than you brought. For modest spenders this is simply the cost of Vegas's unique entertainments, but for some the loss can be hard to take. If your losing gets seriously out of control, you may find yourself on Vegas's darker side – a city of thriving pawnshops willing to give the unlucky cash for just about any object of value they can offer. There is also a network of counseling facilities to help problem gamblers recover.

Pawnshops

More than one Las Vegas taxi driver has talked of driving some unfortunate gambler to McCarran International Airport only to be told that his fare has no money, and been obliged to accept a watch or a wedding ring as payment. But for some big losers there is one stop before that taxi ride: the pawn shop. There are seven pages of pawn shops listed in the Yellow Pages, some with half a dozen branches or more, and many emphasizing that they are open 24hrs a day. It is just what a down-on-his-luck gambler might most want to hear.

If you are staying in a towering Strip casino hotel, you will notice that none of the rooms has a balcony – or a window that opens. This is a response to the fact that when the first skyscraper hotels opened on the Strip, an alarming number of guests would take fatal plunges from the upper-floor windows after disastrous nights of gambling.

Pawnbroker ads invariably include a long list of what they will loan money on, ranging from rifles and shotguns to tools, camcorders, and paintings. A few specialize in automobiles, with one firm promising that you can drive your car away just so long as you leave them the title. But jewelry tops the charts at most shops.

Surprisingly, between 80 and 90 percent of pawnshop customers return to redeem their items. By law, shops must keep items for 120 days before disposal, allowing redemption by the customer within that grace period. Standard interest is 10 percent, though some places charge more, as much as they can in a few establishments.

In most places in the United States, pawnshops are to be found in poor neighborhoods because that's where the customers are, but in Vegas not only are pawnshops a mere stone's throw from the Strip, but customers cut across all income levels and social classes. Habitual gamblers are more

likely to face ups and downs than ordinary people, hence their need for this 24-hour service industry.

Compulsive gambling

Compulsive gambling is an emotional illness that remains hidden until the consequences begin to affect the financial and emotional security of the gambler and his family. Early warning signs include: losing time from work or family; borrowing money to gamble; gambling to escape worry; selling personal possessions to get gambling money; and lying about the time and money spent on gambling.

One thing that might help is the Innovative Gaming Corporation of America's technology, which allows gamblers to program a set limit on their ATM cards at a casino kiosk, then use them in slot machines that "lock up" when the limit is reached. The gambler is not allowed to

Right: pawnshops will convert anything into cash, even sports trophies.

take a break from them, your ability to make decisions will probably be clouded, thus lowering your odds of winning.

3-Set Limits

The smartest way of gambling in Las Vegas is to set a limit for yourself that is based on what you think a night of entertainment is worth. Withdraw this money in cash and stick to this limit. The smart gambler will also immediately set aside this limit from any big winnings they may make before betting again, thus ensuring they at least break even at the end of the night.

4-Stay Sober

Free drinks are a nice perk of gambling in Vegas, but are likely to cloud your judgement. Do not fool yourself into thinking it improves your ability. Casinos do not give away alcohol to make their customers become better gamblers. Their motivation is obviously quite the opposite.

5-Know When to Walk Away

There is no such thing as a lucky streak on a slot machine. They hit jackpots at random, and there is no need to stay there until it cashes out.

6-Know When to Run

If you win big: LEAVE!

use the card again for 5–10 days. There are several organizations that provide counseling and services to problem gamblers.

National Council on Problem Gambling
4340 South Valley View Boulevard, Suite 220, 89103; tel: 369-9740 or 800-522-4700; www.ncpgambling.org
Provides literature for gamblers and family members of problem gamblers as well as organizing speakers to help recovering gamblers and operating a 24-hr helpline staffed by trained counselors. All calls confidential.

Gamblers Anonymous
Tel: 888-442-2110; www.gamblersannonymous.org

Runs dozens of group therapy meetings that incorporate the organization's famous 12-step program to recovery.

How to keep from losing your house

1-Don't Bet It

Pawnshops seem willing to exchange cash for deeds to houses or cars, but if you are even considering this option, you probably need to phone one of the helplines listed above. Casinos are more scrupulous, but will happily allow you to over extend yourself by offering to cash your paycheck.

2-Take Breaks

Slots in particular are very hypnotic, and if you do not

Movies

L as Vegas magic is the magic of illusion, and many of its spectacular displays are the work of experts from the movie business. The puffy clouds and sunsets inside shopping arcades, the millions of megawatts of artificial light outdoors, the pyramids and volcanoes, and the sea battles of TI make the town look like a Hollywood blockbuster set. The gold and the glitter, the instant flips of fortune, and the fantasy façades also offer endlessly rich plot potential. All this has kept Sin City in the movies and in the business of movies. The fact that Vegas is just a short hop in a private jet from Hollywood helps, too.

Made in Vegas

From the days of the silents, Las Vegas had starring roles in movies like *The Hazards of Helen* and John Ford's 1932 film *Airmail*. Edwin L. Mann's 1946 film *Lady Luck* was a moral tale about the irresistible lure of gambling. In 1960, both Marilyn Monroe and Clark Gable played their last movie roles in John Huston's *The Misfits*, much of it filmed in the Nevada desert. Arthur Miller's script about a disillusioned divorcée was uncannily prophetic of the Monroe-Miller marriage.

Ocean's 11, also made in 1960, was the famous Rat Pack saga, directed by Lewis Milestone and shot when Frank Sinatra, Dean Martin, Sammy Davis Jr, and Peter Lawford could spare time from carousing. Though the film wasn't highly rated, it made respectable enough ticket sales for a follow-up, *Robin and the Seven Hoods*. *Ocean's 11* was remade in 2001 with George Clooney, Matt Damon, and Julia Roberts topping a stellar bill, and featured several interiors shot in the Bellagio.

Every year since 1997, the Las Vegas Film Critics Society has presented its Sierra Awards in 19 categories and issued a list of the year's top 10 films. Made up of print, media, TV and Internet critics from the Las Vegas area, the society has 11 members.

Elvis Presley wooed Ann-Margret from the Sahara in the Strip all the way to Lake Mead and Mount Charleston in *Viva Las Vegas* (1964), a famous pairing rumored to be mirrored off screen, too.

In 1971, Sean Connery went Downtown to Fremont Street as James Bond in *Diamonds Are Forever*, which critic Leonard Maltin described as a "colorful comic book adventure."

A SET FOR SCI-FI DRAMA

Vegas has served as the backdrop for cheesy sci-fi movies as well. In *The Amazing Colossal Man* (1957) Las Vegas came under attack from an Army officer who grew 60ft tall after surviving an atomic explosion, but the

Below: the Rat Pack made two films together, the original *Ocean's 11* and the poor follow up *Robin and the Seven Hoods*.

LAS VEGAS STORY
VINCENT PRICE with HOAGY CARMICHAEL

Left: *Las Vegas Story* has a familiar Vegas plot: memory, regret, tragedy, and a second chance.

actor. The movie was remade in 2000, set in Vegas and Seattle, and starred Sylvester Stallone killing lots of people.

AN EASY BACKDROP

Many top movies have used Vegas as a made ready setting, or even as a sturdy plot device. Dustin Hoffman won an Oscar for his role in *Rain Man* in 1988, which co-starred fresh-faced Tom Cruise, and featured a scene filmed in the Pompeiian Fantasy Suite of Caesars Palace. Actor Nicolas Cage is a virtual Vegas veteran, having starred in several local movies: the 1992 comedy *Honeymoon in Vegas*; the dark 1995 drama *Leaving Las Vegas*; two years later, *Con Air*; and the following year, *Snake Eyes*.

Lavish high-roller suites and turns of the tables provided the setting for Adrian Lynn's *Indecent Proposal*

assault came from elsewhere in Tim Burton's wild 1996 sci-fi fantasy, *Mars Attacks*. The movie brought to town a galaxy of stars including Pierce Brosnan, Annette Bening, an extraordinary cameo from Tom Jones, and no fewer than two roles for Jack Nicholson. In that film, the Las Vegas Strip was spectacularly demolished.

In the same year, the special effects were about the only stars of *Independence Day* to survive with reputations intact.

Rick Moranis reprised his goofy scientist role from *Honey, I Shrunk the Kids* in *Honey, I Blew Up the Kid* (1992) where his two-year-old son becomes 150ft high and grows even larger when he comes near electricity. In Las Vegas…well, you can imagine.

MOB ON FILM

The mob of course received a lot of attention in celluloid. In 1972 and 1974, parts 1 and 2 of Francis Ford Coppola's *The Godfather* trilogy were partly filmed and set locally. The saga of the Cor-

leone family includes references to the Mob's attempts at legitimacy in the Nevada gaming business. The movie also features the now-legendary tale of a Hollywood producer who finds the head of his favorite horse tucked up under his silk sheets as a timely reminder to employ a certain skinny, Italian-American crooner.

Warren Beatty played a highly romanticized Benjamin "Bugsy" Siegel while conducting an on-screen romance with his soon-to-be wife Annette Bening in Barry Levinson's *Bugsy* in 1991.

Martin Scorsese's *Casino* (1995), starring Robert de Niro and Sharon Stone, is a brutally comic tale of mobsters hustling their way into the casino business, much of it filmed in the Strip's Riviera casino. *Get Carter* was a classic British gangster movie made in 1971, and it confirmed Michael Caine's status as a powerful screen

Right: Bond's only Vegas appearance so far has been *Diamonds are Forever*.

Above: until the release of *Bugsy*, the owners of the Flamingo had been a little coy about the casino's associations with Mr Siegel, but interest in the movie persuaded them to open the Bugsy Celebrity Theater.

(1993), where Woody Harrelson rashly encouraged screen wife Demi Moore to spend a night with tycoon Robert Redford for a million dollars, and lived to regret it, until the last reel, of course.

Johnny Depp took lots of narcotics and trashed a hotel room as a reporter covering a prosecutors' war-on-drugs convention in the 1998 film version of Hunter S. Thompson's *Fear and Loathing in Las Vegas*, filmed partly in the Riviera, Circus Circus, and Stardust hotels.

In the 1997 *National Lampoon's Vegas Vacation*, Chevy Chase et al reprised their roles as the Griswold family on the road in this fourth installment of the hit "Vacation" franchise, with its views of the Strip in the mid-1990s and a funny sequence on Hoover Dam.

Controversial because of rape scenes, lesbian and straight simulated sex, gratuitous nudity and bad writing, the 1995 show-biz melodrama *Showgirls*, filmed at the recently demolished Stardust, is often ranked as one of the worst movies of all

time but also enjoys cult popularity on DVD. Vince Vaughn and Jon Favreau spent a weekend womanizing in Vegas – specifically, outside the Stardust and inside the Fremont downtown – in the 1996 indy surprise hit, *Swingers*. Favreau returned to the scene in 1998 with the much darker *Very Bad Things*, about the worst that can happen in Vegas.

The 2001 remake of *Ocean's 11* unleashed a veritable gush of television documentaries with Las Vegas as the backdrop. Barely a week goes by without one of the networks shooting in town. The Nevada Film Office assists hundreds of films, music videos, and multimedia productions every day of the week.

William H. Macy plays the unluckiest man alive in *The Cooler*, a gritty, violent, yet charming meditation on the nature of luck in old-time Vegas. For his role as a mobbed-up casino boss, Alec Baldwin was nominated for both an Oscar and a Golden Globe for Best Supporting Actor in 2004.

Movie Theaters

With the closing of the budget-priced Tropicana Cinemas, Las Vegas no longer has an independently owned movie theater in the entire city. It does have quite a few large complexes operated by the national chains, and many of them are in casino hotels, large and small, providing a handy place to park the kids while parents gamble or shop. Here are a few of the best.

Regal Village Square 18
9400 West Sahara Avenue; tel: 221-2283; www.regmovies. com; bus: 204
One of the three largest movie theater complexes in Vegas, this 18-screen facility features THX certified auditorium sound systems and an arcade room.

Regal Boulder Station
4111 Boulder Highway; tel: 221-2283; www.reg movies.com; bus: 107

Regal Sunset Station 13
1301 West Sunset Road; tel: 221-2283
These two Regal Theatres complexes in outlying casino hotels show first-run movies in venues that boast state-of-the-art projection and sound

The fictional Montecito Resort, setting of the television series "Las Vegas," seems to move from one part of the Strip to another each season, judging from the actual hotels visible through the window of the CEO's office. While the Montecito's decor is patterned after the Mandalay Bay, the interior shots are actually taped on one of the world's largest sound stages – a fully re-created casino – in Culver City, California. The cost of shutting down any casino long enough to film the show makes shooting on location in Vegas prohibitive.

Above: William H. Macy's character in *The Cooler* has the ability to ruin other gamblers' good runs, a valuable asset to casino owners.

systems. Tickets are discounted before 6pm.

Century Suncoast 16
9090 Alta Drive; tel: 341-5555; www.centurytheatres.com; bus: 207
This 16-screen facility in the Suncoast Hotel offers stadium seating.

Brendan Las Vegas 14
4321 West Flamingo Road; tel: 507-4849; www.brendentheatres.com; bus: 202; map p.138 A2
Located in the Palm Casino Resort, this 14-screen complex is the scene of the annual CineVegas Film Festival. It features comfortable high-back rocker-style seats and wall-to-wall curved screens.

Galaxy Neonopolis
450 East Fremont St; tel: 383-9600; www.cvarthouse.com; map p.134 B4
The 12-screen theater and entertainment complex not only shows first-run mainstream films but also presents the ongoing CineVegas Art House screening series, featuring the best in foreign, cult, documentary, and "truly independent" American movies.

West Wind Vegas Drive-In
4150 West Carey Avenue; tel: 646-3565
The last drive-in movie theater in Vegas has five screens and shows first-run films nightly year-round.

Festivals

CineVegas International Film Festival
Brenden Las Vegas 14; www.cinevegas.com; 138 A2
With actor-director Dennis Hopper as its Creative Advisory Board chairman, Cine-Vegas has been presenting its annual film festival at the Brenden Theatres complex in the Palms Hotel each June since 1998. The festival producers also sponsor a second CineVegas festival annually in January.

NeonFest
5868 South Pecos, Suite 300; www.neonfest.com
The annual three-day gay, lesbian, bisexual, and trans-gendered film event is held at the Onyx Theater in Commercial Center during Pride Week in late September or early October. Admission to all screenings is free.

Dam Short Film Festival
508 California Avenue, Boulder City; tel: 293-4848
On the first weekend in February, short features from the University of Nevada at Las Vegas Short Film Archive Department are shown at the American Legion Hall in Boulder City. Admission is free.

Below: the updated *Ocean's 11* traded in the Rat Pack for Brad Pitt and George Clooney.

Museums and Galleries

Until tycoon Steve Wynn put his art collection on display at the Bellagio, it had never occurred to anyone that resorts could draw customers with culture. This revelation inspired other casino art museums and moved the city to create a downtown arts district. Vegas also has nature and history museums where you can learn about the desert and the people who lived here in ancient times. Then there are only-in-Vegas museums dedicated to everything from King Tut to Houdini.

Art

Arts Factory
107 East Charleston Boulevard; tel: 676-1111; www.thearts factory.com; free; bus: 206; map p.134 B2

The 18b Arts District got its name when the city designated this 18-block area just south of Downtown as the official art studio neighborhood. Car repair garages and used furniture stores still outnumber storefront art galleries in the 18b, but there are a lot of hidden-away workspaces. The hub of the art district, the Arts Factory is a converted brick warehouse. Once you find the way in through a black side door, you can wander among visual artists' studios. The arts district bursts into vibrant life on the first Friday of every month from 6–9pm, when studios and galleries throughout the 18b hold receptions and special events for local artists and arts-oriented businesses. Crowds of around 15,000 visitors gather in the district for these First Friday festivals.

Bellagio Gallery of Fine Art
Bellagio, 3600 Las Vegas Boulevard South; tel: 693-7871; Sun–Thur 10am–6pm, Fri and Sat 10am–9pm; entrance charge; monorail: Bally's/Paris Las Vegas, bus: Deuce; map p.138 B3

Art gets a lot of attention at Bellagio, where former owner and big-time art collector Steve Wynn started the art-museums-in-casinos craze in 1998 with the Bellagio Gallery of Fine Art. The gallery opened with great fanfare and a well-regarded collection, including paintings by Renoir, Monet, Van Gogh, Rembrandts and Picasso. Each year, the gallery presents world-class exhibitions of artworks and objects from internationally acclaimed museums and private collections. There is an entrance fee even to hotel guests (though a smaller fee than the Guggenheim).

Left: Vegas a city of culture? Surprisingly so.

Boulevard South; tel: 414-2440; www.guggenheimlasvegas.org; daily 9.30am–7.30pm; entrance charge; monorail: Harrah's/ Imperial Palace; bus: Deuce; map p.138 B4

The Guggenheim Hermitage is a partnership with Russia's renowned Hermitage Museum in St Petersburg and the Solomon R. Guggenheim Foundation, which operates leading modern art museums in New York and other major cities around the world. The 63,700-sq. ft Las Vegas exhibition space has no permanent collection of its own but shows touring exhibits from both institutions.

Works of the 19th- and 20th-century artists like Picasso, Renoir, Rothkos and renowned controversial photographer Robert Mapplethorpe, as well as classic treasures from the pyramids of ancient Egypt, to the Kremlin's secret art collection, have been displayed here.

Many of the paintings on display at the Bellagio Gallery of Fine Art are acknowledged to be among the individual artists' greatest masterpieces, including Rubens's beautifully preserved 17th-century depiction of Salome presented with the head of John the Baptist, and Edgar Degas' Impressionist pastel of a stage ballerina.

City of Las Vegas Galleries

The Bridge Gallery, 400 East Stewart; tel: 229-4674; Mon–Fri 9am–6pm; free; bus: 207; map p.134 B4

On the second floor of the Las Vegas City Hall, these galleries show rotating exhibits of paintings and photographs by Las Vegas artists. The city also showcases local artists at the Twin Lakes Gallery in Lorenzi Park (3341 West Washington Avenue, tel: 229-6601) and at the West Las Vegas Arts Center (947 West Lake Mead Boulevard, tel: 229-

4800), which focuses on African-American artists.

Dust

1221 South Main Street; tel: 880-3878; www.dustgallery.com; Wed–Sun noon–5pm; free; map p.134 B2

One of the choicer galleries in the 18b Arts District, Dust represents postmodern painters, sculptors, photographers, and installation artists, about half local residents and the other half from New York, Boston, and Los Angeles.

Godt-Cleary Arts

1217 South Main Street; tel: 452-2000; www.gcarts-lv.com; Tue–Sat 10am–6pm; free; map p.134 B1

A leader among the art establishments in the 18b Arts District, this large gallery exhibits works by more than 60 recent and contemporary artists, including David Hockney, Jasper Johns, and Andy Warhol. It also has the best selection of fine art books, exhibition catalogs, and monographs.

Guggenheim Hermitage Museum

The Venetian, 3355 Las Vegas

Left: Bellagio's gallery was the first of its kind on the Strip.

Below: even the new Wynn Resort's lobbies and corridors are filled with valuable pieces of modern art.

97

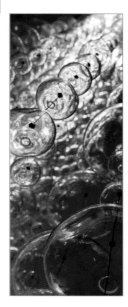

Left: glassworks, especially by artist Dale Chihuly, are very popular in Las Vegas.

Art League in 1950 by a group of volunteers who believed in the need for a local arts venue. Its out-of-the-way location on the west side of the city means you may find yourself completely alone amid all the art. There's also a desert sculpture garden.

S² Art Center

1 East Charleston Boulevard; tel: 868-7880; Mon–Sat 10am–6pm; free; bus: 206; map p.134 B2

Next door to the Art Center in the 18b Art District, S² moved from New York to Las Vegas in 2001. Owner Jack Solomon spent many years as the exclusive lithographer for the painter and illustrator Norman Rockwell, and with art-quality flatbed presses on site, you can often watch artists mixing ink, printing lithographs and hanging them up to dry.

Wynn Art Collection

Wynn Las Vegas, 3131 Las Vegas Boulevard South; tel: 693-7871; daily 9am–7pm; entrance charge; bus: Deuce; map p.136 B1 C1

Steve Wynn, the billionaire developer who parlayed an

The state-of-the-art gallery space was designed by architect Rem Koolhaas. Its exterior and interior walls are covered with panels of Cor-Ten steel, never used before as the structure of a museum gallery. The streamlined, textured metal is meant to evoke the velvet walls of the St Petersburg Hermitage while providing a contrast with the over-the-top architecture of the Venetian.

Las Vegas Art Museum

9600 West Sahara Avenue; tel: 360-8000; www.lasvegasartmuseum.org; Tue–Sat 10am–5pm, Sun 1–5pm; entrance charge; bus: 204

About 10 miles west of the Strip in the Sahara West Library building, the Las Vegas Art Museum is an affiliate of the Smithsonian Institute. It has no permanent collection of its own, but shows Smithsonian touring exhibits. It was founded as the Las Vegas

interest in an old Glitter Gulch casino to build the Mirage and the Bellagio, is credited with introducing fine art to Vegas. He sold both hotels to MGM Grand in 2000 but kept some of the Bellagio Gallery of Fine Art paintings to add to his personal collection. Works owned by Wynn are now exhibited at his newest hotel. The collection includes works by Van Gogh, Vermeer, Gauguin, Turner, and Andy Warhol. He originally planned to name the new hotel after the centerpiece of the collection, Picasso's "Le Rêve," but contented himself with using the name for a spectacular stage show instead. Works from Wynn's collection, some of them valued at upwards of $30 million, are on exhibit in the hotel for a moderate entrance fee. The Picasso painting is absent for restoration since Wynn accidentally poked a hole in it with his elbow in 2006.

High Stakes Art (S² Art Center, 1 East Charleston Boulevard, tel: 868-7880) is a unique studio-gallery that specializes in art prints and paintings on paper created especially for poker enthusiasts, with works by top area artists such as Larry Grossman, Craig DeThomas, Waldemar Swierzy, and Matt Rinard as well as reproductions of old gambling-theme movie posters and vintage advertisements for European casinos.

History

Atomic Testing Museum

755 East Flamingo Road; tel: 794-5151; www.atomictestingmuseum.org; Mon–Sat 9am–5pm, Sun 1–5pm; entrance charge; bus: 202; map p.137 E1

of the region. Tours begin in Anna Roberts Parks Exhibit Hall with a timeline of Southern Nevada stretching from prehistoric times through the 20th century.

The history of southern Nevada is shown in exhibits that begin with a diorama of the desert as it was 12,000 years ago, with petrified logs on sandy wastes, tortoises, cacti, and a tall extinct beast described as a camelope. A Pauite Indian camp is displayed, with rabbit pelts woven into a blanket, baskets, and other finely detailed craftwork.

The pioneer life of trappers, farmers, and ranchers is represented by a woman sitting in her kitchen beside a big spinning wheel, along with a baby in a rocker. Other exhibits are diverse:

there's Fanny Soss's 1930 dress store, the first local shop with window mannequins, as well as a depiction of the notorious Block 16, the downtown Las Vegas area where low-class saloons and gambling dives abutted on the Arizona Club, with its second-floor brothel. Singer Ella Fitzgerald donated two of her dresses to the collection, which includes items from the Tropicana, the Hacienda, and the Thunderbird.

Houdini Museum
The Venetian, 3355 Las Vegas Boulevard South; tel: 796-0301; daily 9am–7pm; free; monorail: Harrah's/Imperial Palace; bus: Deuce; map p.138 B4

The tiny but fascinating Houdini Museum exhibits personal letters, posters, photos, and such props as handcuffs and shackles the legendary magician escaped from. Fun for any age, it is sponsored

Revisit (from a safe distance) the days when Vegas locals used to pack picnic lunches and go watch the above-ground nuclear bomb tests at the Nevada Test Site north of the city *(see p.101)*. Visitors walk through a replica of an underground testing tunnel to view a spectacular multisensory presentation about atomic testing. Also on display are a fragment of the Berlin Wall, old-time Geiger counters, and atomic kitsch.

Carroll Shelby Museum
6915 Speedway Boulevard; tel: 643-3000; Mon–Fri 8am–5pm; entrance charge

Located on the grounds of the Las Vegas Motor Speedway, this museum displays a range of performance cars, including 35 years of Cobras, built by racing legend Carroll Shelby, who became the first auto manufacturer in Las Vegas.

Clark County Museum
1830 South Boulder Highway; tel: 455-7955; daily 9.30am–4pm; entrance charge; bus: 107

The museum can be reached by taking the Boulder Highway route into Henderson. In the lobby are shelves of interesting books about Native Americans and the geology

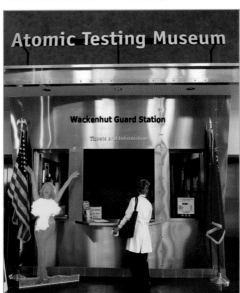

Left: Houdini's Magic Shops are located throughout the strip, but the only museum is in the Venetian *(see p. 99)*.

by the half-dozen Houdini's Magic Shops in resort shopping malls along the strip.

Howard W. Cannon Aviation Museum

SEE CHILDREN P.57

King Tut Museum

Luxor, 3900 Las Vegas Boulevard South; tel: 262-4555; daily 10am–11pm; entrance charge; bus: Deuce; map p.139 C1

Everything on display in this museum is a reproduction of artifacts from King Tut's tomb. Even the muraled stone chambers of the tomb itself are faithfully re-created just as they were found by archeologist Howard Carter in 1922. A 15-minute self-guiding audio tour tells you all about it.

Las Vegas Natural History Museum

SEE CHILDREN PP.57–58

Lost City Museum

721 Moapa Valley Boulevard (Highway 169), Overton; tel: 397-2193; daily 8.30am–4.30pm; entrance charge; map p.16

This state-run museum preserves artifacts from the 1,200-year-old Pueblo Grande de Nevada, which was submerged by the water of Lake Mead after Hoover Dam was built.

It exhibits some of the beads, polished shells, pottery, baskets, and, intriguingly, bone gambling counters, salvaged by archeologists during construction of the dam. The museum also has artifacts tracing Native American inhabitants of the area from archaic hunters 10,000 years ago through the Paiute people of more recent times.

Marjorie Barrick Museum

University of Nevada Las Vegas, 4505 South Maryland Parkway; tel: 895-3381; Mon–Fri 8am–4.45pm, Sat 10am–2pm; free; bus: 109; map p.139 E4

Live lizards, sharp-toothed Gila monsters, a tortoise, and a thin, red snake greet visitors from inside glass cases in the lobby, and in the museum are sandy dioramas of Mojave desert life. Stuffed birds, from sandpipers to pelicans, decorate an oasis filled with cholla cactus, desiccated wood, and a tiny kit fox. In another room are three large bears: black, polar, and grizzly.

There are also exhibits on the Southern Paiute Native Americans, including turquoise belts, rugs, and baskets, pottery, and an explanation of the weaving process, with samples of the natural dyes brazilwood and cochineal. Alongside are Mexican masks, colorful Guatemalan *huipiles* (embroidered blouses), and Mayan ceramics that resemble contemporary pottery. Pierced ears were common, one exhibit explains, because it was believed that without them passage to the "other world" would be impossible. There is an explanation of the pictures in a reproduction of the Codex Barbonicus, an ancient pictorial manuscript that stretches for several feet, and a display of prewar Vegas slot machines and Hoover Dam exhibits.

Behind the museum is the delightful Xeric Garden (from the Greek word *xeros*, meaning dry), with cacti, desert plants, and a bird-watching verandah. Ask for the pretty, free brochure that identifies and describes all the plants, an activity miles away in spirit from the jangling slot machines of the Strip.

Old Las Vegas Mormon Fort State Historic Park

500 East Washington Avenue; tel: 486-3511; daily 8.30am–4.30pm; entrance charge; map p.12

At the corner of Las Vegas

Below: an ambitious sign of intent at the Old Mormon Fort State Park.

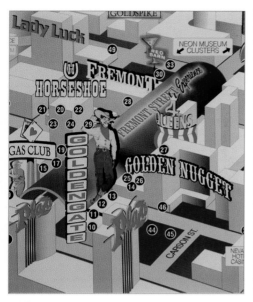

Left: this 3-D map at the Old Mormon Fort Park amalgamates all the buildings that have existed in Downtown Vegas for the last 50 years.

museum, which explores the history of arid but interesting southern Nevada.

Even though it is off the beaten track, the museum is well worth a visit, if only for its mining exhibit and the relics from the days when Las Vegas was still a dusty frontier town. The boots of Rex Bell, the local rancher turned movie star who became governor and married movie star Clara Bow, accompany his picture. The natural history section of the museum includes skeletons of mammoths and other prehistoric mammals as well as dioramas showing present-day wildlife, with explanations of how both ancient and modern animals adapted to survive in the harsh desert.

Nevada Test Site
Frenchman Flat; tel: 295-0944; www.ntshf.org; map p.14
Group tours of the Department of Energy's nuclear weapons proving ground 65 miles northwest of town, used for atmospheric testing from 1951 to 1992, are offered about once a month.

Rhyolite
State Highway 190 leads past the ruins of Rhyolite, near the boundary of Death

Boulevard and Washington Avenue is one of the state of Nevada's most venerable buildings, the Old Mormon Fort, in what is officially the Old Las Vegas Mormon Fort State Historic Park. The fort was built by Brigham Young's pioneers in 1855 to protect missionaries and settlers en route to California. Inside the high adobe walls, a reconstructed tower looks over a plaza deserted except for a broken-down wagon and the iron pegs for throwing horseshoes.

The only surviving part of the original structure is the building nearest to the little creek, rising from underground aquifers a few miles west, supplied a water source running through the fort, nourishing the poor soil in which the hopeful missionaries planted potatoes, tomatoes, squash, grapes, peaches, barley, and wheat. Some of these same plants are grown today on the

museum premises in a demonstration garden.

After the Mormons left, a miner named Octavius D. Gass acquired the site along with other land to assemble a sizable ranch. It was subsequently bought by Archibald Stewart, whose widow Helen ran the ranch after her husband was killed in 1884 and later sold the property to the railroad. The site on which the Stewart home stood is scheduled for excavation to unearth any secrets that may lie buried underneath.

Nevada State Museum and Historical Society
Lorenzi Park, 700 Twin Lakes Drive; tel: 486-5205; daily 9am–5pm; entrance charge
"Work your claim until you have all the gold from it and do not gamble away the money," and "Do not make gold the most important thing in life," were among the nuggets of advice offered to miners in an 1853 letter in the

Between the years 1951 and 1992, there were more than 1,000 announced nuclear tests at the Nevada Test Site, the United States' primary testing location for the country's nuclear devices. Most of these tests took place underground and the site is now covered with subsidence craters as a result. There may have been other, unannounced tests.

Valley National Park, about 2hrs' drive north of Las Vegas. Rhyolite was a prosperous mining community at the beginning of the 20th century but was abandoned in 1916. It is now a ghost town, better preserved than most because it has been refurbished as a movie set several times over the years – first in 1925 and most recently in 2005 for the sci-fi film *The Island*.

Walker African American Museum

705 West Van Buren Avenue; tel: 647-2242; daily 10am–6pm; entrance charge

The museum's collection includes more than 10,000 artworks, dolls, books, figurines, autographs, and records.

Miscellaneous

Boulder City/Hoover Dam Museum

1305 Arizona Street; tel: 294-1988; www.bcmha.org; open daily 10am–5pm, Sun

---

At the Boulder City/Hoover Dam Museum, an educational film shows how hard previously unemployed men had to work during the Depression era to construct the dam. So-called "muckers" shoveled out after each explosive blast with short-handled spades called banjos for just $4 a day.

---

noon–5pm; entrance charge; map p.16

A life-size climber conquers a canyon wall in the museum, offering an imaginative demonstration of the day-to-day tasks of building the dam. It's a pleasant little museum where you can play your part in an old debate by casting your vote for the name "Hoover Dam" or "Boulder Dam."

An ancient switchboard allows visitors to plug in and listen to residents reminisce about the old days. Exhibits re-create the historical context

of the dam project, which took place in the depths of the Great Depression, making this remote outpost in the Nevada desert one of the few places in America where unemployed men could find jobs. The museum and a gallery showing the work of local artists are located inside the historic Boulder Dam Hotel.
SEE ALSO ACCOMMODATIONS P.31

Lied Discovery Children's Museum
SEE CHILDREN P.58

Madame Tussaud's

The Venetian, 3355 Las Vegas Boulevard South; tel: 492-3690; www.mtvegas.com; call for hours; entrance charge; monorail: Harrah's/Imperial Palace; bus: Deuce; map p.138 B4

Dozens of contemporary celebrities are portrayed in wax at this "interactive wax attraction" near the hotel's entrance. Not only are there mannequins of prominent figures from George Washington and Abraham Lincoln to Frank Sinatra, Wayne New-

---

Below: the Fremont Street Experience is Downtown's biggest attraction and includes a collection of vintage neon signs and this extravagant light show.

Above: the Imperial's owner was renowned for his antique cars, which are now on show as the Imperial Palace Auto Collection.

ton, and Julia Roberts, but visitors are invited to touch their hair, skin, and clothing and even to have their photos taken with Elvis and sing a duet with Britney Spears.

Imperial Palace Auto Collection

Imperial Palace, 3535 Las Vegas Boulevard South; tel: 794-3174; daily 9.30am–9.30pm; entrance charge; monorail: Harrah's/Imperial Palace, bus: Deuce; map p.138 B4/C4

An animated figure of John Wayne stands beside the Duke's silver 1931 Bentley, welcoming guests to the impressive 200-car collection. Priceless motors include a $50 million array of 1930s Duesenbergs; Liberace's 1981 Zimmer with a candelabra hood ornament; Howard Hughes' baby-blue Chrysler; a 1929 Isotta Fraschini of the type seen in *Sunset Boulevard*; and a replica of Karl Benz's 1886 three-wheeler, said to have reached speeds of up to 8mph.

Also on show are cars formerly owned by Hitler, Kruschev, and many US presidents. The blue-and-white 1976 Cadillac for which Elvis Presley paid $14,409 – including extras like brass hubcaps – and Marilyn Monroe's 1955 Lin-

coln Capri convertible, in which the screen goddess clocked up only 26,000 miles, are cars that have motor-mad fans eating their room vouchers with envy.

Neon Museum

Fremont Street; tel: 229-5366; www.neonmuseum.org; map p.134 B3

Not actually a building but a collective title for the old neon signs that have been hung all around Downtown, the "museum" has plans for a future indoor exhibit hall. In the meantime, the Old Las Vegas Mormon Fort State Historic Park has agreed to hang some of the signs in its visitors' center. Some of the more colorful exhibits hang on an 85-ft tower in Neonopolis's interior plaza. These recall the 1920s era of Thomas Young's Electric Sign Company (Yesco), whose clients included owners of the now-defunct Thunderbird and Hacienda hotels as well as the Tropicana and the Sands. Today, however, many of the neon signs are indoors, beckoning gamblers to the slot machines.

Many of the historic neon signs here have been

"curated" from other cities: Hunick's Lounge was an Orange biker bar back in the 1950s, the Hunt's Red Car motel sign came from Compton, California.

Star Trek: The Experience

Las Vegas Hilton; 3000 Paradise Road; tel: 697-8700 or 888-462-6535; daily; www.startrekexp.com; monorail: Las Vegas Hilton, bus: 108; map p.137 C3

This permanent attraction guarantees to bring you face to face with the heroes of all the Star Trek series. Of course many are just impersonatorse in costumes, but the virtual reality technology and special effects could convince you otherwise. There is also the chance to dine at the "real" Quark's Bar and Restaurant and shop for memorabilia at the Star Trek Store.

Right: Vegas Vic still stands proud, but his booming voice has been silenced.

Pampering

Self-indulgence can take many forms, and the resorts of Las Vegas are there to cater to nearly every possible whim in that regard. Gambling, seeing stunning stage shows, or even just riding a rollercoaster may get your juices flowing and offer powerful distractions from the real world back home, but they will not do much to reduce your stress level, and surely that is part of what a vacation should be about? Here we list places that sell relaxation, pure and simple, as affordably as any other Vegas adventure, but with less over-stimulation than a night on the casino floor.

Along the Strip

A growing number of Vegas resort hotels offer in-house spa services, typically including a menu of various massage treatments and facials. Among the best Strip hotels with full spas are:
Bally's, tel: 967-4366
Caesars Palace, tel: 731-7776
Excalibur, tel: 597-7772
Flamingo, tel: 733-3535
Harrah's, tel: 369-5189
Las Vegas Hilton, tel: 732-5648
Imperial Palace, tel: 731-3311
MGM Grand, tel: 891-1111
Monte Carlo, tel: 730-7777

Many of Las Vegas's resort hotels now have spas that feature special premium treatments, such as the luxurious caviar and champagne facials (yes, they are rubbed directly on your face). Such superior facilities also feature top-quality saunas, whirlpools, steam rooms, and cold plunge pools.

New York New York, tel: 740-6955
Paris Las Vegas, tel: 946-4366
Stratosphere, tel: 380-7777
Tropicana, tel: 739-2680

Spa Resorts

Some Vegas resorts put spa services among their top priorities; some even include "spa" in the hotel names.
Aquae Sulis
J.W. Marriott Resort and Spa, 221 North Rampart Boulevard, tel: 869-7807 or 877-869-8777, www.marriott.com
Aquae Sulis, the ancient Latin name for Roman baths, is all about the soothing and healing powers of water. Before their treatments, guests are encouraged to spend time in the ritual room with its scented rainfall showers, and then further mellow out in a dimly lit relaxation room filled with soft music and water sounds. Open to non-guests.
Canyon Ranch Spa Club
Venetian, 3355 Las Vegas Boulevard South; tel: 414-3610 or 877-220-2688; monorail: Harrah's/ Imperial Palace; bus: Deuce; map p.138 B4

The largest spa facility on the Strip (69,000 sq ft), the Venetian's renowned two-story spa and fitness center has more than 60 treatment rooms. Open to non-guests with reservations 30 days in advance.
Hibiscus Spa
Westin Casuarina, 160 East Flamingo Road; tel: 836-9775; bus: 202; map p.139 C4
The 15 treatment rooms are used for a range of services such as Reiki, pregnancy massage, and deep-tissue sports therapy. Open to non-guests.
Nurture
Luxor, 3900 Las Vegas Boulevard South; tel: 730-5720; bus: Deuce; map p.139 C1
Partake of luxurious Egyptian rituals at the fall-hued spa off the West Tower's pool area. Hotel guests only.
The Rock Spa
Hard Rock Hotel, 4455 Paradise Road; tel: 693-5554 or 800-473-7625; bus: 108; map p.139 D4
Designed for young, active patrons, it has a fitness area filled with driving rock music. Step into the spa area, and rock walls block the music, leaving only the soothing

Left: cooling off in a plunge pool.

7777; bus: Deuce; map p.139 C1/D1

A tropical beach motif pervades this 30,000-sq. ft facility, where the treatment menu features delights like the Surf and Sand, a skin treatment with salts and bath gels. Open to non-guests on weekends.

Out-of-town spas

Mount Charleston Spa
The Hotel on Mount Charleston, 2 Kyle Canyon Road; tel: 872-5374; map p.14
An upscale rustic resort with fantastic mountain views. Guests only.

Ritz-Carlton Spa
Lake Las Vegas, 1610 Lake Las Vegas Parkway; tel: 567-4700
The most exclusive of three golf resort hotels, on the landscaped shore of Lake Las Vegas. Open to non-guests.

Spa at Green Valley Ranch
2300 Paseo Verde Parkway, Henderson; tel: 617-7570 or 866-782-9487; map p.16
A luxury resort, well removed from Vegas tourist zones yet within 20 minutes drive of the Strip. Open to non-guests.

sounds of running water as you relax in a whirlpool bath. Open to non-guests.

The Spa at The Four Seasons

3960 Las Vegas Boulevard South, tel: 632-5000; bus: Deuce; map p.139 D1
The Spa at The Four Seasons is in such demand that you are urged to make reservations at least two weeks ahead. Exotic Asian treatments top the spa menu, including a Thai herbal poultice massage. Open to non-guests with reservations.

Spa at the Palms

The Palms, 4321 West Flamingo Road; tel: 942-7777 or 866-725-6773; bus 202; map p.138 A2
This three-story spa with its gorgeous roof-top pools offers more than 30 types of massage and a variety of treatments, as well as classes in Pilates and yoga by candlelight. Open to non-guests.

Spa at the Wynn

Wynn Las Vegas, 3145 Las Vegas Boulevard South; tel: 770-3900; bus: Deuce; map p.136 C1
With 45 treatment rooms, the Spa at the Wynn is one of the bigger and busier relaxation

facilities on the Strip. Luxury reigns here. Open to non-guests Monday–Thursday.

Spa and Salon Bellagio

3600 Las Vegas Boulevard South; tel: 693-7111 or 888-987-6667; monorail: Bally's/ Paris Las Vegas, bus: Deuce; map p.138 B3
This elegant spa offers hydrotherapy treatments and fine waxing. Massages in its 56 treatment rooms include shiatsu, aromatherapy, and tandem. Hotel guests only.

Spa Mandalay

Mandalay Bay, 3950 Las Vegas Boulevard South; tel: 632-

Below: relaxation may not seem Vegas's *modus operandi*, but state of the art spa facilities are available.

Restaurants

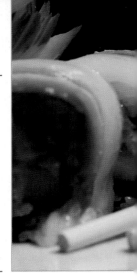

Dining in Vegas casinos was, until recently, mostly in the infamous buffet style. Now, in the upscale resorts, your host is more likely to be a celebrity chef. Vegas buffets still pack in the crowds, but the better ones have evolved to offer almost gourmet selections. The larger hotels feature a wide range of options to fit every budget, plus every fast-food chain imaginable. Food enthusiasts will want to check out the possibilities among the non-hotel restaurants that have sprung up along Paradise Road, in Chinatown and elsewhere, catering to mostly local crowds. Here's a sampler of the dining Vegas has to offer.

Southern Strip

AMERICAN

America

New York-New York, 3790 Las Vegas Boulevard South; tel: 740-6451; 24 hours; $$; bus: Deuce; map p.139 C2

Philly cheese-steak sandwiches from Pennsylvania and buffalo wings from New York are always favorites, as are Texas chile, Southern chicken-fried steak and Santa Fe smothered chicken.

The Burger Bar

Mandalay Bay, 3950 Las Vegas Boulevard South; tel: 632-7777; daily 10.30am–11pm; $–$$$; bus: Deuce; map p.139 C1

Burgers to suit all tastes and pockets can be found here, from the $60 Kobe burger with foie gras and truffles, to buffalo burgers, veggie burgers, and dessert burgers with a donut base topped off with cheesecake, chocolate, or peanut butter and jelly.

Charlie Palmer Steakhouse

Four Seasons Hotel, 3960 Las Vegas Boulevard South; tel: 362-5000; daily 5.30–10.30pm; $$$$; bus: Deuce; map p. 139 D1

Celebrity chef Charlie Palmer presents most of his signature dishes here, like wood-grilled filet mignon and an astonishing 48-oz New York strip steak. Seafood or family-style side dishes are available to non-carnivores. Premises are spacious, with a clubby atmosphere accented by rich polished wood.

Cheesecake Factory

Caesars Palace Forum Shops, 3750 Las Vegas Boulevard South; tel: 792 6888; daily 11.10am–11.30pm; $$; monorail: Flamingo/Caesars Palace, bus: Deuce; map p.138 B3/B4

Part of a popular national chain, "The Factory" is a cavernous restaurant with a huge menu offering a variety of food. Sunday brunch (not buffet) is delicious. Though you might be tempted to sit mall-side, do not, as the statue water show is pretty noisy and can be disruptive.

Craftsteak

MGM Grand, 3799 Las Vegas Boulevard South; tel: 891-7318; Sun–Mon 5.30–10pm, Tue–Thur 5–10pm, Fri–Sat 5–10.30pm; $$$$; monorail: MGM Grand, bus: Deuce; map p.139 C2

Using simple ingredients flown in fresh daily from small

Below: steak and the all-Amerian steakhouse have been given a gourmet makeover at Craftsteak.

Left: there is a large number of fine Pacific Rim restaurants in Vegas, serving everything from the finest sushi to dramatic Teppanyaki grills.

Nero's

Caesars Palace, 3570 Las Vegas Boulevard South; tel: 731-7731, daily 5–11pm; $$$; monorail: Flamingo/Caesars Palace, bus: Deuce; map p.138 B3/B4

This extraordinary steak-house, with its imposing neo-Roman modern design and pink chandeliers, serves a full range of beef and seafood dishes including a ribeye lollipop-cut steak and a 2lb Maine lobster, and has an extensive wine list.

Prime

Bellagio, 3600 Las Vegas Boulevard South; tel: 693-7111; daily 5–10pm; $$$$; monorail: Bally's/Paris Las Vegas, bus: Deuce; map p.138 B3

Dark wood panelling and dining booths secluded by ornate tapestry curtains create a romantic setting in which to savor master chef Jean-Georges Vongerichten's works of culinary art. Though it styles itself as a steakhouse, the menu features only a couple of beef dishes among more creative offerings such as seared tuna au poivre with wasabi-mashed potato and steamed bok choy.

Sir Galahad's Prime Rib House

Excalibur, 3850 Las Vegas Boulevard South; tel: 597-7448; Sun–Thur 5–10pm, Fri–Sat 5–11pm; $$$; bus: Deuce; map p.139 C1/C2

The buffet tradition began in the 1940s at the El Ranch, Vegas Hotel, when the owner, Beldon Katleman introduced an "all you can eat for a dollar" Midnight Chuch Wagon Buffet to keep customers in his casino after the second floor show ended. The idea was copied by other casinos, then extended to include breakfast, lunch, and dinner.

family farms, award-winning chef Tom Colicchio creates striking presentations of flavorful dishes including the house specialty, grilled Kobe skirt steak. There is an extensive wine list.

Emeril's New Orleans Fish House

MGM Grand, 3799 Las Vegas Boulevard; tel: 891-7374; daily 5.30–10.30pm; $$$; monorail: MGM Grand, bus: Deuce; map p.139 C2

Whether it is scallops from Maine, pike from the Midwest, or chicken from Alabama, celebrity chef Emeril Lagasse "bams" it up with Creole-Cajun flair in a setting that is more Bourbon Street than Vegas Strip. Especially tasty is the house specialty, New Orleans barbecued shrimp.

ESPN Zone

New York New York, 3790 Las Vegas Boulevard South; tel: 933-3776; daily 11am–11pm; $$; bus: Deuce; map p.139 C2

This entertainment complex has a sports theme, with 165 HD TVs blaring games that compete for your attention while you fill up on all-American fare like ribs and chicken sandwiches in the Zone's Studio Grill, where fans stand up and cheer in mid-meal.

House of Blues

Mandalay Bay, 3950 Las Vegas Boulevard; tel: 632-7607; daily 7.30am–midnight; $$; bus: Deuce; map p.139 C1/D1

The restaurant at the House of Blues offers a variety of moderately priced dishes for every taste, from macaroni and cheese to wild mushroom penne, as well as eye-openers like eggs Benedict, breakfast burritos, and Cajun pigs in blankets. For Sunday brunch, tuck into grits and hickory-smoked bacon to the sound of live gospel music.

SEE ALSO LIVE ENTERTAINMENT P.86–7

Prices for an average three-course meal with wine:
$ under $20
$$ $20–$30
$$$ $30–$40
$$$$ more than $40

Buffet selection can run to 40 or 50 items and include salads, fruits, roast beef, baked ham, fried chicken, vegetables, coffee, and an array of desserts. Although subject to change, prices average $10 for breakfast, $12 for lunch, and $18 for dinner. At night some hotels offer bacon-and-egg breakfasts for just a dollar or two. Expect to stand in line for a long time, regardless of the hour.

The house specialty is aged prime rib, carved tableside, offered with a choice of old-fashioned soups or salad. For non-beef-eaters, there are Atlantic salmon, Maine lobster, and Alaskan king crab legs, plus English trifle for dessert.

Stage Deli

MGM Grand, 3799 Las Vegas Boulevard South; tel: 893-4045; daily 7am–9pm; $–$$; monorail: MGM Grand, bus: Deuce; map p.139 C2

This spiffy replica of Manhattan's Stage Deli, which has been a New York landmark for more than half a century, serves pastrami (or corned beef or brisket) sandwiches on rye that are so authentic Easterners may forget they are not back home.

FRENCH

Eiffel Tower Restaurant

Paris Las Vegas, 3655 Las Vegas Boulevard South; tel: 948-6937; daily 5.30–10pm; $$$$; monorail: Bally's/Paris Las Vegas, bus: Deuce; map p.138–9 C3

Chef J. Joho's gourmet Gallic entrées are served in an elegantly contemporary atmosphere. Specialties include *tournedos Rossini* with foie

gras and truffle sauce and a spectacular seafood platter.

L'Atelier de Joel Robuchon

MGM Grand, 3799 Las Vegas Boulevard South; tel: 891-7349; Mon–Thur 5–10.30pm, Sat–Sun 5–11.30pm; $$$$; monorail: MGM Grand, bus: Deuce; map p.139 C2

Very expensive even for a Las Vegas signature restaurant, L'Atelier serves either à la carte, with entrees like suckling pig confit and sea bass on a bed of baby leeks, or from *degustation* and *decouverte* menus that offer arrays of tasting portions. The setting is dramatically hip.

Le Cirque

Bellagio, 3600 Las Vegas Boulevard South; tel: 693-8100; daily 5.30–10pm; $$$$; monorail: Bally's/Paris Las Vegas, bus: Deuce; map p.138 B3

Le Cirque has creative gourmet entrées such as black-tie scallops (tied with black truffles), *consommé de boeuf* with foie gras ravioli, roasted duck with a honey-spice fig glaze, and roasted lobster in a port-wine sauce. After all this culinary splendor, enjoy luscious desserts. Jacket and tie are mandatory for men.

Les Artistes Steakhouse

Paris Las Vegas, 3655 Las Vegas Boulevard South; tel: 946-3908; daily 5.30–10.30pm; $$$; monorail: Bally's/Paris Las Vegas, bus: Deuce; map p.138–139 C3

French-inspired versions of steak and seafood fare, such as a bone-in filet mignon with Bearnaise sauce accompanied by a stuffed Provencale tomato, are served in one of the city's most fascinating

Right: enjoy the passing crowds or the Bellagio dancing fountains across the Strip from the charming French restaurant Mon Ami Gabi.

restaurant settings, its walls covered by dozens of French Impressionist paintings.

Mon Ami Gabi

Paris Las Vegas, 3655 Las Vegas Boulevard South; tel: 944-4224; brunch Sat–Sun 11am–3pm, lunch Mon–Fri 11.30am–3.45pm, dinner Sun–Thur 4–11pm, Fri–Sat 4pm–12am; $$–$$$; monorail: Bally's/Paris Las Vegas, bus: Deuce; map p.138–139 C3

Specialties on the menu include lemon chicken paillard, steak Bearnaise, and trout Grenobloise.

Picasso

Bellagio, 3600 Las Vegas Boulevard; tel: 693-7223; Wed–Mon 6–9.30pm; $$$; monorail: Bally's/Paris Las Vegas, bus: Deuce; map p.138 B3

A feast for the eyes and the stomach: French food is served in a room designed by Pablo Picasso's son, Claude, with paintings on the walls by papa estimated to be worth $50 million. Diners can choose between a four-course *prix fixe* menu and a five-course chef's *degustation* menu. Both change daily.

ITALIAN

André's

Monte Carlo, 3770 Las Vegas Boulevard South; tel: 730-7955; daily 4–11pm; $$$$; bus: Deuce; map p.138 C2

Elegant dining featuring award-winning chef André Rochat's gourmet cuisine and world-class wine cellar. The ambience is of a Renaissance chateau.

Bertolini's

Caesars Palace Forum Shops, 3570 Las Vegas Boulevard South; tel: 735-4663; daily 11am–midnight; $$; monorail: Flamingo/Caesars Palace, bus: Deuce; map p.138 B3/B4

This upscale Italian-style trattoria offers delicious Italian entrées and wood-oven

Above: the Eiffel Tower Restuarant has a romantic view of the Strip from the 11th floor.

pizza. Most patrons choose to dine "outdoors" near a huge (and loud) fountain.

Café Bellagio

Bellagio, 3600 Las Vegas Boulevard South; tel: 693-7223; 24 hours; $$$; monorail: Bally's/Paris Las Vegas, bus: Deuce; map p.138 B2

The Italian menu says "gourmet restaurant" more than "café," with sea bass ravioli, rack of lamb and giant shrimp.
SEE ALSO BARS AND CAFÉS P.32

Olives

Bellagio, 3600 Las Vegas Boulevard South; tel: 693-7223; daily 11am–10.30pm; $$$; monorail: Bally's/Paris Las Vegas, bus: Deuce; map p.138 B2

Enjoy tasty Mediterranean food with a great view of the dancing waters of "Lake Bellagio" and Paris Las Vegas's Eiffel Tower at designer Jeffrey Beers's chic pizza and pasta restaurant.

Osteria del Circo

Bellagio, 3600 Las Vegas Boulevard; tel: 693-8150; daily 5.30–10.30pm; $$$$; monorail: Bally's/Paris Las Vegas, bus: Deuce; map p.138 B2

Le Cirque's little sister has a light-hearted feel and great views of the Bellagio's fountain display. A circus motif forms the backdrop for outstanding wood-oven Tuscan cuisine, from octopus and

calamari stew to roasted venison tenderloin.

Penazzi Italian Ristorante

Harrah's, 3475 Las Vegas Boulevard South; tel: 369-5000; Wed–Sun 5.30–10.30pm; $$$$; monorail: Harrah's/Imperial Palace, bus: Deuce; map p.138 B4

Simple decor complements one of the finest Italian dining experiences in the city. Chef Gabrielle Penazzi tantalizes the palate with old family recipes such as *rollatini di soghiole alla don*, a rolled filet of sole stuffed with crab meat and poached in tomato-caper sauce. Penazzi also features an oyster bar.

PACIFIC RIM

Ah Sin

Paris Las Vegas, 3655 Las Vegas Boulevard South; tel: 946-4663; Wed–Sun 5.30–10.30pm; $$$; monorail: Bally's/Paris Las Vegas, bus: Deuce; map p.138 C3

This new Pacific Rim Asian restaurant offers indoor and outdoor dining "family style," meaning fixed-price multi-course dinners to be shared

Prices for an average three-course meal with wine:
$ under $20
$$ $20–$30
$$$ $30–$40
$$$$ more than $40

109

by more than one person. A typical dinner includes lobster spring rolls, hot and sour soup, tangerine spiced beef, and tropical sorbet.

Aureole

Mandalay Bay, 3950 Las Vegas Boulevard South; tel: 705-7133; daily 6–10pm; $$$$; bus: Deuce; map p.139 C1/D1

Celebrity chef Charlie Palmer's version of his New York classic is architecturally arresting (a three-story wine tower and a pond with swans). The excellent seafood menu is complemented by an outstanding wine list.

Bradley Ogden

Caesars Palace, 3750 Las Vegas Boulevard South; tel: 731-7410; daily 5–11pm; $$$$; monorail: Flamingo/Caesars Palace, bus: Deuce; map p.138 B3/B4

The Bay Area celebrity chef of whom this restaurant is the namesake was named Best California Chef by the James Beard Foundation. His Las Vegas location, at once colorful and stiffly formal, presents a changing five- to nine-course tasting menu

Below: Spago's master chef displays his creations.

that focuses mainly on seafood, with a sample of Kobe beef or bison thrown in, and wine pairings. The whole experience takes about three very expensive hours.

China Grill

Mandalay Bay, 3950 Las Vegas Boulevard South; tel: 632-7404; daily 5.30pm–midnight; $$$$; bus: Deuce; map p.139 C1/D1

The large portions served here are intended for sharing. Mouth-watering favorites include the Shanghai lobster served with ginger, curry, and spinach, or sake-marinated "drunken" chicken. The architecture and decor are stunning, with an open kitchen, multilevel dining areas and a planetarium ceiling.

Chinois and Spago

Caesars Palace Forum Shops at 3750 Las Vegas Boulevard South; tel: 737-9700; daily 3–11pm; $$$; monorail: Flamingo/Caesars Palace, bus: Deuce; map p.138 B3/B4

Wolfgang Puck offers Chinese with a Gallic attitude. Specialties include Shanghai lobster with coconut curry sauce, stir-fried string beans, catfish, duck, and much more. A few steps away, a branch of Puck's California-inspired Spago – the first signature restaurant on the Strip – presents an imaginative array of entrées as well as a tasting menu.

Drai's

Bill's Las Vegas, 3595 Las Vegas Boulevard South; tel: 737-0555; daily 5.30pm–midnight; $$$; monorail: Flamingo/Caesars Palace, bus: Deuce; map p.138 C3/C4

Ex-Hollywood producer Victor Drai brings an upscale ambiance to this beautiful room. Dishes include seared jumbo scallops with citrus ginger sauce, artichoke, asparagus, and tomatoes.

Above: most of the seafood for sushi is flown in daily from California, but some travels even further having been caught in South American or Australian waters.

Fusia

The Luxor, 3900 Las Vegas Boulevard South; tel: 262-4000; Sun–Thur 6–10.30pm, Fri–Sat 5pm–1am; $$$; bus: Deuce; map p.139 C1

Even the most jaded of pan-Asian epicures are sure to find something new and unique on the menu of chef Gerald Trujillo's new restaurant, where presentations emphasize spice, color, and aroma. Try the spiced Indonesian crab stack or the Nigiri-style sushi.

Hyakumi Japanese and Sushi Bar

Caesars Palace, 3750 Las Vegas Boulevard South; tel: 731-7731; daily 11am–3pm and 5–11pm; $$–$$$$; monorail: Flamingo/Caesars Palace, bus: Deuce; map p.138 B3/B4

More than 40 varieties of fresh sushi and sashimi are prepared by master chefs with flashing knives. Those who do not like raw fish can order beef, chicken, and fish dishes cooked on a teppan grill in the center of their table.

Jasmine

Bellagio, 3600 Las Vegas Boulevard South; tel: 693-7111; daily 5.30–10pm; $$$; monorail:

Bally's/Paris Las Vegas, bus: Deuce; map p.138 B3
Sparkling chandeliers, stately columns and elegant European furnishings and views of the hotel's spectacular fountain show set the stage for contemporary Hong Kong, Cantonese, Szechuan, and Hunan cuisine. Minced squab in lettuce petals and rose dew lamb chops are among the offerings.

Mizuno's Japanese Steak House
Tropicana, 3801 Las Vegas Boulevard; tel: 739-2713; daily 5–10.45pm; $$$; monorail: MGM Grand, bus: Deuce; map p.139 C2/D2
The Tropicana offers traditional teppan-style dining with specialties that range from teppanyaki vegetables to the Emperor's Dinner, a feast of lobster tail, filet mignon, giant shrimp, and boneless chicken breast.

Nob Hill
MGM Grand, 3799 Las Vegas Boulevard South; tel: 891-7220; Sun–Thur 5.30–10pm, Fri–Sat 5.30–10.30pm; $$$; monorail: MGM Grand, bus: Deuce; map p.139 C2/D2
Award-winning San Francisco chef Michael Mina evokes the culinary traditions of the City by the Bay in this warm, intimate restaurant. Main courses include North Beach Cioppino and Japanese snapper with butternut squash risotto and chanterelle mushrooms. There is a unique lobster tasting menu featuring four different lobster dishes, fruit, cheese, and wine pairings.

Prices for an average three-course meal with wine:
$ under $20
$$ $20–$30
$$$ $30–$40
$$$$ more than $40

Above: the food in Vegas can be as showy as the Strip, with effort even going into the buffets' displays

Noodles
Bellagio, 3600 Las Vegas Boulevard South; tel: 693 8131; daily 11am–2am; $$; monorail: Bally's/Paris Las Vegas, bus: Deuce; map p.138 B3
A modern Tony Chi-designed Pan-Asian noodle shop in the heart of Las Vegas. The Modernist touches are elegantly trendy, and the variety of menu selections is vast and authentic, featuring noodle, rice, and congee specialties from Japan, China, Thailand, and Vietnam, as well as Hong Kong-style barbecue. Dim sum is served Fri–Sun 11am–3pm.

Wolfgang Puck Bar & Grill
MGM Grand; 3799 Las Vegas Boulevard South; tel: 891-3019, Sun–Thur 11.30am–10.30pm, Fri–Sat 11.30am–11.30pm; $$; monorail: MGM Grand, bus: Deuce; map p139 C2
Light and airy in hues of cream and tan, this circular restaurant surrounds a kitchen dishing up high-class pizza and all-American cooking with a California twist.

Signature dishes include duck bratwurst sausage and truffled potato chips with blue cheese.

Wolfgang Puck's Trattoria del Lupo
Mandalay Bay, 3950 Las Vegas Boulevard; tel: 740-5522; Sun–Thur 5–10pm, Fri–Sat 5–11pm; $$$; bus: Deuce; map p.139 C1/D1
Trattoria del Lupo means "restaurant of the wolf." The first Italian restaurant opened by the ubiquitous Mr Puck, this eatery is full of antiques and unique lighting fixtures and even includes an exhibition pizza station. Although known for pizzas, there are also delicious classic and contemporary Italian dishes on the menu, from three-color arugula salad to braised lamb ossobuco with pears, gorgonzola cheese, and watercress.

RUSSIAN
Red Square
Mandalay Bay, 3950 Las Vegas Boulevard; tel: 632-7407;

111

Above: do not miss the chance to try one of Vegas's trademark buffets, they really are an experience unlike any other.

Sun–Thur 5–11pm, Fri–Sat 5–12pm; $$$; bus: Deuce; map p.139 C1/D1

A consistent winner in Las Vegas Weekly's "dining with a scene" list, Red Square is the place to dress up (warmly), roll up to the long bar of solid ice, and partake of as much top-of-the-line vodka shots as possible. Afterwards it's only a short walk to a table to dine on Russian dishes like salmon *kulebyaka* and *stroza-pretti stroganoff*. Assorted Russian caviars make fine, if expensive, appetizers.

SOUTH AMERICAN
Rumjungle
Mandalay Bay, 3950 Las Vegas Boulevard South; tel: 632-7408; daily noon–4pm and 5–10pm; $$$; bus: Deuce; map p.139 C1/D1

Rumjungle's exotic dining choices include fish, fowl, and grilled meats that are marinated in fruits, tropical spices, and rum. Check out the Cuban coffee smoked ribs with guajillo salsa appetizer.

SOUTHWEST
Mesa Grill
Caesars Palace, 3570 Las Vegas Boulevard South; tel: 731-7731; Mon–Fri 11am–11pm; Sat–Sun 10.30am–11pm; $$$; monorail: Flamingo/Caesars Palace, bus: Deuce; map p.138 B3/B4

Southwest nouveau fare is featured at this picnic-casual restaurant by TV personality and cookbook author Bobby Flay. Specialties include sweet potato tamales with crushed pecan butter and ancho chile-honey glazed salmon.

SOUTHERN STRIP BUFFETS
Island Buffet
Tropicana, 3801 Las Vegas Boulevard South; tel: 739-2222; daily 7.30am–10pm, Sat–Sun champagne brunch 7.30am– 2.30pm; $$; monorail: MGM Grand, bus: Deuce; map p.139 C2/D2

Located off the main gaming area with views of poolside gardens, this buffet offers a generous selection of food choices including hand-carved roast beef, turkey, and ham. After 4pm, dinner features all-you-can-eat prime rib and shrimp.

Le Village Buffet
Paris Las Vegas, 3655 Las Vegas Boulevard South; tel: 946-7000; daily 7am–10pm, Sat–Sun champagne brunch 11am– 3.30pm; $$; monorail: Bally's/Paris Las Vegas, bus: Deuce; map p.138 C3

Something completely different in Strip buffets, Le Village offers dishes from each of the five French provinces at a station with a façade patterned after the rural architecture of that region.

Patrons can dine "outside" in the "Village Square" or inside by the fireplace.

Below: Rumjungle serves exotic food, but is just as popular for a stylish drink.

Above: at NASCAR Café the theme is more of an attraction than the food.

Roundtable Buffet
Excalibur, 3850 Las Vegas Boulevard South; tel: 597-7777; daily 8am–10pm; $; bus: Deuce; map p.139 C1/C2
This is one of the less expensive all-you-can-eat buffets on the Strip, which may explain why it's full much of the time. It seats 1,400 people, and accounts for a goodly portion of the 10 million meals a year served at the Excalibur. The food choices are predictable.

Northern Strip

AMERICAN
Delmonico Steakhouse
The Venetian, 3355 Las Vegas Boulevard South; tel: 414-3737; daily 11.30am–1.45pm and 5–10pm; $$$; monorail: Harrah's/Imperial Palace; bus: Deuce; map p.138 B4
Emeril Lagasse dishes up delicious Creole flavors in his personal steakhouse. Twelve-foot oak doors and vaulted ceilings set the stage for specialties such as New Orleans gumbo and grilled pork chops with bacon-wrapped shrimp and bourbon smashed sweet potatoes.
House of Lords Steakhouse
The Sahara, 2535 Las Vegas Boulevard South; tel: 737-2401; daily 5–10pm; $$; mono-rail: Sahara, bus: Deuce; map p.136 B3/B4
Waterfalls and plush seating highlight the cozy ambiance, while the menu features prime beef and seafood as well as the restaurant's signature bone-in ribeye steak.
NASCAR Café
2535 Las Vegas Boulevard South; tel: 737-2111; Sun–Thur 11am–9pm, Fri–Sat 11am–10pm; $; monorail: Sahara, bus: Deuce; map p.136 B3/B4
This two-level restaurant features NASCAR stock cars, sports screens, and auto merchandise. The food is as typically American as you can get, with burgers, steaks, chicken, ribs and salads.
Peppermill Inn
2985 Las Vegas Boulevard South; tel: 735-4177; 24 hours; $; bus: Deuce; map p.136 B2
Dwarfed by the surrounding highrises, the Peppermill is among the last survivors of old-time Vegas and has been used as a location for many movies, including *Casino (see p.93)*. The relaxing Fireside Lounge has soft seats by a flaming pool. The fare – classic American diner food – is served up in gigantic portions calculated to rival any all-you-can-eat casino buffet.

Right: dressed for a pit stop.

THE Steak House
Circus Circus, 2880 Las Vegas Boulevard South; tel: 794-3767; Sun–Fri 5–10pm, Sat 5–11pm, Sun champagne brunch 9.30 and 11.30am, and 1.30pm; $$; bus: Deuce; map p.136 B2/B3
Steaks aged 21 days and cooked to perfection over mesquite wood on an open grill. A display case shows customers the cuts of beef available. Seafood is also served. The dark wood and brass decor is surprisingly subdued for Circus Circus.
Tiffany's
White Cross Drugstore, 1700 Las Vegas Boulevard South; tel: 444-4459; 24 hours; $; bus: Deuce; map p.134 B1
This genuine old-fashioned drugstore lunch counter was the first round-the-clock eatery in Vegas when it opened in the 1950s. Today, caught in a time warp, it's still the place to go for budget meals – not only burgers but also Old World fare like pita bread gyros and satisfying corned beef and cabbage.
Top of the World
Stratosphere Tower, 2000 Las Vegas Boulevard South; tel: 380-7711; Mon–Sat 5pm–3am, Sun 11am–3pm; $$$; Deuce; map p.136 B4
Revolving 360 degrees every

113

Above: book a table in time to catch sunset at Stratosphere's Top of the World – it is fabulous.

Prices for an average three-course meal with wine:
$ under $20
$$ $20–$30
$$$ $30–$40
$$$$ more than $40

1hr 20min, this restaurant 800ft high offers the best view of the Strip in town. Colorado rack of lamb, Muscovy duck, and lobster and crab ravioli are among the house specialties.

ITALIAN
Alex
Wynn Las Vegas, 3131 Las Vegas Boulevard South; tel: 770-3300; Sun–Thur 6–10pm; $$$$; bus: Deuce; map p.136 B1/C1
Run by chef Alex Stratta, this fine dining establishment carries Mediterranean-Continental food to new heights of haute-cuisine with elaborate multi-course *prix fixe* dinners that combine seafood appetizers with meat and wild game entrées and exquisite desserts.

Canaletto
Venetian Grand Canal Shoppes, 3355 Las Vegas Boulevard South; tel: 733-0070; daily 11.30am–11pm; $$–$$$$; monorail: Harrah's/Imperial Palace; bus: Deuce; map p.138 B4
While master chef Luigi Bomparola's regional Italian cuisine varies from wonderful to just okay, the experience of dining by the waterside while sitting in the middle of a desert is the one to write home about. Five separate dining rooms provide intimacy.

Onda
The Mirage, 3400 Las Vegas Boulevard South; tel: 791-7223; daily 5–10.30pm; $$; bus: Deuce; map p.138 B4
This "ristorante and wine lounge" has consistently been voted Las Vegas's Best Italian Restaurant in newspaper surveys. The menu mixes regional and classic Italian dishes with North American innovations, featuring selections such as capellini with scallops, veal marsala, and softshell crabs.

PACIFIC RIM
AquaKnox
The Venetian, 3355 Las Vegas Boulevard South; tel: 414-2220; Sun–Thur 5.30–11pm, Fri–Sat 5.30–11.30pm; $$$; monorail: Harrah's/Imperial Palace; bus: Deuce; map p.138 B4
Celebrity chef Tom Moloney, formerly with the Wolfgang Puck restaurant empire, flies seafood in fresh daily from around the world to prepare dishes like tuna tataki and tartare and wild Tasmanian sea trout, served in a cool, ocean-hued setting.

Japonais
The Mirage, 3400 Las Vegas Boulevard South; tel: 791-7223; Sun–Wed 5–11pm, Thur–Sat 5–11.30pm; $$$; bus: Deuce; map p.138 B4
This Japanese restaurant is a partnership between two chefs, sushi master Jun Ichikawa and hot foods chef Gene Kato. A house specialty is "the rock," thin-sliced marinated beef cooked on a slab of hot granite at the table.

Pho
TI – Treasure Island, 3300 Las Vegas Boulevard South; tel: 894-7223; Sun–Thur 11am–midnight, Fri–Sat 11am–3am; $$; bus: Deuce; map p.136 B1
Elaborate noodle soups and spring rolls are the specialties at the only Vietnamese restaurant on the Strip, located within the hotel's casual coffee shop.

Postrio
Grand Canal Shoppes at The Venetian, 3355 Las Vegas Boulevard South; tel: 796-1110; café daily 11.30am–10pm, dining

room 5.30–10pm; $$$; mono-rail: Harrah's/Imperial Palace; bus: Deuce; map p.136 B4
Wolfgang Puck's San Francisco-style eatery serves modern US cuisine with Mediterranean and Asian accents. Try the signature dish, mesquite-grilled *côte de boeuf*, or for lunch in the café, duck confit pizza with Bartlett pears and blue cheese.

NORTHERN STRIP
BUFFETS
Circus Buffet
2880 Las Vegas Boulevard South; tel: 734-0410; breakfast: Mon–Fri 7am–2pm, brunch: Sat–Sun 7am–4pm, dinner: daily 4.30–10pm; $; bus: Deuce; map p.136 B2/B3
One of the largest buffets on the strip, with more than 50 items, this buffet serves more than 10,000 people a day via three serving lines. (Its record is 17,600 diners on one busy day.) Though it has undergone a recent facelift, Vegas locals still steer clear of the place due to its past reputation for a horrid lack of quality. Kids love it.
Cravings Buffet
The Mirage, 3400 Las Vegas Boulevard South; tel: 891-7374; daily 7am–10pm; Sat–Sun brunch 8am–3pm; $$$; bus: Deuce; map p.138 B4
An excellent, international, all-you-can-eat feast, Cravings features 11 cooking stations and a wide selection of foods prepared with the freshest ingredients. The overall quality, fabulous salad selection, and delicious desserts make this one of the top buffets on the Strip.
World's Fare Buffet
Riviera, 2901 Las Vegas Boulevard South; tel: 734-5110; daily 6am–2pm and 4–10pm; $; bus: Deuce; map p.136 B2
A cut below the average Strip buffet in both quality and

price, the World's Fare offers the usual international buffet choices, including Chinese, Mexican, Italian, barbecue, and "Made in America."

Beyond the Strip
AMERICAN
Big Al's Oyster Bar
The Orleans, 4500 West Tropicana; tel: 365-7111; Sun–Thur 11am–10pm, Fri–Sat 11am–midnight; $$; bus: 201; map p.138 A1
Creole and Cajun-style shucked oysters and clams, voodoo mussels, shrimp, scampi, bouillabaisse, and pasta grace the menu at this pseudo-Louisianan restaurant. You would pay twice as much for much the same food at one of Emeril

Legasse's signature Cajun restaurants on the Strip.
Golden Steer Steakhouse
308 West Sahara Avenue; tel: 384-4470; daily 4.30–11pm; $$$; bus: 204; map p.136 B3
For nearly half a century, the Golden Steer has been serving seafood and tasty steaks to locals and visitors in the know, including Vegas legends like Frank Sinatra and his Rat Pack, Elvis Presley, and John Wayne. There are historic photos on the walls, and the waiters wear tuxedos. The atmosphere resembles that of an old-time bordello.
Mr Lucky's 24/7
Hard Rock Hotel, 4455 Paradise Road; tel: 693-5000; 24 hours; $; bus: 108; map p.139 D4
Mr Lucky's is an "always

Below: the Vegas location of the critically acclaimed New York and Chicago restaurant Japonais is equally stylish.

Left: buffets cover all culinary classes from ketchup to cakes.

Waiters present enormous uncooked steaks, whole lobsters, and fresh vegetables tableside for your inspection before ordering. The Cajun-style sirloin is moderately fiery, and the house specialty, a 24-oz porterhouse steak, is huge.

Ruth's Chris Steak House
3900 Paradise Road; tel: 791-7011, Mon–Fri 11am–11pm, Sat–Sun 4.30–11pm; $$$; bus: 108; map p.137 D1

Ruth Fertel opened her first restaurant in New Orleans in 1965; now these reliable, good-value steak houses can be found all over the country. The fare is USDA prime steak, seafood and New Orleans-inspired appetizers.

The Tillerman
2245 East Flamingo Road; tel: 731-4036; daily 5–10pm; $$; bus: 202; map p.10

Seafood is the main attraction at this family-owned spot that's been around for more than 20 years. East coast oysters – hot and cold – are a specialty.

The Voodoo Café
Rio, 3700 West Flamingo Road; tel: 247-7800; daily 5–11pm; $$; bus: 202; map p.138 A3

High atop the Rio, with a view overlooking all of Las Vegas, this rooftop restaurant serves up spicy Creole and Cajun specialties, including daily specials and a "ménage a trios" of filet mignon, lobster, and prawns, with bananas Foster for dessert.

FRENCH
Alizé
The Palms, 4321 Flamingo Road; tel: 951-7000; Sun–Thur 5.30–10pm, Fri–Sat 5.30–10.30pm; $$$$; bus 202; map p.138 A2

The current doyen of Vegas restaurateurs, celebrity chef André Rochat ascends to the top (literally) of the Palms Hotel to present his award-winning French cuisine and excellent wine list. Alizé serves exquisitely tantalizing fare such as pan-seared Muscovy duck with peach and foie gras tart tatin, duck confit and peach emulsion.

Pamplemousse
400 East Sahara Avenue; tel: 733-2066; daily 5.30–10.30pm; $$$; bus: 204; map p.136 C4

One of Las Vegas's most romantic restaurants for more than 30 years, Pamplemousse combines the ambience of a French country inn with an assortment of ordering options. You can select from the regular menu (not printed, only recited tableside by the waiter), an "epicurean" five-course *prix fixe* dinner, or a "gourmet" menu shared by a minimum of 10 guests.

GREEK
Paymon's Mediterranean Cafe and Lounge
4147 South Maryland Parkway; tel: 731-6030; daily 11am–3am; $$; bus: 109; map p.137 E1

Greek favorites include flaming *saganaki* (fried cheese squares) and *spanakopita* (cheese and spinach pie). There are also Middle Eastern dishes such as Persian *fesenjan* (chicken breast in walnut and pomegranate sauce). Dancing optional.

INDIAN
Shalimar Fine Indian Cuisine
3900 Paradise Road; tel: 796-

open" hotel restaurant that breaks the mold. It has a welcomingly festive atmosphere, with faux tiger skin upholstered booths and views of the casino floor. The menu offers standard American classics such as burgers, steak, pizza, and pasta, as well as one of the best selections of vegetarian fare.

Morton's of Chicago
400 East Flamingo Road; tel: 893-0703; daily 5–11pm; $$$; bus: 202; map p.139 D4

Prices for an average three-course meal with wine:
$ under $20
$$ $20–$30
$$$ $30–$40
$$$$ more than $40

0302; Mon–Fri buffet 11.30am–2.30pm, dinner daily 5.30–10pm; $$; bus: 108; map p.137 D1

The emphasis is on tasty chicken and lamb dishes from the tandoori oven.

ITALIAN

Battista's Hole in the Wall
4041 Audrie Street; tel: 732-1424; daily 5–10.30pm; $–$$$; map p.138 C4

This casual Italian has 30 years' worth of celebrity photos and mementoes. It offers pasta, seafood, or veal, including all the wine you can drink. The accordion player is a local legend.

Chicago Joe's
820 South 4th Street; tel: 382 5637; Mon–Fri 11am–10pm, Sat 5–10pm, closed Sun; $–$$; map p.134 B2

A tiny restaurant in a former Downtown home, Joe's has been serving tasty southern Italian pastas and shellfish for more than 30 years. Besides the usual marinara and similar sauces, you can order pasta with calamari sauce or snails.

Jazzed Café & Vinoteca
8614 West Sahara Avenue; tel: 798-5995; Sun–Thur 4–11pm, Fri–Sat 4pm–midnight; $$; bus: 204;

This tiny, elegant, candlelit café serves carefully crafted Tuscan and other Italian specialties—risotto, pastas, and salads—complemented by an extensive wine list, all to the strains of cool jazz, late into the night.

PACIFIC RIM

Benihana Village
Las Vegas Hilton, 3000 South Paradise Road; tel: 732-5111; Sun–Fri 5:30–10pm, Sat 5–11pm; $$; monorail: Las Vegas Hilton, bus: 108; map p.137 C3

This Asian eatery is set in an elaborate garden complete with simulated gentle rain. Energetic chefs entertain by

cooking Japanese food in front of the diners. A favorite splurge is hibachi lobster tail and filet mignon.

Hamada of Japan
598 East Flamingo Road; tel: 733-3005; Mon–Fri 11am–4am, Sat–Sun 4pm–4am; $$; bus: 202; map p.137 D1

A lounge, sushi bar, and dining room combine to make this a major Japanese food experience. Watch your own food being cooked at the teppan tables. Hamada also has locations in the Flamingo and Rio hotels.

Lotus of Siam
953 East Sahara Avenue; tel: 753-3033; Mon–Fri 11.30am–2.30pm, Mon–Thur 5.30–9.30pm, Fri–Sun 5.30–10pm; $$; bus: 204; map p. 137 C4

Justin Gold of Gourmet magazine has called this the "single best Thai restaurant in North America." The voluminous menu includes not only the full range of coconut curry dishes but also little-known cuisine of north-eastern Thailand such as kang-ka-noon, spicy young jackfruit curry with your choice of pork, chicken, or smoked fish flakes.

Mayflower Cuisinier
4750 West Sahara; tel: 870-8432; Mon–Fri 11am–3pm, Mon–Thur 5–10pm, Fri–Sat 5–11pm, closed Sun; $$; bus: 204; map p.10

Contemporary California-style Chinese cuisine with French influences sets this one apart. Typical of the mixed-culture cuisine is the kung pao seafood medley of shrimp, scallops, and salmon. Patio dining is available.

Nobu
Hard Rock Hotel, 4455 Paradise Road; tel: 693-5090; daily 6–11pm; bus: 108; $$–$$$$; map p.139 D4

At this Nobu Matsuhisa restaurant, the sashimi has South American flair, and the menu features inventive Japanese fare like Kobe beef carpaccio, and tiradito with chile paste and cilantro.

SOUTHWEST

Dona Maria Tamales Restaurant
910 Las Vegas Boulevard South, tel: 382 6538; daily 8am–11pm; $; bus: Deuce; map p.134 B2

Below: food is constantly refreshed on the long buffet counters.

Dona Maria's is an authentic Mexican restaurant, specializing in tamales with a choice of fillings, ranging from hot pork to mild chicken or chile-and-cheese. There are also familiar Mexican standards like enchiladas, burritos, and chile rellenos.

Lindo Michoacán
2655 East Desert Inn Road; tel: 735-6828; Mon–Wed 11am–10pm, Thur–Fri 11am–11pm, Sat–Sun 9.30am–11pm; $$; bus: 213

This authentic Mexican restaurant serves elaborate south-of-the-border cuisine from the state of Michoacán. Specialties include dishes rarely seen in the US, such as *birria de chivo* (roasted goat meat in a beer and chile sauce) and *lengua en pipian* (beef tongue in a pumpkin seed sauce).

Pink Taco
Hard Rock Hotel, 4455 Paradise Road; tel: 693-5000; Sun–Thur 11am–10pm, Fri–Sat 11am–midnight; $$; bus: 108; map p.139 D4

This Mexican restaurant's name comes from the house specialty, Baja-style shrimp tacos. Other fare includes dishes rarely found north of the border, such as *sabana de pollo* (thin-sliced seared chicken) in *chimichurri*.

Rincon de Buenos Aires
5300 Spring Mountain Road; tel: 257-3331; Tue–Thur 9am–9pm, Fri–Sat 9am–10pm, Sun–Mon 9am–8pm; $$; bus: 203

This small mall restaurant, with its comfortable interior in sharp contrast to its stark façade, is the first Argentin-

ian restaurant in Vegas. Try the *parillada*, a huge sizzling platter of mixed meats, and leave room for one of the sexy desserts.

Z'Tejas
3824 Paradise Road; tel: 732-1660; Mon–Thur 11am–10pm, Fri–Sat 11am–11pm; $$; bus: 108; map p.137 D1

No ordinary Tex-Mex restaurant, Z'Tejas has elevated Southwestern cooking to an art form. Appreciative diners enjoy jalapeño chicken pasta, vegetable enchiladas, blackened catfish tacos, and other spicy selections, served in an elegant atmosphere.

BUFFETS BEYOND THE STRIP
Carnival World Buffet
Rio, 3700 West Flamingo Road; tel: 252-7777; Mon–Fri 7am–10pm, Sat–Sun 7.30am–10pm; $$; bus: 202; map p.138 A3

Located in the Rio casino, basically 11 different buffets for one price, it includes Mexican, Mongolian grill, Chinese, American, and Italian serving stations.

Feast Buffet
Palace Station, 2411 West Sahara Avenue; tel: 367-2411; daily 7am–10pm, Sat–Sun brunch 7am–4pm; $; bus: 204; map p.136 A2/A3

The innovator of a modern buffet trend, the Feast was responsible for the live-action cooking now found in buffets citywide. Redesigned in December 2006, the buffet features made-to-order omelets, multiple ethnic food stations, and a smorgasbord of desserts, and low prices that make this one of the buffet bargains in town.

Left: cheap and plentiful food is used to tempt diners Downtown.

Downtown

AMERICAN

Bay City Diner
Golden Gate Hotel, 1 Fremont Street; tel: 385-1906; 24 hours; $$; map p.134 B3

Located in the oldest hotel in town, this diner has long been famous for a deal that's hard to beat: shrimp cocktails for 99¢. Since they started making this offer in 1959, they have served more than 25 million shrimp.

Binion's Ranch Steakhouse
Binion's, 128 East Fremont Street; tel: 382-1600; daily 5–11pm; $$$; map p.134 B3

Some of the best beef in the West comes through this steakhouse. There is also seafood, including the restaurant's signature dish, chicken-fried lobster. The restaurant enjoys a great view of the city.

Hugo's Cellar
Four Queens, 202 Fremont Street; tel: 385-4011; daily 5–10pm; $$; map p.134 B3

Tucked away downtown, the restaurant has a romantic, New Orleans atmosphere. You can create your own salad from a tableside salad cart. The culinary accent strongly favors seafood, such as swordfish with crab meat and shrimp sauce.

Triple 7 Restaurant and Brewery
Main Street Station, 200 North Main Street; tel: 385-7111; daily 11am–7am; $–$$$; map p.134 B4

Among copper-clad brewing pots, choose between five kinds of burger, gourmet pizzas, barbecue ribs, or pale-ale battered shrimp. There's also a sushi bar, but the real attraction is the beer.

FRENCH

André's French Restaurant
401 South Sixth Street; tel: 385-

Above: authentic Mexican food at El Sombrero Café.

5016, Mon–Sat 6–11pm, closed Sun; $$$$; map p.134 B3

The original restaurant that spawned chef Andre Rochat's exclusive dining establishments in the Palms and the Monte Carlo is rustic and friendly, located in a 1930s-vintage building that was one of Vegas's earliest family homes. Classic cuisine such as sole meunière, rack of lamb, and outstanding soufflés is served in an ambience of country charm.

ITALIAN

Stefano's
Golden Nugget, 129 Fremont Street; tel: 385-7111; daily 5.30–11pm; $$$; map p.134 B3

Good wines, singing waiters, and classic dishes lashed with garlic and sauces make this pleasant eatery unmistakably Italian. The lobster-tail Milanese is outstanding.

SOUTHWEST

El Sombrero Café
807 South Main Street; tel: 382-9234; Mon–Sat 11am–10pm, closed Sun; $; map p.134 B2

This small, family-run Mexican eatery serves well-prepared, authentic versions of conventional Mexican-Southwestern food.

DOWNTOWN BUFFETS

The Buffet
Golden Nugget Hotel, 129 East Fremont Street; tel: 385-7111; Mon–Fri 7am–10pm, Sat–Sun brunch 8am–3.30pm, dinner 3.30–10pm; $–$$; map p.134 B3

This set the modern standard. An elegant dining room offers a variety of well-executed, all-you-can-eat fare.

Garden Court Buffet
Main Street Station, 200 North Main St; tel: 387-1896; daily 7am–10pm; $–$$; map p.134 B4

A relaxing buffet experience under high ceilings, surrounded by marble and brick. Multiple food stations allow diners to sample everything, from wood-fired pizzas to Mexican and Asian dishes. After 4pm, the buffet serves steak on Tuesdays, filet and scampi on Thursdays and seafood on Fridays and Saturdays.

Prices for an average three-course meal with wine:
$ under $20
$$ $20–$30
$$$ $30–$40
$$$$ more than $40

119

Shopping

In old-time Vegas, only the bare minimum of retail stores were tolerated. Casino owners believed that every dollar spent shopping was a dollar less to be gambled, and lost. But beginning with the MGM Grand's shopping mall in the 1970s, Vegas entrepreneurs realized that high-fashion shopping gave winners a second chance to leave their money behind, and shoppers would splurge with impunity while spouses were gambling. Today, Las Vegas's array of stores rivals that of Beverly Hills or Palm Beach. Casinos try to out do each other with their shopping arcades, and stand-alone malls have sprung up along the Strip.

Casino shopping

Most of the larger resort casinos have shopping areas that provide guests with almost everything they'll need, but a boutique in a hotel other than your own may have the perfect souvenir to remind you of your Las Vegas visit.

Appian Way and Forum Shops

Caesars Palace, 3570 Las Vegas Boulevard South; tel: 731-7110; monorail: Flamingo/Caesars Palace, bus: Deuce; map p.138 B3/B4

Marked by a replica of Michelangelo's *David*, Appian Way is more low-key than the Forum shops, with boutiques predominating, including Cartier Jewelry and Bernini Couture. The most popular stores here are those offering memorabilia of the top Caesars concert performers, Céline Dion and Elton John.

Stores in the casino shopping centers open various hours. As a general rule, most of the stores open at 10am and close between 5–10pm, though some stay open until midnight.

Above: the Forum Shops complex is monumental and vast, with huge replicas of ancient Roman sculptures and fountains.

By contrast, the Forum Shops are said to have the highest revenue per square foot in America.

Avenue Shops

Bally's, 3645 Las Vegas Boulevard South; tel: 739-4111; monorail: Bally's/Paris Las Vegas, bus: Deuce; map p.138 C3/C4

One of the smaller hotel shopping malls, with just 23 stores and several restaurants, the Avenue Shops boast a handful of clothing and jewelry stores, as well as specialty shops like Chocolate Heaven, Houdini's Magic Shop, and Las Vegas Harley Davidson. There's also a wedding chapel.

Carnaval Court

Harrah's, 3475 Las Vegas Boulevard South; tel: 369-5000; monorail: Harrah's/Imperial Palace, bus: Deuce; map p.138 B4

At this quite modest shopping area in Harrah's, the emphasis is on novelty and fun. Here you will find shops like Desert Colors (chile pepper motif clothing), Hippy-Chic (tie-dyed clothing), Show Me the Money (money motif clothing) and Goldfather's (gold-plated and silver jewelry), along with hot dogs, water massages, and an oxygen bar.

Circus Circus Shops

2880 Las Vegas Boulevard South; tel: 734-0410; bus: Deuce; map p.136 B2/B3

Good for kids' stuff, the sizable mezzanine-level shopping area has themed stores like Nothing But Clowns,

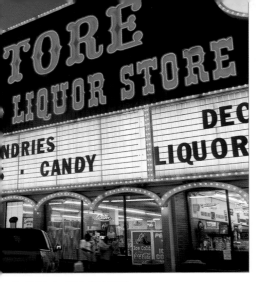

Left: Las Vegas shopping has come a long way since its early days when t-shirts were the must have souvenirs.

Harrah's/Imperial Palace; bus: Deuce; map p.138 B4
Tromp l'oeil ceilings painted and floodlit to simulate the natural sky have become commonplace in themed hotel shopping arcades, but few are as convincing or awe-inspiring as the decor of the Venetian's Grand Canal Shoppes. This is a big, upscale mall complete with singing gondoliers and "living statue" mimes, set in a grand-scale replica of St Mark's Square. Especially noteworthy here are the art galleries, such as the Bernard K. Passman Gallery, Regis Galerie, and Ancient Creations. Other stores include Burberry (apparel), Davidoff (tobacco), Sephora (beauty products), and no less than 14 fine jewelry stores.

Las Vegas Hilton Stores
3000 Paradise Road; tel: 732-5111; www.lvhilton.com; monorail: Las Vegas Hilton, bus: 108; map p.137 C3
If hotel heiress Paris Hilton were to go on a Vegas shopping spree, she would be unlikely to pick the Hilton. There's no faux architecture

The Forum Shops complex is the largest shopping mall in Las Vegas, as well as the most exclusive, with signature boutiques by Gianni Versace, Estee Lauder, De Beers, Harry Winston, Kate Spade, Armani, Polo Ralph Lauren, Jimmy Choo, and a host of others, as well as many fine restaurants and high-end art galleries.

Sweet Tooth, and Circus Kids. Also scattered through the hotel are more adult-oriented stores like the Marshall Rousso men's and women's clothing boutique, Time Tunnel watch store, and the Circus Spirits liquor store. The biggest store in the hotel is Exclusively Circus Circus, offering an array of Circus Circus logo products like T-shirts, mugs, mats, jackets, and sunglasses, often at surprisingly steep prices.
Castle Walk
Excalibur, 3850 Las Vegas Boulevard South; tel: 597-7777; bus: Deuce; map p.139 C1/C2
You will find lots more kids' stuff at this medieval-themed

shopping arcade, where the motto is "Shoppe 'Til You Droppe." Children's souvenirs are available at Kids of the Kingdom and a more general array of Vegas souvenirs can be found at the Vegas Store. Also among the 17 shops are specialized outlets like Merlin's Mystic Shop, which sells Christmas decorations year-round and Dragon's Lair, featuring dragon-themed gifts and crystals.
Grand Canal Shoppes
The Venetian, 3355 Las Vegas Boulevard South; tel: 414-4500; www.grandcanal shoppes.com; monorail:

Below: colorful accessories for a night out.

or skylike ceiling here, and not much in the way of exclusive boutiques. What you will find is essentially an array of specialized hotel gift shops including Kidz Clubhouse, Candy Mania, Paradise Gift Shop, Landau Jewelers, Charisma Apparel and Footwear, the Pool Store, and Regis Salon. The one unique store here is Star Trek: The Experience, where you can choose from the largest selection of Trekkie memorabilia on the planet.

Le Boulevard
Paris Las Vegas, 3655 Las Vegas Boulevard South; tel: 946-7000; monorail: Bally's/Paris Las Vegas, bus: Deuce; map p.138 C3

Though this mall is not especially large, its atmosphere – Old Paris architecture, cobblestone streets and a pale blue sky wispy with clouds –

makes for fun strolling. Here you'll find Le Boutique, which shows clothing and jewelry from designers including Gucci, Fendi, Cartier, and Hermes. Then there's La Cave, a specialty gourmet food store with premium French wines and cheeses. Les Enfantes is a boutique exclusively for the kids, highlighting characters from French children's books.

Mandalay Place
Mandalay Bay, 3930 Las Vegas Boulevard South; tel: 632-7777; bus: Deuce; map p.139 C1/D1

The shopping area at Mandalay Bay is small and select, with most stores tying into other features of the resort. For instance, the House of Blues Company Store offers logo merchandise and limited edition folk art reproductions; Pearl Moon has designer

The MGM Grand is the hotel that pioneered upscale shopping in Las Vegas (or at least its predecessor, since the original burned down long ago), and it has a mixed bag of stores, restaurants, and fast-food joints on a long walkway from the parking lot, with other shopping zones scattered throughout the hotel.

swimwear and beachwear; and the Shark Reef Shop has aquatic-theme souvenirs.

TI Shops
TI – Treasure Island, 3300 Las Vegas Boulevard South; tel: 894-7111; bus: Deuce; map p.136 B1

The TI doesn't need much in the way of on-site shopping, since its new pedestrian bridge connects the hotel to the neighboring Fashion Show Mall (see p.123–4), which has more than 200 stores. Still, scattered through the resort are a number of tie-in gift shops.

Star Lane Shops and Studio Shops
MGM Grand, 3799 Las Vegas Boulevard South; tel: 891-7777; monorail: MGM Grand, bus: Deuce; map p.139 C2

Among the hotel's attractions are stores that have multiple locations in various strip hotels, such as Houdini Magic, Photo Magic, and Las Vegas Harley Davidson. There are also unusual specialty stores like the Pearl Factory, where you can watch cultured pearls being retrieved and buy them in settings of your choice.

Street of Dreams
Monte Carlo, 3400 Las Vegas Boulevard South;

Left: Wynn Esplanade has gone out of its way to raise the bar on Las Vegas shopping.

tel: 791-7777; bus: Deuce; map p.139 C2

Street of Dreams is essentially a cluster of hotel gift shops, including a $10 Boutique, Lance Burton's Magic Shop, the Monte Carlo Collections (home and garden decor), and the Monte Carlo Beach Club (swimsuits, beachwear), plus Lunettes, a boutique that carries eyewear from 70 top designers.

Street of Shops

Mirage, 3400 Las Vegas Boulevard South; tel: 791-7111; bus: Deuce; map p.138 B4

Designed to resemble an exclusive European shopping boulevard, the Street of Shops presents a small selection of fine designer boutiques such as DKNY. You can buy a Rolex at the Watch Boutique or golf gear, from clubs to full virtual golf simulators, at Shadow Creek at the Mirage. The most unusual store on the "street" is Secret Garden, where you can shop for a wide variety of Siegfried & Roy merchandise.

Tower Shops

Stratosphere, 2000 Las Vegas Boulevard South; tel: 380-7777; bus: Deuce; map p.136 B4

A great place for retail highs. Here you will find an unusual selection of shoes and purses at Avanan and South American sweaters and rugs at Alpaca Pete's. Cleo's sells

> The Stratosphere is quite a distance from the main concentration of Strip resorts and shopping malls. Fortunately for shopping buffs, it has an intriguing, diverse and, for the most part, moderately priced shopping area of its own. It was renovated in 2004 and you'll feel like you're wandering the streets of New York, Hong Kong, and Paris.

Above: some of the best shopping in Las Vegas can be found in the huge malls, many of which include entertainment and dining facilities.

toe rings, ankle bracelets, and terrycloth slippers.

Via Bellagio

Bellagio, 3600 Las Vegas Boulevard South; tel: 693-7111; monorail: Bally's/Paris Las Vegas, bus: Deuce; map p.138 B3

Though smaller than the Forum Shops at Caesars, the Bellagio's shopping walk offers as stellar a lineup of designer boutiques as any in Vegas. Polished marble columns and mosaic floors set the scene for individual collections from Armani, Chanel, Dior, Fendi, Gucci, and many more.

Wynn Esplanade

Wynn Las Vegas, 3131 Las Vegas Boulevard South; bus: Deuce; map p.136 B1/C1

The Wynn doesn't really need its own high-end shopping area, since it is right across the street from the Fashion Show Mall (see right), but it hosts not only stores like Graff Jewelers, Manolo Blahnik footwear, and Chanel, Dior, Gaultier, de la Renta, Vuitton, Malone, Leiber, and La Flirt boutiques, but also Wynn's own signature shops. The centerpiece of the shopping area is a Ferrari-Maserati dealership showroom.

Shopping malls

Boulevard Mall

3528 South Maryland Parkway (between Flamingo and Desert Inn roads); tel: 732-8949; daily 10am–9pm; bus: 109; map p.137 E2/E3

Vegas's oldest mall has 170 stores. Anchored by Sears, Dillard's, Macy's, and JC Penney, other stores include Charlotte Russe, The Children's Store, and Gap.

Fashion Outlets of Las Vegas

Primm, Nevada (around 35 miles south of Las Vegas on Interstate 15); tel: 874-1400; www.fashionoutletlasvegas.com; daily 10am–8pm

This upscale mall houses factory outlets with classy names like Escada and Burberry. Shuttle buses run several times a day from the MGM Grand on the Strip (tel: 888-424-6898); there's also a helicopter service if you're feeling flush. Stores include Versace, DKNY, Gap, Burberry, Polo Ralph Lauren, and Escada.

Fashion Show Mall

3200 Las Vegas Boulevard South (at Spring Mountain Road); tel: 369-0704; www.thefashionshow.com; Mon–Fri 10am–9pm, Sat til

123

7pm, Sun noon–6pm; bus: Deuce; map p.136 B1
Stores include Ann Taylor, Dillards, Louis Vuitton, Macy's, Neiman Marcus, and Saks Fifth Avenue.

Galleria at Sunset
1300 West Sunset Road (intersection of Sunset/Stephanie roads), Henderson; tel: 434-0202; www.galleriaatsunset.com; Mon–Sat 10am–9pm, Sun 11am–7pm; map p.16
This recently opened suburban shopping mall is located in the upscale Green Valley area, and houses a selection of interesting specialty stores as well as a massive food court. Stores include Ann Taylor, Bebe, Chevy's, Dillards, Eddie Bauer, JC Penny, and Victoria's Secret.

Las Vegas Outlet Center
7400 Las Vegas Boulevard South; tel: 896-5599; Mon–Sat 10am–9pm, Sun 10am–8pm
Said to be the world's largest factory outlet mall, with more than 130 stores, this indoor center has stores for Calvin Klein, Adidas, Nike, Reebok, Tommy Hilfiger, Liz Claiborne, and countless others. It is accessible from the Strip

Left: Fashion Show Mall, the premier mall on the Strip, has more than 200 stores and restaurants.

and elsewhere via CAT buses.

Las Vegas Premium Outlets
375 South Grand Central Parkway; tel: 474-7500; www.premiumoutlets.com/lasvegas; Mon–Sat 10am–9pm, Sun 10am–8pm
On the way to downtown Las Vegas, with good discounts on upscale fashions. It has a food court and pedestrian courtyards. Among its 120 stores are Dolce & Gabbana, Benetton, and Guess.

Specialty shops
ANTIQUES
Funk House
1228 South Casino Center Boulevard; tel: 678-6278; www.thefunkhouselasvegas.com; open daily 10am–5pm; map p.134 B1
This unusual antiques shop specializes in artifacts from the 1950s era, including art, furniture, rugs, and more. They also rent props for movies set in old-time Vegas.

BOOKS AND MULTIMEDIA
Albion Book Company
2466 East Desert Inn Road; tel: 792-9554; daily 10am–6pm; bus: 213
The largest used book store in Nevada, Albion stocks about 100,000 volumes, specializing in mysteries, poetry, sci-fi, and historical subjects.

Dead Poet Books
937 South Rainbow Boulevard; tel: 227-4070; daily 10am–6pm; bus: 101
The stock of this independent mall bookstore includes new, used and rare books.

Gamblers Book Shop
630 South 11th Street; tel: 382-7555; www.gamblersbook.com; Mon–Sat 9am–5pm; map p.135 C2
This is the world's largest bookstore devoted to gambling and sports betting books, videotapes, and software. Learn about card strategies, cheating, and just about every other gambling-related subject imaginable.
SEE ALSO GAMBLING P.73

Reading Room
Mandalay Bay, 3950 Las Vegas Boulevard South; tel: 632-7800; daily 10am–6pm; bus: Deuce; map p.139 C1/D1
This small store carries a range of bestsellers and classics, as well as useful gambling books and collectors' limited editions.

Tower/Good Guys/ WOW! Multimedia Superstore
4580 West Sahara; tel: 364-2500; daily 10am–10pm; bus: 204

Left: the eye-catching Fashion Show Mall complex has a movable stage with retractable runways, state-of-the art video, and lighting and sound equipment to enhance runway fashion shows.

Above: unique Vegas souvenirs, from dice to slot machines, are available everywhere.

This combined effort overwhelms in every way. There is a huge electronics and computer selection featuring a home theater room and a classical listening room, plus innumerable aisles of records, books, software, CDs, and the city's largest selection of periodicals and magazines. At the fulcrum is a coffee bar and café under a giant-screen TV flanked by CD listening stations.

CLOTHING
The Attic
1018 South Main Street; tel: 388-4088; www.atticvintage.com; Mon–Sat 9am–5pm; map p.134 B2
Maybe the most famous vintage store in America, this collection of clothes, appliances, and knick-knacks serves a willing audience with its selection of period clothing, and items used in movies. Plan on spending a long time here.

Begay Indian Jewelry
1311 Nevada Highway, Boulder City; tel: 293-4822; daily 10am–6pm; map p.16
Navajo craftspeople create attractive goods including everything from gold and sil-

ver. Located on Highway 95/93 towards Hoover Dam.

Designer Shoe Warehouse
Best in the West Shopping Center, 2100 North Rainbow Boulevard; tel: 636-2060; www.dswshoe.com; Mon–Sat 9am–9pm; Sun 10am–7pm; bus: 101
This huge shoe market displays more than 2,000 styles of shoes, and has 30,000 pairs in stock.

TOBACCO
Las Vegas Cigar Company
3750 Las Vegas Boulevard South; tel: 262-6140; www.lvcc.com; daily 10am–6pm bus: Deuce; map p.138 C2
Seeds of Cuban origin, grown in the Dominican Republic and Ecuador, produce the premium tobacco used to hand-roll the fine Cuban look-alikes sold here.

Paiute Tribal Smoke Shop
1225 North Main Street; tel: 387-6433; daily 10am–6pm
This shop sells tax-free tobacco products at some of the lowest prices in town from its drive-through window.

VEGAS SOUVENIRS
Bonanza Gifts
2460 Las Vegas Boulevard South; tel: 385-7359; daily 8am–midnight; bus: Deuce; map p.136 B4
Styling itself as "the World's Largest Gift Shop," this longstanding Vegas landmark is the place to buy souvenir gambling paraphernalia such as used cards, dealer's visors, and poker chips, as well as snow globes, rubber chickens, and a wealth of other tasteless mementos.

Gamblers General Store
800 South Main Street; tel: 382-9903; www.gamblersgeneralstore.com; daily 9am–6pm; map p.134 B2
This centrally located supplier of slots, gaming tables, and other accoutrements, sells everything from "How to Win at Blackjack" videos to full-size wooden roulette wheels. Most items can be shipped.

Serge's Showgirl Wigs
Commercial Center, 953 East Sahara Avenue; tel: 732-1015; www.showgirlwigs.com; daily 10am–6pm; bus: 204; map p.137 C4
The largest wig showroom in the entire US, with a helpful staff and a selection of 2,000 wigs to try on. Selections range from $130 to more than $1,500.

Just a word of warning. At the time of going to press, all the stores in this section have premises in the mall or shopping arcade listed, but if you're interested in visiting a specific shop, be sure to telephone ahead first or check on the internet to make sure that the place you want to see has not moved or closed. Things change quickly

125

Transportation

Getting to Las Vegas is easy. The international airport lands an average of one jetliner per minute, 24hrs a day. Getting around the tourist zones is even easier. Since the majority of visitors do not rent cars – major resorts are so self-contained that visitors often find they have little use for rental vehicles – finding public transportation within the tourist zones is never a problem. If you want to investigate the fabulous desert landscapes nearby, which most tourists miss, you will certainly want to either rent a car or book one of the many tours that explore the region by jeep, van, helicopter, or small plane.

Getting there by air

Domestic flights to and from Vegas are not at all difficult to find. Las Vegas is a hub for AmericaWest and Southwest Airlines and also serves most other national airlines with flights not only from every major city but also from many small Western towns, where entertainment-starved workers routinely spend their weekends in Vegas. Matters become a bit more tricky if one is searching for direct flights from abroad.

From the UK only Virgin Atlantic (www.virginatlantic.com), BMI and MAXjet (www.maxjet. com) fly directly to Las Vegas, though virtually all European airlines connect to Las Vegas through New York, Miami, or other international hubs. International airlines that serve McCarren Airport include AeroMéxico, Air Canada, Aviasca, Korean Air, Mexicana, and Philippine Airlines, among others.

AIRPORTS
McCarran International Airport
5757 Wayne Newton Boulevard; tel: 261-5211; www.mccarran. com; map p.139 E1
The hub for air travel into and out of southern Nevada, though flights are hardest to book on short notice on Fridays (inbound) and Sundays (outbound).

McCarran Airport is about 2 miles from the Strip and about 6 miles from downtown Las Vegas. A taxi ride from McCarran to the Strip costs about $10; the fare to Downtown can run up to $20. A shuttle bus service (Bell Trans, tel: 739-7990) runs continually from the airport and costs much less. CLS Transportation (tel: 740-4040) also runs airport limousines round the clock. The public bus company, Citizens Area Transit (CAT), also serves the airport, though there is no direct bus between the airport and the Strip; you must change from an airport bus (Route 108/109) to a Strip bus (Route 301/302). Most major resorts also have airport shuttles, often complimentary.

Getting there by bus
Greyhound
Information line: 800-231-2222; www.greyhound.com
Downtown depot, 200 South Main Street; tel: 382-5468; map p.134 B3
The national bus line operates daily services to Las Vegas from Los Angeles, San Francisco, San Diego, and Phoenix. There are several inexpensive hotels and motels within walking distance.
GotoBus
Tel: 800-354-2101; www.gotobus.com
This independent bus company operates daily shuttle

McCarren International Airport is one of the world's busiest airports. In 2006, a total of 46 million passengers passed through its terminal, and more than 600,000 passenger flights took off and landed.

Some airborne sightseeing excursions to the Grand Canyon and elsewhere take off from the North Las Vegas Airport, 2730 Airport Drive, tel: 261-3800. Public transportation is limited, and the North Las Vegas Airport is best reached by cab.

Left: a vintage arrival on Interstate 15.

strictly enforced, and drivers can turn right on a red light when it is safe to do so. One difference about Nevada roads is the center lane, which is not used for travel but for left-hand turns only.

Nearly every major hotel has free valet parking with an attendant who, although optional, is usually rewarded with a tip of $1 or $2 per car every time you park.

Avis
5164 Rent A Car Road; tel: 261-5591 or 800-822-3131; www.avis.com

Budget Car and Truck Rental
5188 Paradise Road; tel: 736-1212 or 800-922-2899; www.budgetvegas.com

Hertz Rent A Car
5300 Rent A Car Road; tel: 736-4900 or 800-654-3131; www.hertz.com

Taxis

All taxi services in Las Vegas are heavily regulated by the Nevada Taxicab Authority (tel: 668-4000). There are a limited number of companies and

from Los Angeles, Anaheim, and San Diego to Las Vegas and return. Some buses also take in Grand Canyon West and Hoover Dam en route.

Getting There by Car

Around 26 percent of Las Vegas visitors are from Southern California. Those who come by car usually follow Interstate 10 from LA (or I-215 from San Diego) to join I-15 north of Riverside. Traffic on I-15 is fast moving, mainly through desert. The fact that California speed limits are lower for trucks than for cars has greatly reduced accidents on interstates, though not on secondary highways. At Barstow, I-15 is intersected by US 58, which takes travelers from the north-west; this area has many more accidents than the interstates do. From the north, the most direct route is US 95. From the east, Las Vegas travelers exit I-40 to join US 95 at Kingman, Arizona.

Car Rental

Many rental car companies have outlets at McCarran International Airport on the aptly named Rent A Car Road. Some companies also have offices inside hotels, casinos, or resorts.

There is little difference between Nevada driving regulations and other places in the United States. All speed limits are posted, seat belts are required and their use is

Right: McCarran International Airport operates to capacity seven days a week.

the service is metered. Unlike in most cities, Las Vegas cabs are prohibited by law from picking up hailing customers on the street. Not that it does not occasionally happen, but visitors should not feel snubbed if they hail an empty cab but it fails to stop to pick them up

However, there are nearly always lines of taxis at the airport, or by major hotels on the Strip and Downtown; also at some restaurants. Taxis can also be ordered by telephone 24hrs a day. Services include:

Checker Cab
tel: 873-2000.
Lucky Cab
tel: 477-7555.
Virgin Valley Cab
tel: 737-1378.
Yellow Cab
tel: 933-2000.

Trolleys and buses

A trolley on wheels mainly for the convenience of tourists connects many of the Strip resorts with each other. Stations are located at the Stratosphere, Sahara, Circus Circus, Riviera, Las Vegas Hilton, Fashion Show Mall, Treasure Island, Harrahs, Flamingo, Caesars Palace, Ballys, MGM Grand, New York New York, Excalibur, Tropi-

cana, and Mandalay Bay. The trolley no longer goes downtown. The trolley operates from 9.30am– 1.30am on a 2-hr loop system, and a trolley (supposedly) arrives every 15 min, but it is a slow way to get around. Be sure to have the exact fare ($2.50) when you board.

Public transportation is provided by Citizen's Area Transit (CAT) buses. A guide detailing routes, scheduling, and service is available by calling (tel: 228-7433). There are customer-service representatives at that telephone number who can help plan a trip.

CAT operates 5:30am–1:30am daily on residential routes. Some routes run 24hrs a day, and some only during peak service hours Monday to Friday, except major US public holidays.

All buses have electronic fareboxes that accept dollar bills and coins but do not give change. If you plan to transfer to another bus to complete your one-way trip, ask the driver for a transfer.

Monorail

The privately owned Strip Monorail began operation in July 2004. It presently links the Sahara, Las Vegas Hilton, Convention Center, Harrah's,

Flamingo, Bally's, and MGM Grand and connects with the CAT bus routes along the Strip. Tickets cost $5 for one ride, $15 for an all-day pass or $40 for a three-day pass. The monorail operates Mon–Thur 7am–2am, and runs until 3am on Fri and Sat nights. The company hopes to boost ridership by extending monorail service to McCarren International Airport.

On the other side of the Strip, a short, free private monorail system connects the neighboring Excalibur, Luxor, and Mandalay Bay casinos, all three of which are owned and managed by the same development company.

Limousines

A brief stint of traffic-watching along the Strip leads to the inevitable conclusion that Las Vegas must have more stretch limos than anyplace else in the world. Cruising the Strip in a limousine is an exciting way to see the sights and provides the ultimate in traveling luxury. As with taxis, the limousine service in Las Vegas is strictly regulated. However, unlike taxis, limousines are not metered. The cost, usually per-hour, is agreed upon at the time of rental. Expen-

Below: the monorail has proved less successful than expected, primarily because of its high cost relative to other public transportation alternatives along the Strip.

Right: touring the desert by motorcycle.

sive? They cost more than taxis, but a party of four can cruise the Strip in a stretch limo for an hour for about the same price as any quickie roller coaster ride.

Exotic VIP Limos
tel: 837-2666

Highroller Limos
tel: 868-5600.

Jetset VIP
tel: 433-5466.

Las Vegas Limousines
tel: 736-1419.

Presidential Limousine
tel: 731-5577.

Motorcycles

Eagle Rider-Las Vegas Motorcycle Rentals
5182 South Arville Street;
tel: 888-916-7433;
www.eaglerider.com

Las Vegas Harley-Davidson
2605 South Eastern Avenue;
tel: 431-8500; www.lvhd.com

Walking

The Las Vegas Strip is about as pedestrian-friendly as city streets get. Joining the happy (and often drunken) throngs along the wide sidewalks, you can amble, or on weekends be swept away by the crowds, up and down the whole 4-mile stretch of casinos and hotels, crossing the hopelessly traffic-clogged streets on any of the numerous pedestrian overpasses. In fact, during

Helpful CAT phone numbers are 228-7433 for transit information; 676-1500 for RTC administrative offices; and 228-7433 for lost and found. Websites include www.rtc.co.clark.nv.us for general RTC information, and www.catride.com for specific CAT information.

the evening it is often much faster to park your car and walk along the Strip than to drive. In the hot months, from mid-spring through mid-fall, you will want to restrict your outdoor walking to the nighttime hours. If you long for a stroll during the day, avoid the 100-degree heat of the day by choosing an indoor walking area such as the Forum Shops in Caesars Palace. Beyond the Strip, except for a few city parks with walking, jogging, and biking trails, travel on foot is unthinkable due to the maze of freeways and busy, sidewalkless arterials that block your route at every turn.

Charters and tours

Action Tours
175 Cassia Way, Henderson; tel: 566-7400 or 888-288-5200
Off-road vehicle, horseback, and rafting tours to Red Rock Canyon, Death Valley, and others.

Coach USA
4020 East Lone Mountain Road; tel: 644-2233 or 800-559-522; City, Lake Mead, Hoover Dam, and Grand Canyon tours by bus.

Grand Canyon Tour Company
4343 North Rancho Drive #230; tel: 655-6060 or 800-222-6966; City, Hoover Dam, Red Rock Canyon, and Grand Canyon tours by bus.

Grand Tours
tel: 368-5100 or 866-371-8005 Day and night bus tours of the city, Hoover Dam, and Grand Canyon West. Bilingual English-French.

Gray Line Tours
tel: 384-1234 or 800-634-6579 City tours and van tours to Hoover Dam, Lake Mead, and Grand Canyon West, with pickups at all hotels.

Haunted Vegas Tours
Greek Isles, tel: 983-6380 or 800-591-6423
Tour of ghostly sites with tales of celebrity hauntings by an "expert" in the paranormal.

Heli USA Flights
275 East Tropicana Avenue, Suite 200; tel: 736-8787 or 800-359-8727; www.heliusa.com Tours over the Strip, to the Grand Canyon, and other destinations.

Lake Mead Cruises
480 Lakeshore Road, Boulder City; tel: 493-9765
Ccruises on the *Desert Princess* paddlewheeler.

129

Weddings

Las Vegas is a favorite destination not only for gambling and conventions, but also as a mecca of matrimony. Though there are many places for a traditional wedding, it's the extreme and badly themed nuptiuls that Vegas is famous for, where anyone from Elvis to Captain Kirk can conduct your ceremony, and a drive-thru wedding can be arranged for those in a rush. More than 174,000 troths are pledged here every single year. Some of them even last; for those who feel the seven-year itch prematurely, it's only a seven-hour drive to Reno, Nevada, once home of the quickest divorces in the West.

Chapels

Chapel of the Bells

375 East Harmon Avenue; tel: 731-2355 or 800-305-9040; www.weddingbellschapel.com; map p.139 D3

All weddings take place outside in the attractive garden gazebo across from the Hard Rock Hotel. Tom Petty got married here.

Elvis Chapel

727 South Ninth Street; tel: 383-5909 or 800-452-6081; map p.134 C2

The most famous man in Vegas is here every day to celebrate your wedding or vow renewal.

Gay Chapel of Vegas

1205 Las Vegas Boulevard South; tel: 384-0771 or 800-574-4450; www.gaychapeloflasvegas.com; bus: Deuce; map p.134 B2

Part of Viva Las Vegas (see opposite), it conducts ceremonies for same-sex couples.

Graceland Wedding Chapel

619 Las Vegas Boulevard South; tel: 382-0091 or 800-824-5732; www.gracelandchapel.com; bus: Deuce; map p.134 B3

The self-proclaimed King of the Elvis wedding scene.

Las Vegas Wedding Specialists

Suite A101, 4045 South Buffalo Drive; tel: 496-2613 or 888-638-4673; www.lasvegaswedding specialists.com

One of the leading chapels for alternative lifestyle commitment ceremonies. There are also a range of themed and traditional packages.

Little Church of the West

4617 Las Vegas Boulevard South; tel: 800-821-2452 or 739-7971; www.littlechurchlv.com; bus: Deuce; map p.10

The oldest wedding chapel in Vegas, the building looks as if couples had wedded there since Wild West days. Billy Bob Thornton married Angelina Jolie here in May 2000. By coincidence, the chapel is listed on the National Register of Historic Places. Traditional wedding packages only.

The Little White Wedding Chapel

1301 Las Vegas Boulevard South; tel:382-5943 or 800-545-8111; www.alittlewhitechapel.com; bus: Deuce; map p.134 B1

Offering traditional wedding packages only, the Little White Chapel is popular in celebrity circles. Singer Britney Spears married hometown honey Jason Allen Alexander at the Little White Chapel (the marriage was annulled 50 hours later). The Little White Chapel was also chosen for the happy day for Michael Jordan and

Las Vegas weddings have become more a matter of fun than practicality, since only a few states now require a blood test for a marriage license, once the main advantage of a Sin City elopement. Speaking of the changing legal climate, Nevada also used to be the divorce capital of the United States because of an exceptionally short six-week residency requirement, which could be satisfied by a stay at a resort. With today's no-fault divorce laws and simplified jurisdiction requirements, dissolving a marriage is just as easy in several other Western states. Nevada used to have a reputation as an easy place to get an annulment, too, but today court hearings are required and annulments are only granted in rare circumstances.

Left: because love could strike anytime, day or night.

packages are available. The Terrazza Di Sogno package includes use of the terrace for your ceremony and the famed fountains will play one song of your choice, beginning just as the bride and groom kiss for the first time as a married couple.

Canterbury Wedding Chapel
Excalibur, 3850 Las Vegas Boulevard South; tel: 597-7260 or 800-811-4320; www.excalibur.com; bus: Deuce; map p.139 C1/C2
The Excalibur provides a medieval-themed ceremony in addition to numerous traditional packages.

Chapel in the Clouds
Stratosphere, 2000 South Las Vegas Boulevard; tel: 380-7777 or 800-789-9436; bus: Deuce; map p.136 B4
How about saying your vows high above the desert in the Stratosphere's observation decks? At 800ft above street

Mickey Rooney may hold the record for Vegas weddings. He married Ava Gardner at the Little Church of the West in January, 1942. Over the next three decades he made seven return trips to the same chapel, concluding with a marriage to January Chamberlin in 1978.

Juanita Vanoy in 1989. Bruce Willis and Demi Moore were married here, and the chapel beams a live wedding over the Web every few minutes via its Wedding Cam onto the Discovery Channel's Internet site.

Vegas Wedding Chapel
320 South 3rd Street; tel: 933-3464 or 800-823-4095; www.702wedding.com; map p.134 B3
Outdoor weddings in the Valley of Fire, on the rim of Red Rock Canyon or even on a boat on Lake Mead, are a specialty of this business. Uniquely, at their chapel weddings you can have butterflies and doves released after your ceremony.

Viva Las Vegas
1205 Las Vegas Boulevard South; tel: 384-0771 or 800-574-4450; www.vivalasvegasweddings.com;

bus: Deuce; map p.134 B2
Viva Las Vegas now operates two chapels. Their main operation is at the above address and is the largest chapel on the strip. The second location is the historic Hartland Mansion, with its sweeping staircase and grand ballroom. Traditional and themed weddings are available and they are also happy to organize outdoor weddings.

Hotel and casino chapels
Generally speaking, facilities available in Hotels and Casinos are more traditional: in their decor and types of ceremonies, and many of their chapels even close before midnight. Some may even expect participants to be sober. Still it is Vegas, and they can not resist dipping their toes into themed wedding experience, especially since many are in themed resort hotels.

Bellagio
3600 Las Vegas Boulevard South; tel: 693-7700 or 888-987-3344; monorail: Bally's/Paris Las Vegas, bus: Deuce; map p.138 B3
Several Italian-style wedding

Below: tying the neon knot.

Above: reasonable package prices make Vegas a good destination for a "real" wedding too.

level, it's higher above the ground than any other chapel in the country.

Le Chapel de Paris
Paris Las Vegas, 3655 Las Vegas Boulevard South; tel: 946-7000 or 877-650-5021; monorail: Bally's/Paris Las Vegas, bus: Deuce; map p.138 C3
With several packages to choose from, the highlight is a ceremony at the top of the Eiffel Tower. This setting is also available if you just want to propose.

Star Trek: The Experience
Las Vegas Hilton, 3000 Paradise Road; tel: 697-8750 or 800-732-7117; www.startrekexp.com; monorail: Las Vegas Hilton, bus: 108; map p.137 C3
The Las Vegas Hilton provides Intergalactic Federation regalia, hires-out several of the Star Trek characters as witnesses, and lets you have your wedding pictures taken in the Molecular Imaging Chamber, presumably just before you are beamed off the Enterprise for your honeymoon. Packages usually include a ringside seat at the Borg Invasion. Who needs a reception?

TI – Treasure Island
3300 Las Vegas Boulevard South; tel: 894-7700 or 888-818-0999; bus: Deuce; map p.136 B1

The casino's Enchantment wedding ceremony takes place on their notorious pirate ship, with the captain officiating over the occasion. The hotel also has an elegant traditional chapel.

The Venetian
3355 Las Vegas Boulevard South; tel: 866-548-1807; monorail: Harrah's/Imperial Palace; bus: Deuce; map p.138 B4
In addition to the chapel, there are two faux romantic locations to choose from: you can tie the knot on a floating gondola or on a Venetian bridge.

Drive-up weddings

Several wedding chapels provide convenient drive-up services, so the bride and groom don't even need to leave their car. At A Special Memory Wedding Chapel (800 South 4th Street; tel: 800-962-7798 or 384-2211; www.aspecialmemory.com) you can even borrow a pink Cadillac for a drive-through Elvis ceremony. Special indeed. The Little White Wedding Chapel *(see p.130)* also has a wedding window.

For the more upmarket autophile, you can have a limo drive to the scenic backdrop of your choice – and

get married in the back of the stretch. In fact, a few limos come equipped with whirlpools and hot tubs, so the happy couple can bubble and betroth simultaneously.

Vegas Adventure Wedding Chapel
1600 Las Vegas Boulevard South; tel: 888-463-1399 or 212-0220; www.vegasadventureweddings. com; map p.134 B1
In addition to traditional chapel themes and immortal Elvis themed weddings, they specialize in more adventurous nuptiuals. You can say your vows in a helicopter above Hoover Dam or the Grand Canyon (you have to say them loud, though).

Vegas Dream Weddings
tel: 949-0939 or 877-877-7342; www.vegasdreamweddings.com
Another specialist tour organizer that takes advantage of Vegas's beautiful natural surroundings, their packages include transport to sites and ceremonies. Locations include Red Rock Canyon, Mount Charleston, and Area 51, aliens not included.

Making arrangements

Vegas has about 50 wedding chapels, which are open daily from 8am to midnight, and stay open 24 hours on legal holidays. In 2006, the Clark County Marriage Bureau made a significant change to the wedding scene in Vegas by deciding to close at midnight. Previously, you could apply for a marriage license at any time of the night. You can still be married in the wee hours, provided you receive your license before midnight.

The invitation to impulsiveness is taken advantage of by an average of 337 couples every day, with Valentine's Day weekend understandably the busiest time of the year, when as many as 2,000 licenses are issued. Licenses cost $55, cash only and correct change is appreciated.

Prices for weddings vary enormously with the basic ceremony costing as little as $75 and themed packages costing from $200 up.

Under Nevada law, marriage licenses are only issued to couples consisting of exactly one man and one woman who are at least 18 years of age and not nearer of kin than a second cousin,

and neither party can have another living husband or wife. Some legal identification is required, like a driver's license, passport, or birth certificate with photo ID.

If you are a US citizen you must provide your Social Security Number. If you are from abroad, it is a good idea to check with your local authorities to see what documentation may be needed to make your marriage legitimate in your home country.

Divorced applicants must know the month, day, year, and location of their divorce, but you do not need to bring the decree so long as the divorce is final.

Applicants under 18 but over 16 can get married so long as one of their parents or guardians is present at the ceremony for consent.

Clark County Marriage Bureau
200 South 3rd Street, 1st floor; tel: 671-0600; www.co.clark.nv.us/clerk/marriage_information.htm; 8am–midnight daily; map p.134 B3
Applications can be made online.

Above: costume stores help you make your wedding fantasies come true.

Wedding outfits and costume rental

I&A Formalwear
3345 South Decatur Boulevard, Suite 27; tel: 364-5777 or 800-249-5075; www.iaformalwear.com; open Mon–Fri 9am–6pm, Sat 9am–5pm; bus: 103; map p.10
They promise to get you suited and booted in ten minutes and offer several ranges of wedding dresses and tuxedos, plus a service for the last-minute pressing of garments.

Bridal de Paris
2207 Las Vegas Boulevard South; tel: 301-1002; www.bridaldeparis.com; bus: Deuce; map p.136 B4
Reputedly the finest wedding rental outfitter in Las Vegas, they have more than 500 wedding gowns in stock and also do hair and makeup, with package rates that cover the bride, her bridesmaids and her mother.

A-1 Discount Tuxedo and Formal Wear
812 Las Vegas Boulevard South; tel: 382-9906; bus: Deuce; map p.134 B2
The name says it all.

Below: an offer too good to refuse.

A   **B**

↑ Natural History Museum,
Lied Discovery Children's Museum,
Old Las Vegas Mormon Fort H.P.

PEARSON PARK

Verdi Ln.
Biltmore Dr.
Bell Dr.
Tam Dr.
4th Dr.

Bonanza Way
Bonanza Rd

G St.
Adams Av.
F St.
E St.
D St.

Washington Av.
Morgan Av.

12th St.
11th St.
10th St.
9th St.

93

4

Morgan Av.
Gerson Av.
McWilliams Av.

Wilson Av.
D St.
E St.

Wilson Av.

Mesquite Av.
Bus Station
City Hall

3rd St.

Mesquite Av.
7th St.

Bonanza Rd
93
15

Mesquite Av.
F St.

Main Street Station

North Main St
Stewart Av.

California

Gold Spike Hotel

3rd St.

Ogden Av.
7th St.
8th St.

Ogden Av.

Binion's Horseshoe

1st St.

Fremont

Neonopolis

El Cortez

Plaza Hotel and Casino

Las Vegas Club

Fremont Street Experience

Fremont St

95

3

Golden Nugget

Four Queen's

Fitzgerald's

Carson Av.

10th St.
9th St.
8th St.

Interstate Rail Terminal (Amtrak)

South Main St

Casino Center Blvd

Bridger Av.

DOWNTOW

Discovery Dr.

Union Park Development (under construction)

Lewis Av.

Lloyd D. George Federal Courthouse

Lewis A

604

Clark Av.

West Bonneville Av.

East Bonneville Av.

Martin Luther King Boulevard

Clark County Government Offices

Grand Central Parkway

Garces Av.

1st St.
3rd St.
4th St.
6th St.
7th St.
8th St.

Garces Av.
10th St.

2

Alta Dr.
Kenyon Pl.

Las Vegas Premium Outlets

Commerce St

Gass Av.

Casino Center Blvd

Gass Av.

East Charleston Boulevard

DUTTON PARK

Park Paseo

15

Pinto Ln.
Desert Ln.

Hoover Av.

18B ARTS DISTRICT

Coolidge Av.

159

Park Paseo

5th Pl.
7th St.
8th St.

Yu

Valley Hospital

Iron Horse Ct.

3rd St

Park Paseo

Franklin Av.
St

Bearden Dr.
Hastings Av.

California Av.

Shadow Ln.

Colorado Av.

4th St.
3rd St.

Sweeney Av.
Bracken

Griffith

1

University Medical Center

Willow Ln.
Alturas Av.

West Charleston Boulevard
159

1 Mercedes Cl.
2 Richard Ct.
3 Ormsby St

Wall St.

Western Av.

Imperial Av.

Imperial Av.

Main St

Commerce St

Casino Center Bd

Bracken Av.
Griffith Av.

Houssels Av.

Rexford Pl.

5th

Ellen Wy.

Westwood Dr.
Parlor Dr.
Park Cl.

Mercedes Cl.
Jaylar Cl.
Ellis Ln.
Shadow Ln.
1st St.
Charmast

Martin Luther King Blvd
Wall St.
15

Industrial Rd

Utah Av.
Fairfield Av.

Wyoming Av.

Oakey Blvd

Las Vegas Boulevard

Santa Barbara Wy.
Canosa Av.
Rexford Dr.
Bonita Av.

Weldon Pl.

St. Louis W

New York Av.

A   **B**

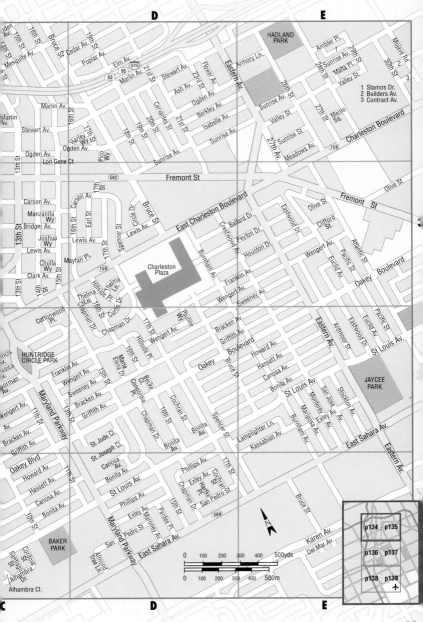

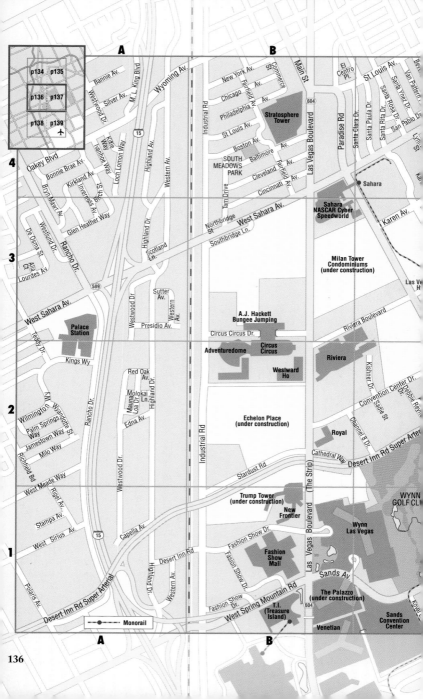

A

B

p134 | p135
p136 | p137
p138 | p139 ✈

4

Bannie Av.
New York Av.
Commerce
Main St
El Centro Pl
St. Louis Av.
Bev...
Wyoming Av.
Fairfield Av.
Chicago
Van Patten...
Silver. St
Westwood Dr.
M. L. King Blvd
Philadelphia St
Santa Ynez Dr.
Santa Rosa Dr.
Santa Paula St
San Pablo St
Industrial Rd
Stratosphere Tower
St Louis St
Paradise Rd
Santa Clara Dr.
Lyn... St
15
Boston Av.
Las Vegas Boulevard
Western Av.
Fairfield Av.
604
Kara...
Oakey Blvd
Baltimore
Bonnie Brae Av.
SOUTH MEADOWS PARK
Cleveland
Sahara
Kirkland Av.
Cincinnati
Highland Dr.
Bryn Mawr Av.
1st St
Inverness Av.
Birch
Loch Lomon Way
Kiele Way
Ivanhoe Av.
Tam Drive
Sahara NASCAR Cyber Speedworld
Karen Av.
Glen Heather Way
West Sahara Av.
Northbridge St
3
De Osma St
Rancho Dr.
Alia Ct
Southbridge Ln.
Milan Tower Condominiums (under construction)
Lourdes Av.
Scotland Ln.
Las Ve... H
589
Westwood Dr.
Sutter Av.
West Sahara Av.
Western Av.
Riviera Boulevard
A.J. Hackett Bungee Jumping
Presidio Av.
Circus Circus Dr.
Teddy Dr.
Palace Station
Adventuredome
Circus Circus
Riviera
Kings Wy
Red Oak Av.
Westward Ho
Kishner Dr.
2
Rancho Dr.
Mauna Loa Dr.
Molokai Ln.
Convention Center Dr.
Wilmington Way
Wyandotte St
Highland Dr.
Echelon Place (under construction)
Debbie Reyn...
Palm Springs Way
Edna Av.
Royal
Sable St
Jamestown Way
Milo Way
Industrial Rd
Channel 8 Dr.
Richland Rd
Cathedral Way
Desert Inn Rd Super Arter...
West Meade Way
Stardust Rd
Rigel Av.
(The Strip)
WYNN GOLF CL...
Westwood Dr.
Stampa Av.
Trump Tower (under construction)
1
West Sirius Av.
New Frontier
Wynn Las Vegas
15
Capella Av.
Fashion Show Dr.
Las Vegas Boulevard
Polaris Av.
Highland Dr.
Desert Inn Rd
Western Av.
Fashion Show Mall
Sands Av.
Fashion Show Dr.
West Spring Mountain Rd
The Palazzo (under construction)
Desert Inn Rd Super Arterial
●━● Monorail
T.I. (Treasure Island)
604
Venetian
Sands Convention Center

A

B

136

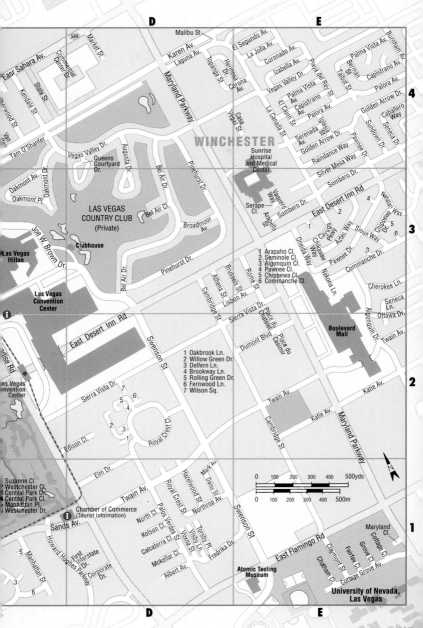

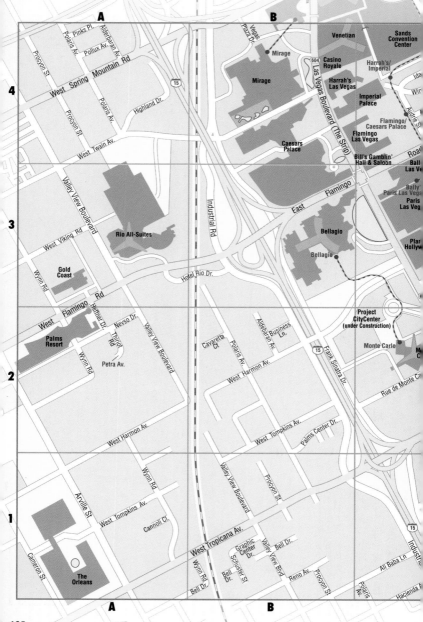

A

B

4

Pinks Pl.
Polaris Av.
Pollux Av.
Alderbaran Rd

Procyon St

West Spring Mountain Rd

Procyon St

Polaris Av.

Highland Dr.

15

West Twain Av.

Vegas Plaza Dr.

Mirage

Mirage

Venetian

Sands Convention Center

604

Casino Royale

Harrah's/ Imperial

Harrah's Las Vegas

Ida

Las Vegas Boulevard (The Strip)

Imperial Palace

Win

Audrie St.

Flamingo/ Caesars Palace

Flamingo Las Vegas

Caesars Palace

Bill's Gamblin' Hall & Saloon

Road

Ball Las Ve

3

Valley View Boulevard

West Viking Rd

Rio All-Suites

Industrial Rd

Flamingo

East

Bally's
Paris Las Vega

Paris Las Veg

Gold Coast

Wynn Rd

Flamingo Rd

Heltner Dr.

Hotel Rio Dr.

Bellagio

Bellagio

Plar Hollyw

2

West

Palms Resort

Wynn Rd

Third Rd

Nevso Dr.

Petra Av.

Valley View Boulevard

Cavaretta Ct.

Polaris Av.

Business Ln.

Aldebaran Av.

West Harmon Av.

15

Frank Sinatra Dr.

Project CityCenter
(under Construction)

Monte Carlo

M C

Rue de Monte Ca

West Harmon Av.

West Tompkins Av.

Palms Center Dr.

1

Arville St.

West Tompkins Av.

Wynn Rd

Cannoli Ct.

Valley View Boulevard

Procyon St

Procyon St

Valley View Boulevard

Bell Dr.

15

Cameron St.

The Orleans

West Tropicana Av.

Graphic Center Dr.

Wynn Rd.

Bell Dr.

Schuster St.

Bell Dr.

Valley View Blvd

Reno Av.

Procyon St

Ali Baba Ln.

Polaris Av.

Industr

Hacienda

A

B

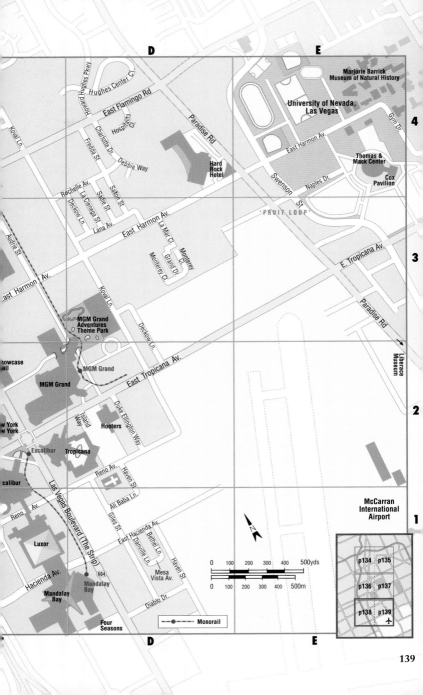

Index